Drowned Landscape

HARRY FOKKENS

Drowned Landscape

The Occupation of the Western Part of the Frisian-Drentian Plateau, 4400 BC – AD 500

1998

Van Gorcum

ROB

Rijksdienst voor het Oudheidkundig Bodemonderzoek

COLOPHON

editor J.F. van Regteren Altena
project manager Ms A. Mars
production coordinator G.H. Scheepstra
English translator Ms N. Forest-Flier
English editors Ms K.E. Waugh & Ms M. de Groot
color map production J.F.M. Schoonebeek, COMP. FORMS.
pre-press & DTP ROB, section Media Producties,
& Casparie Heerhugowaard BV
cover design Chris van Egmond BNO, Casparie Heerhugowaard BV
printed in the Netherlands by Casparie Heerhugowaard BV

© 1998 Van Gorcum & Comp. BV
P.O. Box 43, 9400 AA Assen

Rijksdienst voor het Oudheidkundig Bodemonderzoek
P.O. Box 1600, 3800 b.p. Amersfoort

ISBN 90 2323 305 0

Contents

Notes: The maps I – VIII and I' – VIII' are reproduced at the end of the book (p. 165–182).
The location of the places mentioned in the text is indicated in figures 2 and 3 (p. 14 and 17), the location of the lakes in figure 3 (p. 17), and the location of the rivers and rivulets in figure 17 (p. 42).

Preface

This book first appeared in April 1991 as a doctoral dissertation under the title *Verdrinkend landschap: archeologisch onderzoek van het westelijk Fries-Drents Plateau; 4400 BC tot 500 AD*. It is an account of research into the distribution of finds on the western part of the Frisian-Drentian plateau. In this context a method was developed to allow analysis of distortions of such distribution patterns: map formation analysis. This part of the study, in which the largest amount of time has been invested, ought to be seen as an essential part of each archaeological investigation, both regional and supra-regional. It should be included not only in the analysis of known finds distributions, which is chiefly a matter of interpretation, but also in the preparation of regional investigations and as an aid in archaeological heritage management.

In present practice planning is chiefly based on known findspots, although fortunately changes are on the way thanks to the Stichting Regionaal Archeologisch Archiverings Project in Amsterdam (Stichting RAAP).[1] Little attention is paid to post-depositional processes. This sometimes results in sites coming to light unexpectedly, often when it is too late to save them. A systematic application of map formation analysis can be a strong defence against such problems. It is not inconceivable that within the Netherlands the ARCHIS.[2] project will provide a suitable framework for the application of map formation analysis on a wider scale.

This study started in 1982 as a dissertation project subsidized by the Dutch Organization for Scientific Research (NWO). From January 1981 until June 1983 I worked at Groningen University (Biologisch-Archaeologisch Instituut) full-time on the project. This period came to an end by my appointment at Leiden University (Instituut voor Prehistorie Leiden). I now had to continue the work in my spare time. Luckily NWO allowed the work on the finds catalogue to be continued by P.H. Deckers. I gratefully used the data he collected.

Many other people contributed to the realization of the original dissertation and of the present book. In the first place I want to give credit to my promoter, Professor H.T. Waterbolk, who patiently waited for 10 years until this work was finally finished. I do not think that he agrees in all respects with my interpretation of the data, an indication of the much appreciated freedom he gave me to develop my own ideas.

At the Instituut voor Prehistorie, now the Faculty of Archaeology of the Leiden University, I received much moral and scientific support from its dean, Professor L.P. Louwe Kooijmans and my fellow staff members. Many students participated in coring campaigns, in the inventory of finds and mapping projects. Of those I specially want to thank Hortense André de la Porte-Janss, Mirjam van Ieperen, Erik Jungerius, Dimitri de Loecker, Marie-France van Oorsouw, Jan Albert Schenk, Kees Schinkel, Liesbeth Smits, Liesbeth Theunissen, Monique van Veen, and Dieke Wesselingh for their enthusiastic support.

In the museums, I had the assistance of the keepers and their staff. In the Fries Museum these were G. Elzinga, Dr J. Bos, J. Boschker, and E. Kramer; in the Groninger Museum J. Boersma and J. Wachter; in the Drents Museum Dr W. van der Sanden and J. Beuker; in the

---

1 The Stichting RAAP, in English, Trust for Regional Archaeological Survey, is specialised in non-destructive archaeological investigations, in particular in rural areas.
2 ARCHIS is an abbreviation, in Dutch as well as in English, for archaeological information system. The ARCHIS project is a Dutch archaeological centre of expertise in which participate the Rijksdienst voor het Oudheidkundig Bodemonderzoek and the archaeological departments of the Universities of Amsterdam, Groningen, and Leiden.

Streekmuseum Opsterland Mr De Boer. I am grateful for the fact that they admitted me to their collections and answered many annoying questions. Also several local archaeologists kindly showed me their collections. Of those I want to thank Mr Ley (Leeuwarden) and Mr and Mrs Van der Burg (Selmien) for their benevolence. At several points in time, I have received guidance from my colleagues. P. Cleveringa (Rijks Geologische Dienst, Haarlem) and Dr W.A. Casparie (Biologisch Archeologisch Instituut, Groningen University) helped planning the coring campaign near Joure and interpreting the results. Dr J. Griede, Dr O. van de Plassche, Professor W. Roeleveld (Instituut voor Aardwetenschappen, Vrije Universiteit, Amsterdam), and M.W. ter Wee (Rijks Geologische Dienst, Oosterwolde office) have contributed by discussing palaeogeograhical problems. In this respect, especially Dr van de Plassche has been of great assistance. Professor C. Bakels, E. Drenth, J. Kolen, Professor L.P. Louwe Kooijmans, Professor J.D. van der Waals, and Dr H. Zimmermann were much valued sparring partners in discussions on archaeological and theoretical issues.

An incredible amount of time and energy has been dedicated to the task of producing the maps and drawings for this publication. Since January 1990, when the manuscripts were ready, several draughtsmen have worked on the project. In Leiden, I. Stoepker and H. de Lorm prepared the first draft that was used for the dissertation. Between April 1991 and February 1995 M. Ghars of the Rijksdienst voor het Oudheidkundig Bodemonderzoek in Amersfoort adapted all the drawings for the present version. The planning and supervision of the draught work, by no means an easy job, was skilfully executed by G.H. Scheepstra. Especially the production of the colour drawings has a history of its own, in which M. Ghars and S.J.A. Kuppens, the photographer who had to redo his work over and over again because of our little alterations in size, presentation, etc., were the most important actors.

Last but not least I want to thank my translators and editor. It was a long haul! First I revised my own text and afterwards J.F. van Regteren Altena read my Dutch text with painstaking precision. He cleaned out many inconsistencies that were still present. Subsequently, from 1992 to 1994, the manuscript was translated by Nancy Forest-Flier. This was a difficult task, especially since she was not familiar with the specialised geological and archaeological language that I used. The end result was again scrutinized by J.F. van Regteren Altena and by Karen Waugh and Marieke Groot. Although sometimes his drive for grammatical and technical precision was difficult to put up with, I am very grateful for the work that François has done. When he retires, the ROB will undoubtedly lose one of the best editors in the field.

The text is a slightly revised version of the original dissertation. It was submitted for translation in 1992. Due to problems of different character the translated manuscript could only be sent to the printer in 1997. Publications that appeared after the revision of the book are not considered. The three appendices of the original dissertation, Finds Catalogue, Catalogue of *Terpen* and Coins, and Typology and Dating of Axes of Flint and other Types of Stone, have not been included in the English edition of the book.

Chapter 1

Introduction and objectives

1.1 INTRODUCTION

This study covers an investigation of the archaeological evidence for occupation in an area designated as the western part of the Frisian-Drentian plateau (fig. 1). The Frisian-Drentian plateau is that part of the northern Netherlands in which the substratum was chiefly formed during the Pleistocene, under glacial and periglacial conditions. Little of it is visible on the surface today, since the Frisian part of the boulder clay plateau, in particular, was largely covered with organic and clastic sediments during the Holocene.

The study area is contained more or less within natural borders. The western and northern borders are for the most part defined by the constantly shifting coastline and adjoining tidal flat and peat areas. The eastern border, viewed technically, is formed by the 225 abscissa of the Netherlands National Grid. In landscape terms, this border is formed by the valley of the Peizerdiep, the Fochtelooër and Smildiger Venen, and the valley of the Oude Vaart. The southern border follows the heights of the plateau to the 530 ordinate. The area covers the Province of Friesland and small parts of the Provinces of Groningen, Drenthe, and Overijssel.

The subject central to this study is closely related to the Holocene genesis of the western part of the Frisian-Drentian plateau. The plateau changed slowly but surely from a wooded region to a vast marsh, a broad, impassable zone between the higher sandy grounds and the coast. This 'drowning' of the area should be seen as a long-term development, a process to which the population, over the course of time, had to accustom itself and ultimately had to yield. The central question then is, whether it is possible, with the help of archaeological data, to determine the reactions of the inhabitants of the plateau to the drowning of their territory.

The western part of the Frisian-Drentian plateau has already been discussed in numerous surveys.[1] These

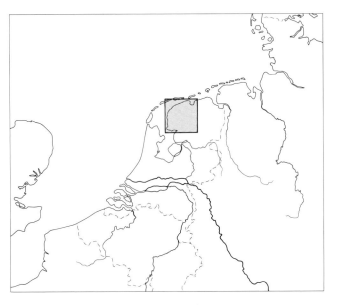

Figure 1 The Netherlands and its surroundings: the location of the study area, the western part of the Frisian-Drentian plateau.

works clearly show that the quality of information derived from most of the finds is low, that is to say, that many of the finds are without context, so-called stray finds. The northern part of the Netherlands is certainly no exception in this respect. On the contrary, this situation should be considered normal inside as well as outside the Netherlands. One of the objectives of this investigation is therefore to determine how to obtain optimal use from such data with low information quality, with the central question as set out above functioning as a restrictive framework.

In terms of chronology, the lower limit chosen is the

1 Pleyte 1877–1902; Boeles 1927; 1951; Elzinga 1964; Waterbolk 1965–66.

◁ Figure 2 The Netherlands: the location of the places, lakes, and peat areas mentioned in the text.

Legend in numerical order (from south to north and from west to east): 1 Baarlo; 2 Venlo; 3 Hoogeloon; 4 Horst; 5 Meerlo; 6 Overloon; 7 Mook; 8 Oss; 9 Molenaarsgraaf; 10 Bergschenhoek; 11 Groenlo; 12 Drakenstein; 13 Hilversum; 14 Laren; 15 Vaassen; 16 Vasse; 17 Spoolde; 18 Swifterbant; 19 Heemse; 20 Urk; 21 Coevorden; 22 De Gaste; 23 Vollenhove; 24 Hoogkarspel; 25 Bovenkarspel; 26 Meppel; 27 Hoogeveen; 28 Aartswoud; 29 Ruinen; 30 Onna; 31 Darp; 32 Havelte; 33 Noordbarge; 34 Kolhorn; 35 Steenwijk; 36 Uffelte; 37 Emmen; 38 Emmerhout; 39 Steenwijkerwold; 40 Uffelterveen; 41 Wijster; 42 Eesveen; 43 Dwingeloo; 44 Oude Mirdum; 45 Valthe; 46 Vledder; 47 Wapse; 48 Bakhuizen; 49 Rijs; 50 Vinkega; 51 Vledderveen; 52 Doldersum; 53 Elp; 54 Balk; 55 Hijken; 56 Tjerkgaast; 57 Tjeukermeer; 58 Fluessen; 59 Slotermeer; 60 St. Nicolaasga; 61 Oldeberkoop; 62 Heegermeer; 63 Nannewijd; 64 Heerenveen; 65 Appelscha; 66 Smilde; 67 Drouwen; 68 Workum; 69 Joure; 70 Oudegaasterbrekken; 71 Oudega; 72 Jutrijp; 73 Oosterwolde; 74 Fochteloo; 75 Oppenhuizen; 76 Akmarijp; 77 Gorredijk; 78 Weper; 79 Fochtelooër Veen; 80 Donkerbroek; 81 Peelo; 82 Sneek; 83 Gasteren; 84 Oldeboorn; 85 Haule; 86 Zeijen; 87 Anloo; 88 Den Burg; 89 Makkum; 90 Bolsward; 91 Wijnjeterp; 92 Een; 93 Bakkeveen; 94 Vries; 95 Witmarsum; 96 Rauwerd; 97 Selmien; 98 Zurich; 99 Wommels; 100 Drachten; 101 Tolsum; 102 Eernewoude; 103 De Legauke; 104 Jorwerd; 105 Wartena; 106 De Leijen; 107 Marum; 108 deleted; 109 Garijp; 110 Opende; 111 Bergumermeer; 112 Leeuwarden; 113 Veenwouden; 114 Visvliet; 115 Grijpskerk; 116 Vrouwenparochie; 117 Tergracht; 118 Steenendam; 119 Kollum; 120 Rinsumageest; 121 Westergeest; 122 Engwierum; 123 Ezinge; 124 Bornwird; 125 Dokkum; 126 Oostrum; 127 Hiaure; 128 Middelstum; 129 Ternaard; 130 Bollingawier.

Legend in alphabetical order: Aartswoud 28; Akmarijp 76; Anloo 87; Appelscha 65; Baarlo 1; Bakhuizen 48; Bakkeveen 93; Balk 54; Bergschenhoek 10; Bergumermeer 111; Bollingawier 130; Bolsward 90; Bornwird 124; Bovenkarspel 25; Coevorden 21; Darp 31; De Gaste 22; De Legauke 103; De Leien 106; Den Burg 88; Dokkum 125; Doldersum 52; Donkerbroek 80; Drachten 100; Drakenstein 12; Drouwen 67; Dwingeloo 43; Een 92; Eernewoude 102; Eesveen 42; Elp 53; Emmen 37; Emmerhout 38; Engwierum 122; Ezinge 123; Fluessen 58; Fochtelooër Veen 79; Fochteloo 74; Garijp 109; Gasteren 83; Gorredijk 77; Grijpskerk 115; Groenlo 11; Haule 85; Havelte 32; Heegermeer 62; Heemse 19; Heerenveen 64; Hiaure 127; Hijken 55; Hilversum 13; Hoogeloon 3; Hoogeveen 27; Hoogkarspel 24; Horst 4; Jorwerd 104; Joure 69; Jutrijp 72; Kolhorn 34; Kollum 119; Laren 14; Leeuwarden 112; Makkum 89; Marum 107; Meerlo 5; Meppel 26; Middelstum 128; Molenaarsgraaf 9; Mook 7; Nannewijd 63; Noordbarge 33; Oldeberkoop 61; Oldeboorn 84; Onna 30; Oosterwolde 73; Oostrum 126; Opende 110; Oppenhuizen 75; Oss 8; Oude Mirdum 44; Oudega 71; Oudegaasterbrekken 70; Overloon 6; Peelo 81; Rauwerd 96; Rijs 49; Rinsumageest 120; Ruinen 29; Selmien 97; Slotermeer 59; Smilde 66; Sneek 82; Spoolde 17; St. Nicolaasga 60; Steenendam 118; Steenwijk 35; Steenwijkerwold 39; Swifterbant 18; Tergracht 117; Ternaard 129; Tjerkgaast 56; Tjeukermeer 57; Tolsum 101; Uffelte 36; Uffelterveen 40; Urk 20; Vaassen 15; Valthe 45; Vasse 16; Veenwouden 113; Venlo 2; Vinkega 50; Visvliet 114; Vledder 46; Vledderveen 51; Vollenhove 23; Vries 94; Vrouwenparochie 116; Wapse 47; Wartena 105; Weper 78; Westergeest 121; Wijnjeterp 91; Wijster 41; Witmarsum 95; Wommels 99; Workum 68; Zeijen 86; Zurich 98.

beginning of the Neolithic and the upper limit the Early Middle Ages. The Neolithic is chosen because, on the one hand, the most radical changes in the landscape have occurred since the Middle and Late Neolithic and, on the other hand, because the investigation is intended to concentrate primarily on sedentary communities. The upper limit is determined by developments in occupation on the sandy grounds. In the Early Middle Ages occupation can be demonstrated in only a single region. Besides a tendency for archaeological evidence of occupation to decline in the 5th and 6th century, landscape developments also played a role in this respect. In the regions which remained inhabited, a general continuity can be seen until the Middle Ages. These regions also form the nucleus for other new developments which fall outside the framework of this investigation.[2]

I.2 OBJECTIVES OF THE INVESTIGATION

The first part of this study focuses on the inventory and evaluation of the available data in museums and private collections. These data form the basis for a number of distribution maps (Chapters I–3; maps I–VIII).
In view of landscape developments on the Frisian-Drentian plateau, it is clear that the archaeological distribu-

2 Waterbolk 1982; 1987a.

tion maps are but a strongly distorted reflection of the actual situation. Therefore, before a critical interpretation of the visible patterns can be undertaken, it is necessary to analyse the severity of the distortion. This means that the problem of site formation must play a significant role in the assessment. Although a great deal of work has been carried out on investigations at the site level (particularly in America), methods for analysing on the regional level are absent. The first part of this study is therefore concerned with devising a method for processing site-formation factors in the analysis of distribution maps. This method has been called map formation analysis (Chapters 4–6).

Only after such an analysis is completed, can the distribution maps be used as a basis for general statements about the occupation history of the Frisian-Drentian plateau. For the regions where the distribution of find-spots can be demonstrated to be a more or less trustworthy reflection of the original occupation, an attempt will be made to describe and to clarify the processes of cultural change. On the one hand, connections are made between these processes and cultural changes of a more general nature. On the other hand, an attempt is made to reveal the extent to which the special situation of a slowly drowning occupation area played a role in specific cultural developments (Chapters 7 and 8).

There are various models which can be used to predict the reaction of cultural systems under such circumstances. With most of these, the reduced carrying capacity of the environment is emphasized, as well as the resulting economic, social, and political tension. One of the models which describes which mechanisms are at work is Waterbolk's theory of adaptation groups.[3] Numerous other models, however, have been formulated to 14describe reactions to environmental stress. Examples of these are intensification of production, tribal wars with the resulting development of social stratification, the appearance of hierarchical means of decision-making and intensified ceremonial behaviour, ecological specification, economic diversification, storage of foodstuffs, surplus conversion, and increased social interaction.[4] The book concludes with a discussion of to what extent these models can be considered applicable to the Frisian-Drentian plateau (Chapter 9).

1.3 GENESIS OF THE STUDY AREA

1.3.1 *Pleistocene*

The boulder clay of the Frisian-Drentian plateau, belonging to the Drente Formation, was deposited as ground moraine in the Saalian by the Scandinavian ice-cap, the southern extent of which reached the Haarlem–Nijmegen line (fig. 4).[5] The southern border of the boulder clay plateau, however, lies along the Gaasterland–Steenwijk–Meppel–Hoogeveen–Coevorden line. This border is characterized by low, ice-pushed boulder clay ridges which have relatively steep slopes in the direction of the ice-marginal valley of the rivers Rhine and Vecht, located along the southern edge of the plateau. The ice-pushed boulder clay ridges of Gaasterland and Steenwijk were formed by the spreading out of glacial snouts during a period when the ice-front was relatively inactive.[6]

The ice-cap coverage which occurred during the Saalian is divided into five phases of advance and retreat. Only in phase II did the ice reach its southernmost limit along the Haarlem–Nijmegen line. The ice-pushed ridges and glacial troughs in the middle Netherlands were also formed during this phase. During phase III, the ice front retreated to the Castricum–Hoorn–Urk–Vollenhove–Ootmarsum line and the ice-pushed ridges of the east Netherlands, among others, were formed. In phase IV, the ice-cap front remained stationary along the Texel–Wieringen–Gaasterland–Steenwijk line, and in some places lobes of ice lying in front of the ice-cap pushed up ground moraines which had been formed during previous phases. The glacial snouts themselves left depressions which in later periods filled up with coversand and peat. An example of this is the depression which now holds the Fluessen and the Heegermeer.[7] The rivers Rhine and Vecht held a western course and eroded a deep valley in front of the ice-pushed ridges which now forms the southern border of the plateau. In phase V, the ice-cap retreated further, just to the north-east of the Dutch territory. Glacier snouts formed the landscape of Westerwolde, while in a north-westerly direction the Hunze eroded a deep valley bounded on the west side by the Hondsrug. In the north and west the transitions are less pronounced. On the north side the plateau drops

3 Waterbolk 1974; 1979; 1987a.
4 Boserup 1965; Carneiro 1970; Johnson 1982; Minnis 1985.
5 Jelgersma & Breewer 1975.

6 The description of the stages of ice-cap coverage is taken from Ter Wee 1962 and Jelgersma & Breewer 1975.
7 Ter Wee 1975.

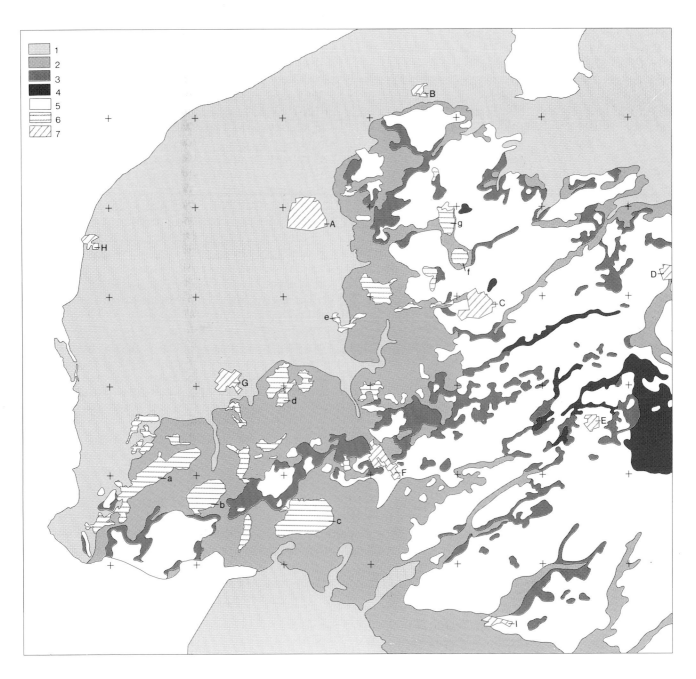

Figure 3 The western part of the Frisian-Drentian plateau: the major physiographic entities and the location of major places and lakes.

Legend: I clay; 2 clay on peat; 3 fen peat; 4 bog peat; 5 sand; 6 lake; 7 built-up area; A Leeuwarden; B Dokkum; C Drachten; D Marum; E Oosterwolde; F Heerenveen; G Bolsward; H Harlingen; I Steenwijk; a Fluessen and Heegermeer; b Slotermeer; c Tjeukemeer; d Sneekermeer; e Pikmeer; f De Leijen; g Bergumermeer.
After Soil Map of the Netherlands Scale I:200 000.

gradually in the direction of the Waddenzee until it reaches the Vrouwenparochie–Leeuwarden–Sneek line. East of this line the plateau lies above 10 m -NAP (Normaal Amsterdams Peil, Dutch Datum Level), to the west a quick transition takes place reaching a zone with depths between 19 and 26 m -NAP.[8] This depression extends to the Sneek–Bolsward–Zurich line. South of this the plateau again rises in the direction of the ice-pushed heights of Gaasterland.

Following the Saalian a warmer period occurred, the Eemian. The melting of the ice-cap caused the sea level to rise to just below the current level, and continental as well as marine sediments were deposited. In the lower parts, west of the Leeuwarden–Sneek line, the sediments were marine, of which the upper side reached depths of 10–15 m -NAP.[9] Continental Eemian deposits are in evidence near Rauwerd, among other places, reaching a depth of 9 m -NAP and can probably also be found in glacial troughs.[10]

During the cold phase which followed, the Weichselian, the Scandinavian ice-cap reached its southernmost boundary in Denmark and north Germany. The largest part of the relief of the plateau as we know it today came into existence in this period.[11] The rivers Drait, Oude Diep, Boorne, Tjonger, Linde, Steenwijker Aa, Oude Vaart had already cut deep courses early in the Weichselian, and as this glacial passed they filled up with sand and peat. According to Ter Wee, the parallel south-west–north-east orientation of the valleys is linked with the direction of ice-cap flow in the Saalian. The rivers thus follow in part the course of older depressions.[12]

The Weichselian deposits belong to the Twente Formation. Their origin could either have been fluvio-periglacial (brook and basin deposits) or aeolian (coversands). In the low regions to the west of the Leeuwarden–Sneek line mostly basin deposits formed, laid on top of Eemian deposits. They consist of fine sand supplied by brooks from the south and south-west as well as probably from the east.[13] The top of these deposits is in general lower than 5 m -NAP. With the exceptions of a few local elevations around Bolsward and Witmarsum, they reach higher levels first to the south from the Sneek–Bolsward–Zurich line and to the east from the Sneek–Leeuwarden line. On these higher parts the Twente Forma-

tion consist of coversands. They cover the boulder clay surface with a layer that varies in thickness from 1 m to 25 m (in depressions) and is responsible for the current topography. The coversands are divided into two phases of deposition. In the Middle Weichselian the loamy Older Coversands were laid down, followed by the Younger Coversands in the Late Weichselian. In this last period, along the edge of the low-lying western part a high belt of Younger Coversands was deposited which even shut off the valleys of the rivers Drait, Boorne, and Tjonger in numerous places.[14]

Under the Weichselian periglacial conditions, which made the formation of aeolian deposits from dry sea and river beds possible on a grand scale, pingos also developed. Today these pingos are still visible in the landscape as *dobben*, round or oval pits with diameters of 350 m maximum. *Dobben* exist in great numbers on the Frisian part of the Frisian-Drentian plateau; however, not all of them are pingos: some are wind-blown depressions filled with peat. Approximately 60 percent of the *dobben* lay between sand-dunes with peat-filled depressions under which a water-tight layer had formed.[15] For this reason, they are important sources for vegetation reconstruction on the higher parts of the plateau.

1.3.2 *Holocene*

After the Weichselian cold period the climate again grew warmer and the Holocene commenced (around 10 000 b.p.). The different ice-caps gradually melted and the sea level rose as a consequence. At first this occurred rather quickly but became more gradual as time passed. The rise of the sea level, which was especially influenced by the melting ice-caps but also affected by the sinking of the sea floor, determined developments in the Holocene. The Holocene developments are divided into transgressive and regressive phases. In a transgressive phase the sea pushes inland; in a regressive phase the continental deposits spread seawards. According to Zagwijn it is possible to trace a cyclic movement in these phases of 300–600 years, linked to climatic fluctuations. A deterioration of the climate would cause a rise in the tidal amplitude, precipitating a transgressive phase. Obviously, local factors and storm tides played as great a role. A lowering in the tidal amplitude made the devel-

---

8 Wensink 1958.
9 Ter Wee 1976.
10 Wensink 1958; Ter Wee 1976.
11 Steenbeek *et al.* 1981.

12 Ter Wee 1975.
13 Ter Wee 1976.
14 Cnossen 1971.
15 Steenbeek *et al.* 1981.

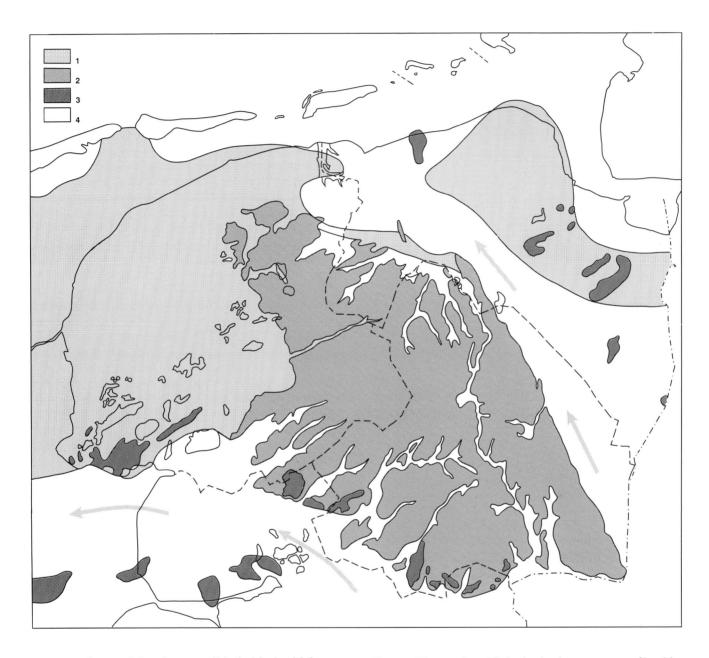

opment of coastal barriers possible behind which peat could expand during regressive phases.[16]

In the past it was believed that transgressions and regressions occurred at approximately the same time along the whole coastline. Detailed regional investigation has made clear, however, that although there is a certain correlation, local circumstances played an important role in the way in which transgressions and regressions have influenced coastal formation. Moreover, today the terms

Figure 4 The northern Netherlands: the occurrence of boulder clay within the Frisian-Drentian boulder clay plateau. Legend: 1 boulder clay deeper than 2 m below the surface; 2 boulder clay less than 2 m below the surface; 3 ice-pushed boulder clay on the surface; 4 prehistoric river valleys of the Vecht (south) and the Hunze (east). After Jelgersma & Breeuwer in Zagwijn & Van Staalduijnen 1975.

16 Zagwijn 1986, 13.

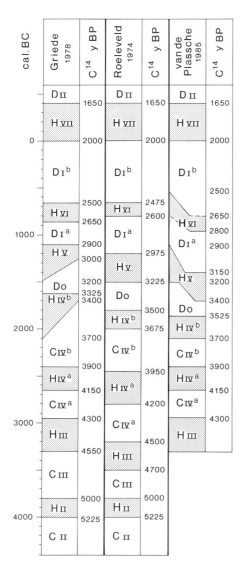

Figure 5 Chronological-stratigraphical division of the Holocene in the northern Netherlands. After Griede 1978 and Van de Plassche 1985.

here, with particular attention given to those occurring in the northern Netherlands.[17] The dates of the various phases are provided in figure 5, in which the chronologies of north-east Friesland and north Groningen are compared with each other, supplemented by the correcting view of Van de Plassche on the north-east Frisian dates.

Roeleveld and Griede distinguish the Wold Formation (the lower peat and the surface peat) and the Groningen Formation (the clastic sediments) in the Holocene which together form the North Sea group. The lower peat lies on top of the older Pleistocene deposits and under the clastic sediments, and began to grow in several places during the Atlantic (after 8000 b.p.). The lower peat of this age occurs only in the north-east of the study area. Pre-boreal peat deposits are evident only in a few deeper-lying depressions, such as in north-west Friesland near Bollingawier.[18] Usually the peat-formation began as oligotrophic, but became mesotrophic or eutrophic as conditions became wetter, or as the peat was broken down by marine transgressions.

The first marine influence is noticeable shortly after 6500 b.p. in the north-east and the outermost north-west of Friesland.[19] In the latter area the sea probably pushed inwards via the Boorne valley, which at that time followed a north-westerly course.[20] In middle Friesland, in the lower areas with poor drainage, bog peat had probably already begun to grow locally.

Hereafter followed a short regressive interval (Holland I) in which (reed) peat formed in some places on the Calais I deposits. This came to an end with the Calais II transgressive interval, during which in any case marine influence increased considerably in the low north-west. Marine deposits from this period are encountered near Jorwerd in a channel of the Boorne.[21]

Zagwijn reconstructs in map 3 of his series of maps illustrating the development of the landscape of the Holocene part of the Netherlands a fenland around the area of marine influence on both sides of the 6 m -NAP level of the Pleistocene surface and round this a rather broad raised bog. However, when we follow the 4.75 m -NAP contour for the inland border of this peat area, the extension of the raised bog in Zagwijn's model is reconstructed too far south and east. This also applies to the reconstruction of his maps 4, 5, and 6.[22]

'transgressive interval' and 'regressive interval' are preferred to emphasize the picture of fluctuations occurring within a general pattern of the rising sea level.

A brief description of the Holocene developments follows

17 This description is chiefly based on the work of Griede 1978, Roeleveld 1974, Ter Wee 1976, and Zagwijn 1986.
18 9.90 m -NAP; Griede 1978, table 8.
19 Calais I deposits; Griede 1978, 82.

20 Ter Wee 1975.
21 Ter Wee 1976, 168, fig. 34.
22 Zagwijn 1986; Roeleveld 1974, 96.

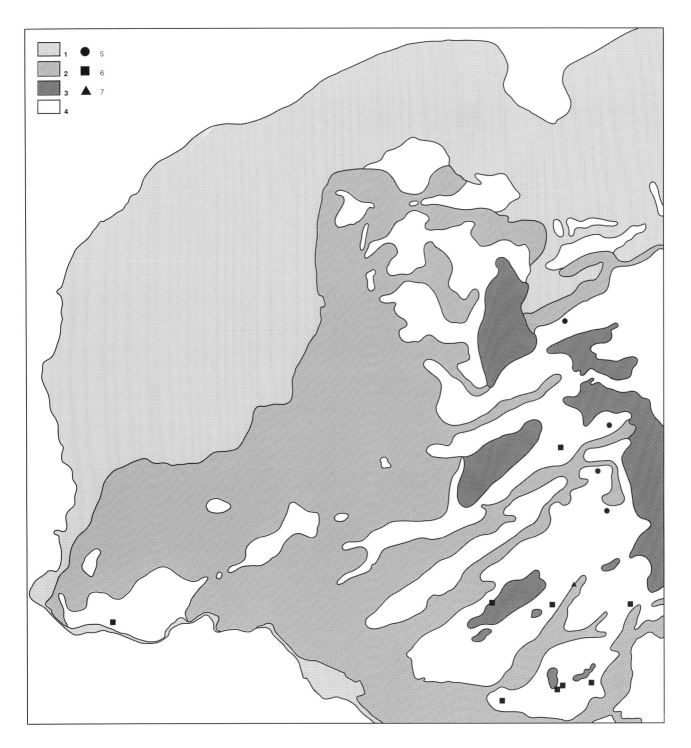

Figure 6 The western part of the Frisian-Drentian plateau: detail from the first archaeological map of the Netherlands.

Legend: 1 clay; 2 fen peat; 3 bog peat; 4 sand; 5 Stone Age findspot; 6 Bronze Age findspot; 7 Iron Age findspot. After Pleyte 1877.

In the north-east the marine influence reached roughly to the Ternaard–Dokkum–Oostrum–Engwierum line, where a narrow peat area divided the tidal flat area from the higher sandy grounds.[23] This situation remained more or less stable until the Calais IVa transgressive interval when the sea, notably in the north-east, pushed further inland, although the rather steep gradients of the subsoil precluded a fast advancement. The developments in the west are difficult to reconstruct for these periods. The date of 4385 ± 130 b.p. for the end of the peat formation at Makkum[24] indicates that locally the marine influence had already penetrated during the Calais IVa transgressive interval. However, the maximum spreading of marine influence most likely dates from the later Calais IVb interval.[25]

During the Holland IVa regressive interval peat formation began on a large scale on the Calais IVa deposits. The great expansion of peat formation seawards, in proportion to the preceding regressive interval, is probably linked to the deceleration in the rise of the sea level.[26] Just as in the north-east, an estuary maintained itself in the western part of Friesland round the former mouth of the Boorne,[27] but the southern extent of the marine influence is not known. In the following transgressive interval (Calais IVb) the sea pushed several kilometres into the peat area in the eastern part of this estuary.[28] The Calais IV deposits reached their maximum extension at the Makkum–Sneek line.[29] In north-east Friesland and north Groningen the peat area was less severely affected and the sea claimed only a small amount of territory. During the Holland IVb regressive interval, the peat expanded in north Friesland over a larger area than in the previous interval.[30] Peat formation also took place in the Lauwerszee area. The depression between Visvliet and Grijpskerk, and possibly the valley of the Oude Riet as well, became a part of the eastern estuary in the Calais IV transgressive interval and probably remained so during the Holland IV regressive interval.[31] Peat formation also extended over the tidal flat deposits in the west and south,[32] although the precise expansions can no longer

be determined due to erosion in the Dunkirk 0 transgressive interval in particular. In this period, according to Zagwijn's reconstruction (map 5), all of Gaasterland was already cut off from the rest of the plateau by bog peat formation. This reconstruction cannot be correct, because the ridge running north of the Tjonger over St. Nicolaasga and Tjerkgaast was not yet covered by peat at this time and formed a rather broad, dry zone.[33]

After this period of rapid peat formation, resulting in what was formerly known as surface peat, a series of new transgressive intervals began: the Dunkirk intervals. The first, the Dunkirk 0 transgressive interval, is characterized as highly erosive, at least in western Friesland. Broad inlets and four wide erosion channels of 15–20 m deep developed, into which sand was deposited.[34] In the north and north-west, the Dunkirk 0 influence was also clearly noticeable; the sea pushed inland via stream valleys. Even so, marine influence was weaker than in the west and the peat area remained unaffected in large areas, particularly in the north.[35] Roeleveld is of the opinion that, through the deceleration in the rise of the sea level and the resulting blockage of the drainage system, the fen peat could have developed inland into bog peat and could thereby expand more vigorously than in the previous period. The deceleration in the rise of the sea level also led to the appearance of new land and the extension of peat formation in the following interval, the Holland V regressive interval.

The gradual development of a habitable salt-marsh area, however, only occurred at the end of the Dunkirk Ia transgressive interval.[36] That period saw an end to peat formation in many regions and the development of extensive salt-marsh areas along the coast.[37] The situation in the west is difficult to reconstruct because the division between the Dunkirk Ia deposits and the Dunkirk II deposits is barely perceptible and no regression levels have developed between them. The Dunkirk Ia transgressive interval must have been one of calm flooding from the Boorne channel, which was still present in the west. The only further indication for this transgressive

23 Griede 1978, fig. 34; Roeleveld 1974, fig. 58.
24 GrN 6138; Ter Wee 1976, 72.
25 Ter Wee 1976, fig. 35.
26 Roeleveld 1974, 99.
27 Griede 1978, 86; Ter Wee 1975, 338.
28 Griede 1978, 86, fig. 37.
29 Ter Wee 1976, fig. 35.
30 Griede 1978, fig. 37.

31 Roeleveld 1974, 100.
32 Ter Wee 1976, 72, fig. 41.
33 See Chapter 3.
34 Ter Wee 1976, 34, fig. 10a; Zagwijn 1986, map 6.
35 Griede 1978, fig. 38; Roeleveld 1974, fig. 62.
36 Roeleveld 1974, 104, note 285.
37 Griede 1978, fig. 39; Roeleveld 1974, fig. 63.

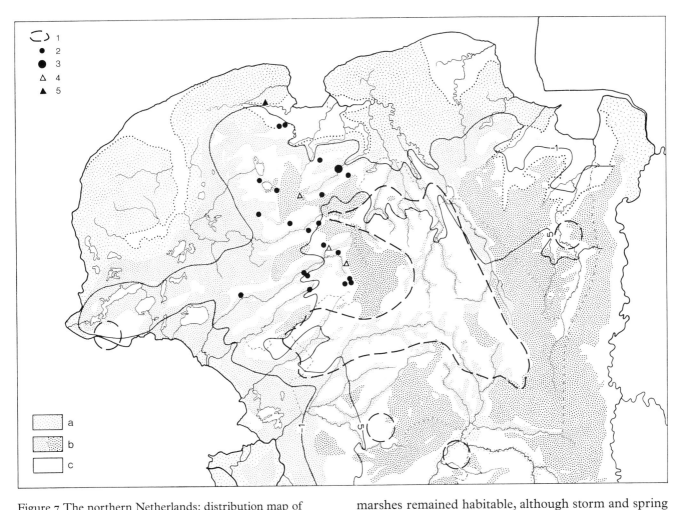

Figure 7 The northern Netherlands: distribution map of Funnel Beaker culture axes in the Province of Friesland. Legend: a clay; b peat; c sand; I area within which graves of the Funnel Beaker culture are found (megalithic and flat graves); 2 flint axe; 3 hoard of flint axes; 4 hammer axe; 5 Rössen-type adze. According to Waterbolk 1965–66, figure I.

interval is the extension along the Workum–Oudega–Jutrijp–Oppenhuizen line.[38] During the Holland VI regressive interval, almost the entire salt-marsh area rose above the high tide level. For the first time, peat formation did not take place and the salt-marshes became suitable for occupation. Peat continued to accumulate only along the land-side of the peat area, perhaps at a faster rate than previously caused by stagnation of the drainage.

During the following transgressive interval the salt-marshes remained habitable, although storm and spring tides may have led to temporary flooding and possibly to local catastrophes. However, by rebuilding houses on the remains of ruined structures which had been levelled with layers of sods, the inhabitants developed dwelling mounds, or *terpen*, which enabled them to adapt to these circumstances. During the Dunkirk Ib transgressive interval, deep channel systems developed in the north and a large section of the peat area became covered with clay sediments (clay on peat in the legend of fig. 3). From this period onwards, the Lauwerszee constituted a permanent part of the tidal flat area.[39] The developments in the west during the Dunkirk Ib transgressive interval are still difficult to determine. A rough reconstruction of the salt-marsh areas from this period can be made based on the distribution of the *terpen*, although this is

38 Ter Wee 1976, 82.

39 Griede 1978, fig. 40.

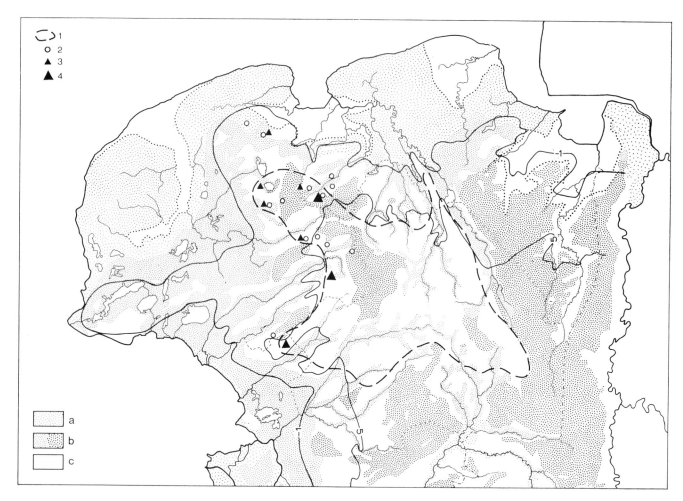

Figure 8 The northern Netherlands: distribution map of the Single Grave culture in the Province of Friesland (with the exception of one findspot). Legend: a clay; b peat; c sand; 1 area within which Single Grave culture graves are found (barrows and flat graves); 2 hammer axe; 3 barrow; 4 group of barrows. According to Waterbolk 1966, figure 2.

no simple matter because of the lack of datable archaeological material from most of the *terpen*. The Middelzee was almost certainly present in rudimentary form, while a precursor of the Marne must also have existed as an erosion channel.[40] The inland border of the peat areas from this period onwards is difficult to estimate, however. The pattern is limited by local circumstances in particular. A more extensive discussion of this can be found in Chapter 3.

40 Cf. Zagwijn 1986, preface and map.

After the beginning of the current era came the Dunkirk II and Dunkirk III transgressive intervals, during which seawater could penetrate inland predominantly via the Middelzee. Since these changes along the coastal area do not fall within the framework of this study (at least they are no longer expressed in the palaeogeographic reconstructions), this last part of the development history will not be discussed.

1.4 SHORT HISTORY OF THE ARCHAEOLOGICAL INVESTIGATION

The western part of the Frisian-Drentian plateau has been the subject of many archaeological studies. Most of these were based on a survey of the data which were kept in the Fries Museum in Leeuwarden. The first publication of Frisian material was offered in the book

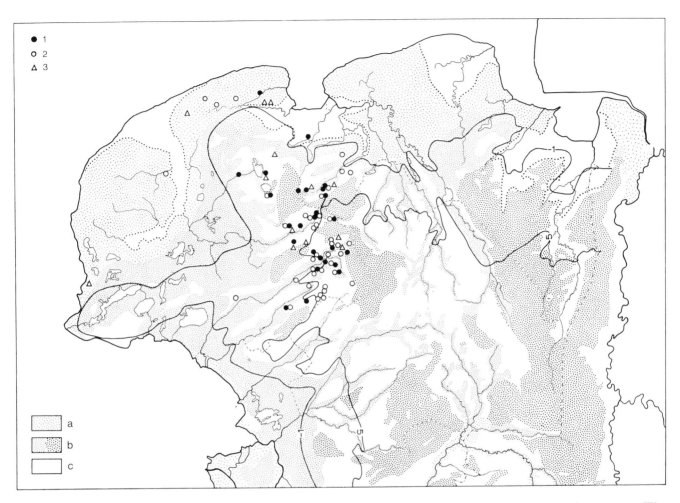

Figure 9 The northern Netherlands: distribution map of the remaining types of axes found in the Province of Friesland. Legend: a clay; b peat; c sand; 1 flint axe; 2 axe of other material; 3 perforated axe or adze. According to Waterbolk 1966, figure 3.

Nederlandsche Oudheden by W. Pleyte.[41] Pleyte's work was chiefly based on the collections in the Rijksmuseum van Oudheden at Leiden (National Museum of Antiquities), where he worked from 1869 to 1903, presiding as director from 1891. However, he also visited and described provincial collections. For this reason his book gives a good overview of the number of findspots from the study area which were known at that time (fig. 6). It will come as no surprise to the Dutch reader

that the bulk of the known finds came from *terpen*. The digging of *terpen* for their phosphate-rich soil, to be used as artificial fertilizer in the lower areas and on the poor sandy soils, was well under way at the time. Of the countless finds which had been dug up since the beginning of the 19th century, many had already been brought into the Fries Museum. In Friesland in 1877 almost nothing was known of the older periods. One megalithic tomb, the *hunebed* from Rijs, had been known since the investigation of 1849.[42] The other *hunebed*, near Finkega, was described at the end of the 18th century, but was destroyed in order for the stone to be used in road construction and its location was forgotten. Van Giffen rediscovered it on the country estate 'de Eeze' near Steenwijk in the Province of Overijssel.[43] Pleyte

41 Pleyte 1877–1902.
42 Janssen 1850; Van Giffen 1924a.

43 Van Giffen 1924b.

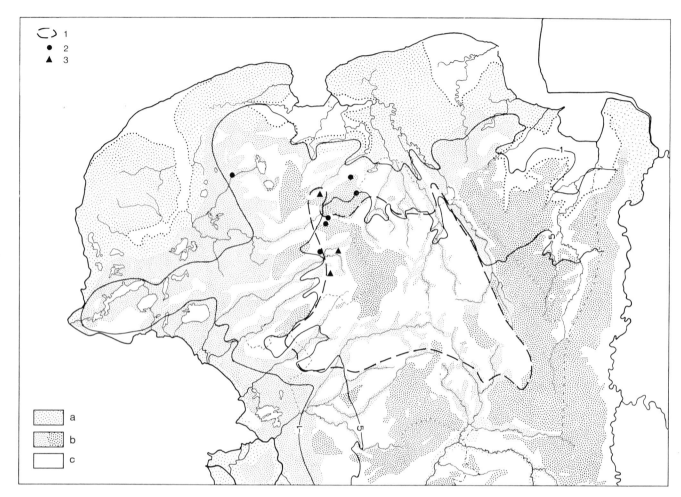

Figure 10 The northern Netherlands: distribution map of the barrows and bronze finds from the Early and Middle Bronze Age in the Province of Friesland. Legend: a clay; b peat; c sand; 1 area within which barrows of the Early and Middle Bronze Age are found; 2 bronze object; 3 barrow. According to Waterbolk 1966, figure 4.

further reported two moraine flint axes from the same period and two 'flint lanceheads', found in the peat near Oosterwolde and Haule, which are now believed to be flint daggers from the Early Bronze Age. Except for the point of a bronze object and a palstave from Marum, no other Bronze Age finds were known. Iron Age findspots were not encountered outside the *terpen* area, although a wooden road and a horse's hide, found in the peat near Appelscha, could be reckoned to belong to this period (or to the Bronze Age). Since neither the finds themselves nor their location can be retrieved, further clarity

in this matter is not available. Pleyte's work is accompanied by the first 'Archaeological Map of the Netherlands', at a scale of 1:200 000 (fig. 6). It is an accurate and valuable document for its time, not least because its topography is a generalized soil map.

In 1927, P.C.J.A. Boeles, curator of the archaeology section of the Fries Museum from 1897 to 1950, presented a new overview in his *Friesland tot de Elfde Eeuw*. He used the collections of the Fries Museum as his most important source, supplemented by finds from the 'Vereeniging voor Heimatstudie der Stellingwerven' in which the well-known amateur archaeologist H.J. Popping played a leading role. However, like Pleyte, Boeles had no training in archaeology and discussion of older occupation on the sandy grounds appears on only 22 of the 295 pages. The second, revised edition of 1951 offered little change in this area. Nevertheless, the number of finds known then which came from the Frisian sandy

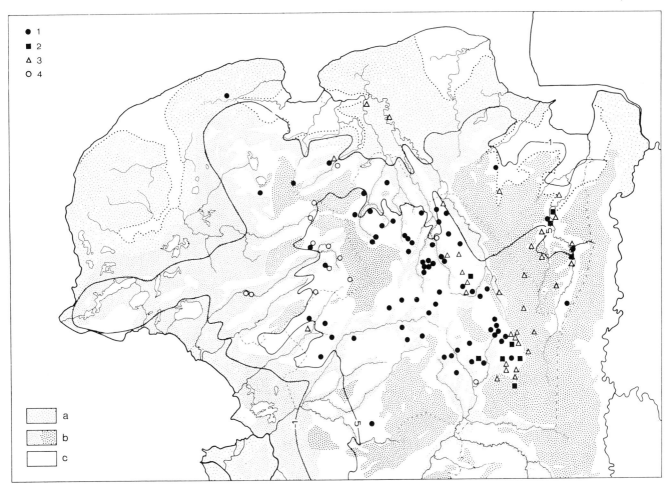

Figure 11 The northern Netherlands: distribution map of the urnfields, stone axes and bronze finds from the Late Bronze Age. Legend: a clay; b peat; c sand; 1 urnfield; 2 urnfield with keyhole-shaped ditches; 3 hammer axe of Muntendam type; 4 bronze find. According to Waterbolk 1966, figure 5.

grounds was too great to summarize here completely. This rapid increase was mostly the consequence of peat and heath reclamations and the activities of three men: Professor A.E. van Giffen, director of the Biologisch-Archaeologisch Instituut in Groningen, H.J. Popping, publisher of the *Ooststellingwerver Courant* and bookseller in Oosterwolde, and J. Siebinga, physician in Marum. The activities of G.H. Voerman from Havelte are regarded as having set the scene for the Drenthe part of the study area, although they cover only a small part of it.

Professor van Giffen had founded the Biologisch-Archaeologisch Instituut in 1920 and was kept informed, mainly by Popping, of new finds and the reclamation of threatened monuments around Oosterwolde. So it happened that during the 1920s Van Giffen investigated an urnfield and a number of barrows which lay in the heath reclamation area. The well-known investigation of the settlements near Fochteloo, discovered during peat reclamation activities, was also a result of Popping's attentiveness.[44] In the region round Oosterwolde Popping was viewed as The Archaeologist and received or bought finds from everybody. He regularly set to work himself, beseeching labourers working on the heath and peat reclamation to warn him if they found anything, and publicizing his findings in the *Ooststellingwerver Courant* and in other separate publications produced by the printers Popping and Van der Meer.[45] The finds were exhibited

44 Van Giffen 1924b; 1929; 1954; 1958.
45 Popping 1929; 1931; 1932a; 1932b; 1933a; 1933b; 1933c; 1934; n.d.

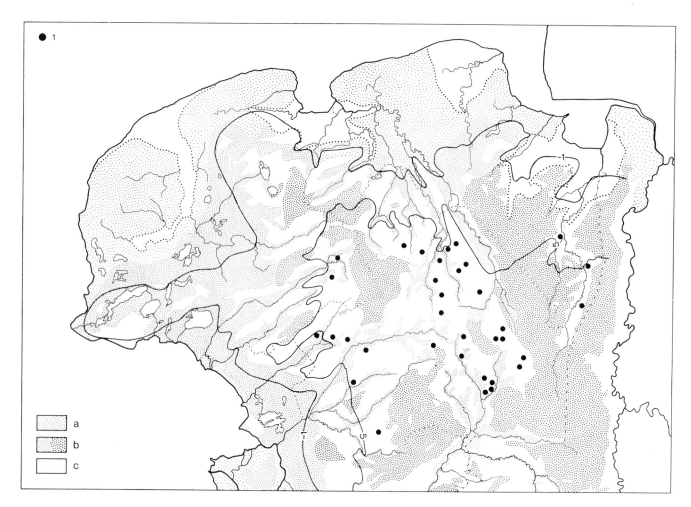

Figure 12 The northern Netherlands: distribution map of Harpstedt type urns. Legend: a clay; b peat; c sand; 1 Harpstedt type urn. According to Waterbolk 1966, figure 6.

in the collection of the 'Vereeniging voor Heimatstudie der Stellingwerven' in the agricultural school at Oldeberkoop[46] or sold to various museums. In connection with this work, Popping maintained extensive correspondence with the directors of the Biologisch-Archaeologisch Instituut, the Fries Museum, and the Rijksmuseum van Oudheden. This correspondence has been preserved in the archives of these institutions; it offers new insight into the find context or findspot of a number of otherwise undocumented finds. Reading the correspondence also reveals how it was possible that this digging in Friesland went back and forth between the Biologisch-Archaeologisch Instituut and the Rijksmuseum van Oudheden. It was a matter of Popping repeatedly changing his loyalties. For a long time he refused to have any contact with Van Giffen because, in Popping's opinion, Van Giffen had been rude to him.[47] Van Giffen had taken him to task over incompetent excavation practices.[48] Popping also believed that Van Giffen had waited too long to react to his urgent find reports. In the period

46 This society was founded by I. Bezema, engineer, and was dissolved in 1931. The collection had already been given on loan to the Fries Museum in 1929 (correspondence Fries Museum).
47 Correspondence BAI 2nd July 1930.
48 This involved an 'investigation' by Popping of a barrow near Langedijke where first a beaker was dug up. Some time later Popping sent in a flint blade which had been recovered from the excavated soil. This demonstration of inaccuracy had infuriated Van Giffen (correspondence Biologisch-Archaeologisch Instituut).

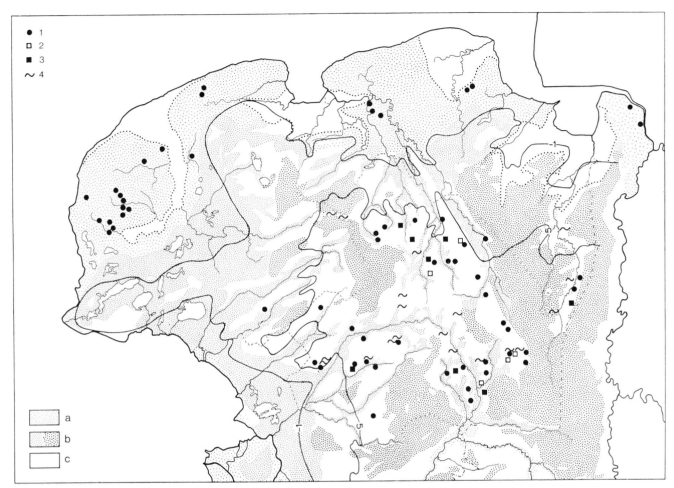

Figure 13 The northern Netherlands: distribution map of the Zeijen culture. Legend: a clay; b peat; c sand; 1 Ruinen-Wommels I and Ruinen-Wommels II type pottery; 2 cemetery with square ditches; 3 cemetery with square ditches with Ruinen-Wommels I type pottery; 4 double podsol. According to Waterbolk 1966, figure 7.

that followed Popping, however, maintained contact with H.J. Holwerda, director of the Rijksmuseum van Oudheden, who, because of existing rivalries within the archaeological world, was all too happy to encroach on Van Giffen's territory. So at the beginning of the thirties we find J.C. Bursch from the Rijksmuseum van Oudhe-

den excavating a number of barrows near Marum.[49] Also in this period a small number of investigations were undertaken by the Rijksmuseum van Oudheden at the Tjonger findspots, which had been discovered and acquired by Popping. When these relationships cooled again, Popping's finds went for a time to the Fries Museum and later to Groningen.[50]

Also important in drawing up a picture of the find distribution is the work of the physician J. Siebinga. Siebinga carried out field-surveys and investigations in the environment of Marum and Drachten. He discovered countless Mesolithic and Neolithic findspots. His collection was acquired by the Fries Museum in 1969. It is also

49 Bursch 1936.
50 That all this did not have a favourable effect on the documentation and storage of various finds should not surprise anyone. The Biologisch-Archaeologisch Instituut in particular

still contains undocumented finds from the Popping collection. Other find assemblages were apparently distributed to various museums.

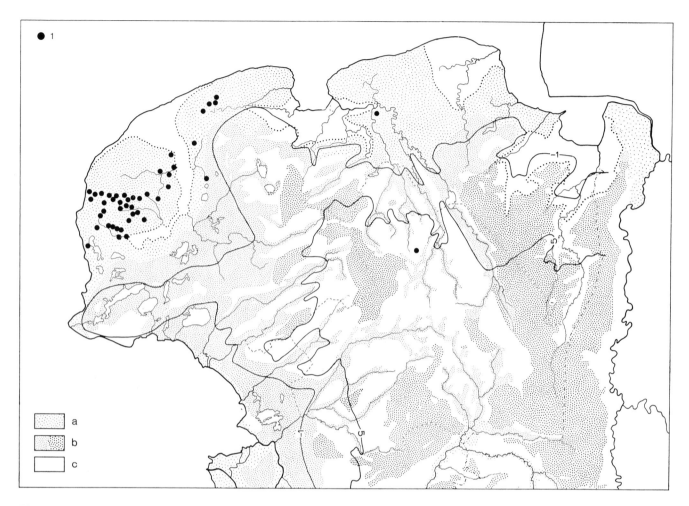

Figure 14 The northern Netherlands: distribution map of the Proto-Frisian culture. Legend: a clay; b peat; c sand; 1 Ruinen-Wommels III type pottery. According to Waterbolk 1966, figure 8.

known that Siebinga received artifacts from third parties, sometimes in exchange for medical treatment.[51] Like Popping, Siebinga published part of his investigations.[52]

During the 1960s, two summaries of the finds from the previous period were written. G. Elzinga, who became Friesland's first provincial archaeologist in 1959 as well as keeper of the archaeological department of the Fries Museum, published in 1964 *Fynsten ût Fryske groûn*.[53] In 1967 H.T. Waterbolk's *The Occupation of Friesland in the Prehistoric Period* appeared.[54] This last article, as the most recent and the most complete survey, formed the point of departure for the present study. For more than twenty years, the conclusions drawn in that article have formed the basis for thinking and writing about developments on the western part of the Frisian-Drentian plateau. For this reason, the trends which appeared to

51 In a daily report of the excavation of a barrow near Een, which in 1936 had already been 'investigated' by A. Bijma (also known under the name 'black Andries'), Van Giffen noted the following: Mr Bijma refused compensation for his help at the excavation of the 3rd of April because 'for his archaeological work he enjoyed free medical care from the physician J. Siebinga in Opende'. Van Giffen was set on the trail of the barrow by beaker sherds from the Siebinga collection, brought in by Bijma.

52 Siebinga 1944.

53 Elzinga 1964.

54 Waterbolk 1965–66.

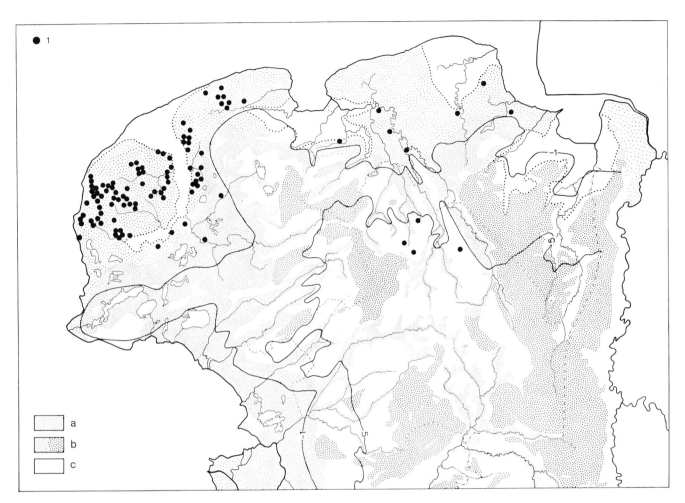

Figure 15 The northern Netherlands: distribution map of the Frisian culture. Legend: a clay; b peat; c sand; 1 *streepband* type pottery. According to Waterbolk 1966, figure 9.

be clearly present in 1966 will be discussed in greater detail below, using the original distribution maps (figs. 7–15) as points of reference.

The first map (fig. 7) shows the findspots of the artifacts which were attributed to the Funnel Beaker culture and one older find: a *Rössener Breitkeil*. A total of twenty flint axes and three knob-butted hammer-axes are known, mostly discovered as stray finds. According to Waterbolk, the distribution map shows that the Funnel Beaker culture occupation remained above the I m NAP contour. Then, in figure 9, the findspots of the artifacts are indicated which could be either of Middle Neolithic or Late Neolithic date. In any case, the picture reveals a

distribution restricted to the eastern part of the area, although the *hunebed* at Rijs (Gaasterland) points to a centre of activity outside the area.

In the period of the Single Grave culture (formerly Protruding Foot Beaker culture in the Netherlands; fig. 8) there was little change. The findspots lie in the same area, but Gaasterland is without finds and the inhabited area appears to have shrunken somewhat. Thirteen hammer-axes, two groups of barrows, and five individual barrows form the total number of datable findspots, apart from a number of flint and stone axes which can be assigned to this and the preceding period (fig. 9) but not to a particular culture.

In the Bronze Age drastic changes occurred: 'The inhabited area continues to shrink in the Bronze Age (fig. 10). Occupation maintained itself only in the Oosterwolde region, a district well drained by small streams and lying on high ground. Elsewhere the population was driven out by the peat-formation and the increase of the sea level.'[55]

The bronze axes and the Hallstatt sword (fig. 10), found in association with water, were interpreted as artifacts which had been lost by traders or smiths on their journeys along the rivers. The barrows all lie above the 5 m NAP contour and are concentrated in the area around Oosterwolde.

The Late Bronze Age showed another and, in a certain sense, contradictory picture (fig. 11). A few urnfields, in De Legauke and in Bornwird, were reported in the low-lying areas. The urnfield in Bornwird was even found to lie at 0 m NAP, the present average sea level. Waterbolk explained these low-lying cemeteries by pointing to developments in the Bronze Age in eastern West-Friesland where occupation from the Middle and Late Bronze Age on a former tidal flat area is known, in particular on top of low ridges, fossil channel, gully, and creek deposits.[56]

No finds are known from the sand regions in Friesland and Groningen from the period in which the urns of Harpstedt type were in use (fig. 12; c. 2600 b.p., beginning in Hallstatt C). Only Drenthe appears to have been inhabited, which, according to Waterbolk, leads to no other conclusion than: 'It can be assumed that peat-formation had reduced the area too drastically for agriculture and stockbreeding to survive. These areas remain more or less uninhabited until the Middle Ages.'[57]

In this period the coastal area was still uninhabited. The first colonization of the salt-marshes can be dated to the period 600–400 cal. BC (fig. 13), when people from the Zeijen culture in Drenthe migrated to the coastal areas of Friesland and Groningen.[58] In the following phase (fig. 14), that of the Proto-Frisian culture, it can be seen how the pottery style in the coastal area developed independently in the framework of the 'terpen culture' and during the Roman period became clearly recognizable as the Frisian culture (fig. 15).

The cultural history described above formed, in 1980, the basis for the formulation of the original premise of this study. The extent to which this picture of development can be maintained, or should be adjusted by the results of the current study, will be discussed in Chapters 8 and 9.

55 Waterbolk 1965–66, 22.
56 The district of West-Friesland is situated north of Amsterdam in the Province of Noord-Holland, not in the Province of Friesland.

57 Waterbolk 1965–66, 27.
58 Waterbolk 1962; Van Gijn & Waterbolk 1984.

Chapter 2

The data base

2.1 INTRODUCTION

The extent of the study area made it impossible to carry out all the forms of investigation which might constitute a regional study today. No field-surveys were conducted and no test excavations pertinent to this study were undertaken. The existing data consist chiefly of museum and literature research. The discussion is quite comprehensive precisely because these data should serve as basis for further investigation.

2.2 THE SOURCES

The primary sources for this investigation are chiefly museum collections. Inventories of these collections were made for the most part after 1985.[1] Of the inventoried collections, the Fries Museum contained the greatest quantity of the finds of importance to this study. An active acquisition policy was followed there, especially while G. Elzinga was connected with the museum as curator of the archaeological department (1965–1988), leading to many purchases and gifts not only of stray finds but also of entire collections, such as the important collection belonging to J. Siebinga of Marum. A second collection of significance to the study area is that of 'De Vereeniging voor Heimatstudie der Stellingwerven', which has been on loan to the Fries Museum since 1929. This collection is made up mainly of finds which were received as gifts from or through the agency of H.J. Popping of Oosterwolde. The greatest part of Popping's own collection is also found in Leeuwarden as well as a large number of W. Wijkel's finds. Wijkel worked in a small area to the south of Oosterwolde.

The collection in the Fries Museum is thus representative of the province and is still being enhanced by the distinction of having a *fynstensiker* (find seeker in Frisian) on staff, a practice which the museum has maintained for many years. The first of these 'find seekers' was P. Mudstra whose appointment in 1960 was mediated by Elzinga and funded by the Grontmij[2] in order to provide archaeological accompaniment to reallotment activities. In 1965 Mudstra was succeeded by J.K. Boschker, who received an appointment at the Fries Museum.[3] In addition to his work with land consolidation, Boschker checks up on other forms of ground activities and find reports, wherever possible. In this respect, Boschker is very well informed about private collections situated in the Province of Friesland. However, no card index exists of these collections, as is the case at the provincial museums of Groningen and Drenthe.

Work in the Fries Museum was hampered by the failure of the card index to indicate where the finds were stored.[4] This made it impossible to check the identifications of the finds. As a consequence, the research was approached in reverse order: all the finds stored in repositories and dis-

---

1 The assistance of L. Smits, who joined in the work for three weeks in 1985 in the context of a student assistantship, should be mentioned in particular. In 1986 and 1987 supplementary work was carried out with the help of E. Jungerius and K. Schinkel, and in 1989 with the help of M.A.F. van Oorsouw and D. Wesseling. The processing of the data involved the work of H. André de la Porte-Janss and M.N.A. van Veen.

2 The Grontmij is a contracting company for, amongst others, reallotment projects.

3 In fig. 16 the doubling of the number of finds in the period 1960–1970 gives a clear indication of Boschker's activities. Elzinga's acquisition policy also contributed to this increase, however.

4 The inventory work at the Fries Museum has had the continued assistance of the curator, G. Elzinga, his staff, and his successors, J.M. Bos and E. Kramer.

play cases were examined, and those which were relevant to the investigation were drawn. The total number of recorded finds in the Fries Museum is smaller than the card index indicates because a number of them remain untraceable and therefore unverifiable.

The flint collections in the Fries Museum also proved to be a difficult problem. Boschker collected and registered a large amount of material, but these data had not yet been incorporated into the card index at the time the inventory was taken. For this reason, use was made of Boschker's own data which he gathered in carefully-kept notebooks and on topographical maps. The dating of the flint assemblages is particularly difficult because, for the most part, they are chronologically mixed. It was finally decided to include in the catalogue[5] those findspots for which relative dating was made possible by the existence of diagnostic artifacts. In addition, findspots without diagnostic artifacts but with flakes of polished axes were always considered to be Middle Neolithic (Funnel Beaker culture). Undated assemblages were not recorded in the catalogue, meaning that dozens of potential findspots do not appear on the distribution maps.

The archaeological collections of the Groninger Museum and the Drents Museum are organized in a comparable way and are easily accessible.[6] The Drents Museum includes the important collection of G.H. Voerman, who conducted a number of field-surveys in the area of Havelte.[7]

Besides the collections of the provincial museums, the collections from the various antiquities' rooms were recorded. In particular the antiquities' rooms in Dokkum, Drachten ('It Bleekerhûs'), Gorredijk ('Streekmuseum Opsterlân'), and Kollum should be mentioned in this connection. In Gorredijk is housed the largest part of the collection of H. van Vliet, who in the 1930s unearthed many finds in the area of Wijnjeterp. Finally, the northern Netherlands finds which are kept in the Rijksmuseum van Oudheden were also included in the inventory.

In addition to the museums, a small number of privately-owned collections were investigated, especially the Ley (Leeuwarden), Minnema (Westergeest), and Van der Brug (Selmien) collections, and a number of finds owned by Vermaning (from the area around Appelscha). Two collections, those of Houtsma and Mudstra, were eliminated from consideration because they

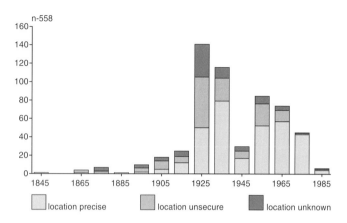

Figure 16 The number of sites discovered in the study area between 1840 and 1990 per ten-year period and divided over three location categories. The scale on the x-axis indicates the mid-point of the ten year periods.

mostly contained artifacts which fell outside the chronological framework of this study. Apart from a few incidental privately-owned finds, the stock of known finds from the Province of Friesland was quite thoroughly investigated. Private collections of finds from the Provinces of Groningen and Drenthe were not investigated more closely because descriptions of these collections can be found in the museums. For the small part of the Province of Overijssel that falls within the study area, use was made only of the filing cards in the Central Archaeological Archive of the Rijksdienst voor het Oudheidkundig Bodemonderzoek at Amersfoort (State Service for Archaeological Investigations) after consultation with A.D. Verlinde, the provincial archaeologist. It is assumed that the number of uninventoried finds is so small that this omission has not led to chronological or geographical lacunae in the data base.

Written documents formed a secondary source of data. This category includes letters, newspaper articles, records, and scientific articles. Findspots or finds encountered in letters or newspaper articles were recorded only when the descriptions were sufficiently specific to enable dating. Sometimes it was possible to identify a described find in a museum, but in a number of cases these remained 'paper' finds. To the 'letters' category belongs correspondence which museums carried on not only

5 The catalogue is published as Appendix 1 in Fokkens 1991.
6 The curators of the Groninger Museum and the Drents Museum, J. Boersma and W.A.B. van der Sanden respectively,

and their staffs, especially J. Wachter and J. Beuker respectively, offered their complete assistance.
7 Jager 1992.

with archaeological institutes and local archaeologists but also with dealers. Thus Van Giffen maintained contact with A.A. Barendsen, a Drachten pharmacist, who regularly reported and sold to Van Giffen finds which he came across in the province. Often Barendsen had bought these from third parties or managed to mediate when they were purchased. A very important and sizeable archive is the correspondence between Popping and the various museums and institutions to which he reported finds. His letters to Van Giffen[8] contain much information on finds and findspots which is not documented elsewhere. The letters archive of the Rijksmuseum van Oudheden also contains much of Popping's correspondence.

Another secondary source of data is the Central Archaeological Archive of the Rijksdienst voor het Oudheidkundig Bodemonderzoek. Among the find reports located here, those which predominate (as far as the study area is concerned) correspond to the Fries Museum card index or were copied from the 'old find archive' at the Rijksmuseum van Oudheden.

Virtually all the finds which were described in annual reports or scientific publications were recorded, even those remaining in the 'paper' stage because the actual finds could not be located in the museums. In these cases, a good description was the criterion for inclusion in the records. Lastly, the data from a number of scientific works were taken over in their entirety. This is the case with the *terpen*,[9] the coins,[10] the Celtic field systems,[11] the urnfields,[12] and the finds around Havelte.[13] For the distribution and dating of *terpen* in Westergo, use was made of data collected by E. Taayke (Groningen) in connection with an investigation of Iron Age occupation in the northern Netherlands. Also used were the data on south-western Drenthe gathered by P.H. Deckers during the second phase of the investigation subsidized by the Dutch Organization for Scientific Research under which investigation the present study was begun.

2.3 QUALITY OF THE DATA

A significant part of the finds in the northern museums and antiquities' rooms were collected during the first decades of this century (fig. 16). This occurred on the one hand in connection with reclamation efforts then being initiated by the government and on the other hand in connection with the fact that, at precisely that time, a number of local archaeologists – Siebinga, Popping, Van Vliet, Voerman – were intensively at work collecting finds. They encouraged labourers and others to report finds and told them what to look out for.[14] Both Popping and Siebinga carried out excavations on their own.

This means that although the amount of data known from certain areas is indeed considerable, these are not representative of the area as a whole. Moreover, the above-named archaeologists had their clear preference for findspots with flint – Popping was the discoverer of the first Tjonger sites – and the artifacts associated with them; they rarely, if ever, collected pottery.

Because most of the finds were unearthed during a relatively early period, the findspot locations are frequently imprecise or even missing entirely. In connection with this, the remaining documentation on context and find-recovery was often fragmentary. In most cases this involved stray finds and verifying investigations never took place. The number of places where excavations were carried out is particularly small. In this respect, the location being peripheral to Groningen – the place of residence of the Biologisch-Archaeologisch Instituut – probably played a role.

2.4 ORGANIZATION OF THE DATA BASE

2.4.1 *Findspot, site, and assemblage*

The basic unit for data collecting in this study is the findspot. In archaeological parlance the concepts of findspot and site are often treated as synonymous. However, there are a number of aspects which make a more careful handling of the terminology advisable. These are connected with the question whether an archaeological site should be considered as that which we as archaeologists come upon, or as the result of human activity in the systemic context. This may sound like an academic question, but the problem posed here is, in my opinion, just as important as the difference between chrono- and lithostratigraphy in geology.

---

8 Kept in the Biologisch-Archaeologisch Instituut.
9 Boeles 1927; 1951.
10 Van Es 1960.
11 Brongers 1976.

12 Kooi 1979.
13 Jager 1992.
14 Also see section 6.5.1.

As an example: when someone finds flint artifacts in a field there is nothing further to conclude but that here we are dealing with an archaeological *findspot* having the character of a flint scatter. How this flint scatter should be interpreted in terms of activities from the past can only be determined after investigation of the spatial distribution and character of the flint and associated artifacts. Then we are talking about a site: an extraction site, a butchering site, a kill site, etc.

Thus in the rest of the study I will continue to speak of findspots when the matter concerns descriptions of finds and find locations. Only when the determination of function is included, i.e. an interpretation of the finds in terms of human behaviour in the systemic context, is the concept of site used.[15] The importance of this distinction will again be underscored in Chapter 4, when the difference will be pointed out between site formation (systemic context) and findspot formation (archaeological context).

When the concept of findspot is used, two aspects should be more closely specified: extent and composition. How far may individual finds, or find locations, lie from each other and still be considered as part of the same findspot? Hamond, in considering *Linearbandkeramik* findspots, assumes that locations lying 350 m apart still belong to the same findspot.[16] Willems and Woltering assume a limit of 100–200 m; these authors, however, deal chiefly with the Iron Age and the Roman period.[17] In a diachronic study such as this one it is impossible to determine a standard value. In general, therefore, each find location is regarded as a findspot unless the location under discussion is part of a settlement area with distinct features.

At a given findspot, more than one assemblage can be found.[18] Sometimes the assemblages date from the same archaeological period (for instance, various seasonal encampments), sometimes from periods far distant from each other. In the former case, it is often difficult to determine, certainly on the basis of superficial finds, whether the evidence points to one or to a number of assemblages. Thus, for example, it is incorrect (although a common practice) to simply interpret the findspot with a relatively large surface as a settlement and one with a smaller surface as an encampment. In each case, the composition of the find assemblage should also be considered. When a findspot includes assemblages from diverse periods the differences usually pose fewer problems, except when the artifacts belong to types that have remained typologically unchanged over a long period. This is the case, for example, with a large category of finds: axes of flint and other types of stone.

2.4.2 *Findspot categories and site-types*

Archaeological reasoning often does not separate findspot categories from site-types. It is common practice to immediately classify an independently-found pot, which would be described as an urn if found in a cemetery, as coming from a destroyed grave. In that case, observation and interpretation are confused and premature conclusions are drawn. Therefore in this study the findspots are first divided into categories that are defined solely on the basis of artifact composition. These assemblages form the basis for the drawing up of site typologies which can vary from period to period, depending on the research problems. The degree of detail by which sites can be classified depends furthermore on the character of the assemblage. Since most of the inventory for the northern Netherlands consists of surface and stray finds with low information quality, it was not possible to draw up a detailed site typology for most periods. Attempts were made in any case to distinguish settlements (large and small), graves, hoards, and arable. The remaining category is registered as undeterminate.

Whenever stray finds are involved it is difficult to determine the site-type; any number of processes can cause an object to end up in the ground. However, in most of the cases of which the cultural context was unknown an attempt was still made to reach a conclusion about site-type by inference. Otherwise about 50% of the finds would have been deemed unallocated and thus left outside consideration.[19] A number of criteria were employed (table 1). First, the ecological context of the findspot was taken into account, usually interpreted in terms of sand–dry–high and water–moor–river valley–low. The reason for this is that almost all settlements and other places of activity, including burials, generally lie relatively high and dry. This is true even for settlements in the *terpen* area. Certain kinds of extraction activities (fishing, etc.) and ceremonial activities (acts involving deposition) are often associated with water and swamp.

---

15 For the definition of the concepts of systemic context and archaeological context see section 4.2 and Schiffer 1972, 157.
16 Hamond 1978.
17 Willems 1981; Woltering 1979.

18 An assemblage is defined by Clarke as 'an associated set of contemporary artefact types' (Clarke 1978, 489).
19 In the legend of the maps I–VIII the difference between observation and interpretation is expressed in symbols.

Table 1 Decision controls for determining the site-type of contextless finds. The table is to be read from top to bottom.

ecological context	high; dry; sand				low; water or peat	
number of artifacts	one artifact		more than one artifact		one or more artifact(s)	
state of artifact(s)	com- plete	incom- plete	com- plete	incom- plete	com- plete	incom- plete
site-type	*grave*	*settle- ment*	*hoard*	*settle- ment*	*votive hoard*	*tempor- ary activity*

In this study it is assumed that votive hoards actually were deposited in a moor, river, or *dobbe*.[20] A mere moist depression found in the proximity of the find is not considered sufficient to fulfill those conditions.[21] Indeed, votive hoards involve the destruction of goods, a gesture which by definition is irrevocable. Closed finds with a hoard character which were not found in such a context must often be interpreted in another way.[22] Stray finds which satisfy the above conditions can also be considered as votive hoards.

A second important criterion in determining the site-type of stray finds is the condition of the artifact: was it complete or incomplete at the time it was deposited? Traces of use, in particular signs of extreme wear and tear, also play a role here. The following reasoning was maintained. Burial finds are comparatively seldom broken or incomplete. The same is true for votive hoards, at least up to the Iron Age. Whole artifacts may also end up in the ground through loss or concealment. In case of a single complete axe (with handle), however, loss is hardly likely, and concealment even less so. On the other hand, axes – both used and worn ones – were frequently provided as personal equipment in graves. Finally, some hoards of complete artifacts can also be interpreted as founders hoards or as commodity hoards.[23]

Conversely, within settlements one can expect to find few whole specimens other than those which are extremely worn. Of course a hasty departure, fire, etc., can account for a complete artifact being left behind, but that cannot be regarded as the norm. Davidsen's investigation of Middle Neolithic v settlements in Jutland brought 167 identifiable fragments of flint axes to light, of which only nineteen were more or less complete.[24] There were remarkably few cutting-edge fragments and, by comparison, many top ends. Davidsen explains this with the thesis that whenever the blade of an axe that was being used in work outside the settlement broke, the handle with the top part was brought back home in order to repair it or replace it, while the cutting-edge became primary refuse.[25] This reasoning is considered applicable not only in the case of hammer axes, axes of flint and other types of stone, and flint daggers, but also for bronze objects. In combination with the ecological context this provides the following matrix of decisions of table 1.

Of course these decision controls are not conclusive. They are merely guidelines to be used to draw closer to the original context with an undeterminable degree of probability. Therefore any indication in the find-recovery which can force a more balanced interpretation is given priority.

Other indicators for settlements are grinding stones, whetstones, pestles, lap stones, etc.; that is, objects which are almost never present in grave or hoard contexts. There is one instance of a grinding stone in a barrow in Exloo, but it formed a part of the stone circle around the burial and not of the inventory.[26] Whetstones for axes also belong to settlements. The numerous whetstones in the Funnel Beaker culture settlements in Denmark[27] and the Netherlands, the Anlo whetstone for example,[28] are indications of this. The work of Steensberg shows that among the people in New Guinea who still use stone axes, sharpening is a settlement activity.[29] Unlike the sharpening of a scythe, which can take place during mowing, axe-grinding is too time-consuming a task to be performed during tree felling. Moreover, it is work

20 Investigations as those by Bradley 1991, Levy 1982, and Von Brunn 1968 provide sufficient cause for this thesis.
21 This in contrast to the opinion of Jager regarding a large axe from Fochteloo (Jager 1981).
22 Compare e.g. Harsema 1979a.
23 Also see the discussion on trade and exchange in Chapter 7.
24 Davidsen 1978, 129 ff.

25 That is, refuse left behind at the place of use (Schiffer 1972). Skaarup's analysis of find material from Stengade supports this hypothesis (Skaarup 1975).
26 Harsema 1979b, 15.
27 Skaarup 1975.
28 Van der Waals 1962.
29 Steensberg 1980.

Table 2 The western part of the Frisian-Drentian plateau: the exactness of location of all findspots, distributed over three classes.

class	description	number of findspots	percentage
code 1	exact location is known	387	58%
code 2	location is known within a radius of 250–500 m	161	24%
code 3	only village name is known	119	18%
	total	667	100%

that requires the use of water, and whetstones are heavy to haul during long journeys.[30]

Finds of single Roman coins in the *terpen* area are also always interpreted as settlement indicators; finds of a number of coins, however, point to hoards.

Complete and nearly-complete pots (broken or whole) are included as grave indicators. For pottery the same rules apply as those shown in table 1.

Finally, there is the remaining category of finds of which the ecological context is unknown. Usually these are the finds with only a village name as an indication of the findspot. These finds are shown on the maps as 'site-type undetermined'.

2.4.3 *Exactness of the location of findspots*

One of the annoying aspects of working with older finds is that the findspot indications are often either vague or completely absent. Since approximately 50% of the finds were discovered before the 1950s, only a vague location is known in a large number of cases (table 2). So quite a bit of time was spent looking for supplementary data on location and context in the archives of the Fries Museum, the Rijksmuseum van Oudheden, the Biologisch-Archaeologisch Instituut, the Groninger Museum, and the Drents Museum. These archives contain correspondence with finders and occasionally rough maps as well. In this way a rather large amount of hitherto unknown information about finds in museums and lost finds has been brought to light.

Next to the archives, maps are an extremely valuable source of information. This is particularly true of the various editions of the Topografische Kaart van Nederland 1:50 000 (Topographical Map of the Netherlands 1:50 000, hereafter referred to as Topographical Map; first edition 1850–1862) but also of the older maps.[31] These maps can be used to trace old, now-forgotten place designations and toponyms.

In addition, the division of the study area in this study is not based on present-day municipal divisions but on medieval divisions in *marken* and village territories.[32] The main reason for this is that the largest part of the finds were discovered during a period when the old territorial divisions were still in common use. The designation of a find location such as 'found directly to the south of the Weper es' can be localized correctly only in that context.

On the maps I–VIII, the exactness of the location of each findspot is shown by use of a code indicating:

code 1 The exact location of the findspot is known.

code 2 The position of the findspot within a village area is known, but not precisely. In practice this mostly means that in the findspot designation a toponym (or a similar sort of description) is indicated. In general, the findspot should be sought within a radius of 250–500 m round the indicated grid values.

code 3 Only the name of the village area is known. In this case the intersection of grid values that lie closest to the nucleus of the village was taken.[33]

These differences are made clear on the maps by the use of the site-type symbols without circles (code 1), within small circles (code 2), and within somewhat larger circles (code 3).

2.4.4 *Information about findspot formation factors*

Considering the analysis of map formation factors, a number of data for each findspot were documented which were used to determine the archaeological visibility indexes (Chapters 5 and 6). The most important of these variables are find-recovery (table 3) and soil use. With respect to find-recovery it should be noted that excavation and documentation studies (for instance Brongers' study of Celtic field systems) were coded as archaeological activities. All field-surveys, in particular

---

30 Many of them weigh more than 5 kg (Fokkens & Schinkel 1990).

31 Schotanus 1664; Schotanus à Sterringa 1718; 1739; Huguenin 1820–24; Eekhoff 1849–59.

32 See section 7.8.

33 Finds which are only described as having been 'found in Friesland' were not considered.

those carried out by local archaeologists,[34] were documented as 'survey'. Furthermore, attempts were made to collect data relating to the matrix in which the finds were discovered. However, in many cases this variable could not be identified because the matrix was undocumented, so further use of it was abandoned. The same was true for the height relative to NAP. Because in a large number of cases the findspot is not precisely known and the height variations can be large (at least in Frisian terms), use of this variable was also discontinued.

2.5 DATING AND PERIODIZATION

The dating of the findspots is based on the system of archaeological and absolute dating currently in use in the Netherlands.[35] The ^{14}C dates are calibrated according to the curves which were published in 1986 in *Radiocarbon*.[36]

Various sources were used in dating the different assemblages on typological grounds. These are generally rough dates. As a rule, pottery can be dated with the greatest precision because it is the basis for most relative dating systems. There is little pottery represented in collections from the Frisian-Drentian plateau, however, which can be primarily attributed to findspot formation processes.

The most important material group is axes of flint and other types of stone from the Neolithic, a category which is difficult to date because the types cannot be sharply defined. During the collecting of data, therefore, a proportionally large amount of time was spent on this problem.[37] Lacking any connection with pottery, a large number of material categories remain difficult to date and to assign to a specific archaeological culture because it is often on the basis of pottery that archaeological cultures are defined.

Since periodization is the basis for distribution maps, the classification was compiled in such a way that the

Table 3 The western part of the Frisian-Drentian plateau: the findspots divided according to the type of find-recovery (digging operations include reclamation activities; Celtic field systems are registered amongst the findspots recovered by field-surveys).

find-recovery	number of findspots	percentage
excavation	115	17.2%
field-survey	136	20.4%
digging operation	116	17.4%
agricultural activity	40	6.0%
dredging work	22	3.3%
construction activity	14	2.1%
unknown	224	33.6%
total	667	100%

least possible number of material groups or archaeological phenomena fall within more than one period. If this was nevertheless the case, a choice was made (in the absence of datable context) for dating in the period in which the occurrence was concentrated. Thus the placing of difficult to date artifact groups on more than one map was avoided.[38] The periodization is briefly represented in the following list.

Early Neolithic B (4900–4200 cal BC; 6000–5300 b.p.) In the southern Netherlands this phase begins with the Rössen culture. In the northern Netherlands, only the Swifterbant culture is known from this period, the last phase of which is dated 5200 b.p.[39]

Middle Neolithic A (4200–3400 cal BC; 5300–4700 b.p.) In the northern Netherlands, the Middle Neolithic A is a period of few known finds, leading to the supposition that at least the higher grounds were uninhabited during this period (see Chapter 8). In the southern Netherlands

34 The term 'local' archaeologist is used throughout the text as a synonym for 'amateur' archaeologist, a concept that, wrongly, has a negative flavour.
35 See Lanting & Mook 1977. The dates are adapted to the new periodization presented in Louwe Kooijmans *et al.* in press.
36 Stuiver & Pearson 1986; Pearson & Stuiver 1986; Stuiver & Becker 1986; Pearson *et al.* 1986.
37 The result of this part of the investigation is recorded in Appendix 3 of Fokkens 1991.

38 An exception was made for the Celtic field systems. These are shown on the maps of the Late Bronze Age and Early Iron Age (map VI) as well as on the map of the Middle and Late Iron Age (map VII) because continuous use of these field systems probably occurred in most areas.
39 Hogestijn's proposal (1990, 163) to call the last phase of the Swifterbant culture the 'Dronten' phase is unwarranted in my opinion. Since Swifterbant is the type-site for this phase, 'Swifterbant phase' should be used.

the Middle Neolithic A is characterized by the Michelsberg culture.

Middle Neolithic B (3400–2900 cal BC; 4700–4300 b.p.) In the northern Netherlands this period begins with the Funnel Beaker culture. Phases 1–5 of this culture fall within the Middle Neolithic B; phases 6 and 7 belong to the Late Neolithic A. After calibration of the radiocarbon dates the overlap of the Funnel Beaker culture and the Single Grave culture (the latter culture is characteristic for the next period), which traditionally has led to so many discussions, becomes smaller and is limited to a few generations at the most. The end of the Funnel Beaker culture (Middle and Late Havelte phases) can now be dated to 2850 cal BC.[40]

Late Neolithic A (2900–2500 cal BC; 4300–3950 b.p.) This period is characterized by find associations from the Single Grave culture. The All Over Ornamented pottery is also included in this period.

Late Neolithic B and Early Bronze Age (2500–1800 cal BC; 3950–3450 b.p. This period begins with the Bell Beaker culture, which makes a smooth transition into the last group of the beaker cultures, characterized by Barbed Wire pottery. Traditionally, the Sögel phase (Montelius I; Reinecke *Bronzezeit* B1 and B2) is included in the Early Bronze Age, although by Lanting and Mook's reckoning the Montelius I Period for the most part stands in the Middle Bronze Age, phase A.[41]

Middle Bronze Age A and B (1800–1100 cal BC; 3450–2900 b.p.) The Middle Bronze Age in the northern Netherlands is traditionally associated with the Elp culture, characterized by barrows with a circular ditch in phase A and with post circles in phase B. The dead are predominantly laid out in an extended supine position. Farm houses are of the Emmerhout and Elp types. Amongst the finds palstaves, flanged axes, and *Kümmerkeramik* are characteristic.[42]

Late Bronze Age and Early Iron Age (1100–500 cal BC; 2900–2450 b.p.) The Late Bronze Age and the Early Iron Age together are also typified as the Urnfield period. The typochronology of the pottery from this period for the northern Netherlands has been dealt with extensively by Kooi.[43] Kooi distinguishes the Elp, the Sleen, and the Zeijen phases, the first two being limited to the Late Bronze Age (1100–800 BC). The Zeijen phase continues into the Middle and Late Iron Age. The development of the Celtic field systems also occurred in the Late Bronze Age, although there are indications that their origin lay in the Middle Bronze Age.[44]

Middle and Late Iron Age (500 cal BC–12 BC; 2450–2000 b.p.) At the end of the Early Iron Age an important development occurred which left its imprint on the following period: the colonization of the clay areas of Westergo and Oostergo. The pottery forms include the Ruinen-Wommels assemblage, characteristic of the Zijen culture. The incidence of Ruinen-Wommels type pottery continues from the middle of the 6th century[45] to the end of the period. In the coastal area a separate style developed which Waterbolk[46] has called the Proto-Frisian culture, with Ruinen-Wommels III type pottery as its distinguishing feature. In this study, the *streepband* pottery of the Frisian culture[47] is attributed to the Late Iron Age although its use continued into the Roman period.[48]

Roman period (12 BC–AD 406; 2000–1650 b.p.) The Roman period begins with the encampment of troops, under Drusus, south of the Rhine. Even north of the *limes* the influence of the Romans, through, among other things, trade, tribute, war, and military service, should not be underestimated. The many Roman coins and the imported goods found in the *terpen* bear witness to this fact. The official departure of the Romans from our country was in AD 406, but in the north the migration period had already begun by then.[49] This period, in which occupation is poorly visible from an archaeological standpoint, forms the termination of this study.

40 Brindley 1986, 105.
41 Lanting & Mook 1977.
42 In line with the Hilversum, Drakenstein, and Laren terminology, the term 'Elp pottery' deserves preference over the term *Kümmerkeramik*, which is so laden with modern value judgment.
43 Kooi 1979.
44 Waterbolk 1985b, 63; also see Chapter 8.
45 Boersma 1988, 34.

46 Waterbolk 1962.
47 The *terpen*, with a distinct pottery style, economy, and house plan design, can rightfully be seen as a single archaeological culture. Since the difference between Proto-Frisian and Frisian cultures is found only in the pottery form, it seems advisable to refer to the entire *terpen* development as the Frisian culture.
48 Lanting & Mook 1977.
49 Van Es, Sarfatij & Woltering 1988.

Chapter 3

Palaeogeography

3.1 INTRODUCTION

The period under discussion in this study covers roughly 5000 calendar years. The changes in landscape which occurred during this period were so drastic that for a reliable study of the various occupation stages and the processes of change involved, palaeogeographic reconstructions are an absolute prerequisite. The ideal would be to study each archaeologically recognizable period in terms of its distinct palaeogeographic circumstances, but that is seldom possible. The restricting factors are the available geological data, in addition to the datability of the archaeological finds. In considering the investigated area from this viewpoint, three studies by respectively Griede, Roeleveld, and Zagwijn are of importance[1]. Table 4 gives an overview of published periodization of this publication. The reconstructions and the mean sea levels are indicated per publication by their respective conventional (b.p.) and calibrated (cal BC/AD) radiocarbon datings.

Table 4 The northern Netherlands: summary of the palaeogeographic reconstructions by Griede, Roeleveld, and Zagwijn respectively of (part of) the area and of the successive mean sea levels according to Van de Plassche, as far as relevant to the current investigation, in relation to the archaeological

archaeological periodization		palaeogeographic reconstruction						mean sea level		
		Griede 1978		Roeleveld 1974		Zagwijn 1986		Van de Plassche 1982		
	b.p.	b.p.	cal BC / AD	b.p.	cal BC	b.p.	cal BC / AD	b.p.	cal BC / AD	MSL -NAP (in cm)
EN	6000–5300	5500	4350 BC	5400	4300 BC	5300	4150 BC	5150	3970 BC	500–490
MN A	5100–4900									
MN B	4900–4300	4400	3050 BC	4400	3050 BC	4400	3050 BC	4600	3350 BC	390–400
LN A	4300–3950	4000	2500 BC					4000	2500 BC	300–320
LN B / EBA	3950–3450			3650	2080 BC	3700	2120 BC	3650	2080 BC	240–250
MBA A / B	3450–2900	3150	1480 BC	3200	1500 BC	3000	1250 BC	3200	1500 BC	170–200
LBA / EIA	2900–2500	2650	c. 800 BC	2600	c. 800 BC			2600	c. 800 BC	120–140
MIA / LIA	2500–1950	2300	c. 400 BC			2300	400 BC	2250	c. 300 BC	110–100
RP	1950–1450	1650	AD 400			1900	AD 50	1650	AD 400	40–50

42

◁ Figure 17 The western part of the Frisian-Drentian plateau: the drainage. Legend: a clay; b peat; c sand; 1 Zwemmer; 2 Lauwers; 3 Kromme Ee; 4 Lits; 5 Drait; 6 Oude Diep; 7 Boorne; 8 Peizerdiep; 9 Tjonger; 10 Linde; 11 Vledder Aa; 12 Steenwijker Aa (below Steenwijk: Steenwijkerdiep); 13 Wapserveense Aa; 14 Dwingelerstroom; 15 Oude Vaart; 16 Ruiner Aa; 17 Wold Aa; 18 Echtenerstroom or Oude Diep; 19 IJssel.

palaeogeographic maps. Basically they relate to the northern and western coastal areas.

The available geological reconstructions do not agree in all cases with what, for archaeological periodization, is the optimal moment. In principle this optimal moment corresponds with a point halfway through an archaeological period. For both the Late Neolithic A and the Roman period in particular suitable reconstructions do not exist. In these cases an interpolation is made between the preceding and the succeeding models, while the extension of the fen peat is related, if possible, to the mean sea level, and the extension of the bog peat to ^{14}C dates. The largest problem was the reconstruction of peat development in the northern Netherlands. From the scarce data that were available, Zagwijn developed a maximum model:[2] on all maps, the occurrences of raised bogs are reproduced almost to their maximum dimensions. This is perhaps sufficient for the scale on which these maps were published and as a national synthesis, but it is not sufficient for the investigation at hand, especially because the development of the coastal peat and the continental raised bogs is of great significance to the habitability of the area. Thus an attempt has been made to reconstruct the peat development on the western part of the Frisian-Drentian plateau as accurately as possible.

3.2 THE STRUCTURE OF THE WESTERN PART OF THE FRISIAN-DRENTIAN PLATEAU

For a reliable construction of the palaeogeographical models, the investigated area must be divided into a number of geographical units. The reason for this is that because of varieties in subsoil, relief, and drainage patterns the development of the continental peat in these regions occurred dissimilarly. The five units are (fig. 17): 1. the western and northern coastal area; 2. the northern sandy area; 3. the central and south-western sandy area; 4. the fluvial area of the rivers Tjonger, Linde, Steenwijker Aa, and Oude Vaat; 5. the eastern border area.

The coastal area includes the tidal flat and salt-marsh zone running the entire length of the Frisian coast. The developments here are closely related to the rise in sea level and the position of coast, islands, and tidal inlets.

The northern sandy area is bordered in the south by the river Boorne and in the east by the Peizerdiep. It forms the watershed between the fluvial area of the Peizerdiep, the Oude Diep, the Lauwers, and the Zwemmer in the east and the Drait and the Boorne in the west (fig. 17). It is a relatively flat area with rather steep gradients along its north-eastern and north-western sides. Here the geographical changes can be more or less directly related to the curve in the rise of the sea level. Oligotrophic peat formation took place on the watershed, especially in the strip to the east of Drachten. This formation probably first began after 1500 cal. BC, considering the presence of finds from the Middle Bronze Age in that area.

The central and south-western area here includes the area south of the Boorne and north of the Tjonger and the Heerenveen–St. Nicolaasga–Oude Mirdum line. This is a region where chiefly peat formation occurred. Influence from the sea did not take place until after the beginning of our era; drainage by rivers was absent. The boulder clay in this area is relatively high and surfaces in large parts of Gaasterland.

To the south of the Heerenveen–St. Nicolaasga–Oude Mirdum line are the river valleys of the Tjonger, Linde, Steenwijker Aa, and Oude Vaart, which provide good drainage for the higher parts of the area. Eutrophic peat formed only in the valleys themselves and in the low area to the south. Bog peat developed in the flat parts north of the boulder clay heights of Steenwijkerwold and Havelte and in the southern part of the area. Even though no absolute dating is available, the impression exists that formation of bog peat was a late development (i.e. since the Middle Iron Age). Indications of this are occupation traces covered by peat (especially Celtic field systems) north of Havelte.

Finally, the eastern border area includes the great Fochtelooër and Smildiger Venen. Hardly any dates exist for the origin of this peat area, but its nucleus, lying on the watershed between the eastern and western parts of the Frisian-Drentian plateau, was certainly formed early on. From the fact that a second-century AD settlement was

1 Griede 1978; Roeleveld 1974; Zagwijn 1986.

2 Zagwijn 1986.

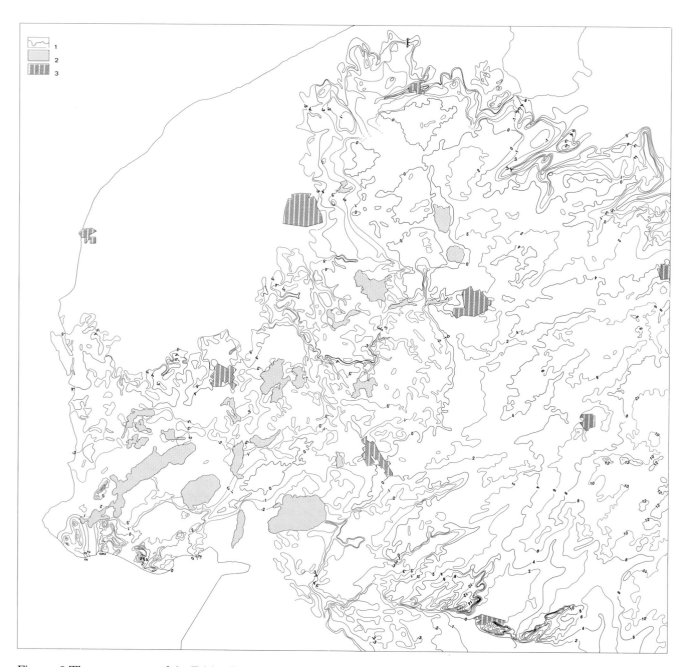

Figure 18 The western part of the Frisian-Drentian plateau:
contours indicating the surface of the Pleistocene deposits.
Contours of this surface deeper than 5 m -NAP are not
indicated. Legend: 1 contour, height in metres; 2 lake; 3 built-
up area.

discovered at Fochteloo,[3] it can be deduced that the maximum (Late Medieval) borders of this peat area had not yet been reached at that time.

3.3 THE CONTOUR MAP OF THE SURFACE OF THE PLEISTOCENE DEPOSITS

In the construction of the contour map of the surface of the Pleistocene deposits (fig. 18), a number of different sources have been used.
– For the northern coastal area: the manuscripts of Griede and Roeleveld's publications[4] and core data from the Rijks Geologische Dienst at Haarlem (Geological Survey of the Netherlands), the latter for the area around Leeuwarden in particular: the connection between the areas of Griede's fieldwork and map sheets 10 E and W of the *Geologische Kaart van Nederland 1:50 000* (Geological Map of the Netherlands 1:50 000, hereafter referred to as Geological Map).
– For map sheets 10 E and W and 11 W: data from the Rijks Geologische Dienst[5] and draft maps for sheet 11 W of the Geological Map. The original hand-coloured versions on a scale of 1:25 000, as are kept at the Rijks Geologische Dienst, Oosterwolde office, were used. Data from the author's own fieldwork were used only for the area around Oldeboorn and Akkrum.
– For the sandy area: spot height maps on a scale of 1:10 000,[6] map sheets of the Topographical Map, and reports from the former Stichting voor Bodemkartering (Soil Survey Institute), now part of the Winand Staring Centrum at Wageningen.[7]
– For the south and south-west: Core data from the Rijks Geologische Dienst, reports from the former Stichting voor Bodemkartering.[8]
The biggest problems in the assembly of the map were the extreme south-western area (sheet 15 W) and the connection of the area of sheet 10 W and E with that of

Griede's fieldwork. Only incidental core data from the Rijks Geologische Dienst were available for this task, while other reports were altogether lacking.[9] The area around the Tjeukemeer was also difficult to reconstruct, in spite of the work of Veenenbos which shed light on a small surface area south of the Tjeukemeer.[10] The reconstructions of the course of the Tjonger and of the Linde in the subsoil are based on unpublished core data from the Rijks Geologische Dienst. In view of the palaeogeographical reconstructions related to the mean sea level, the contours below NAP were reconstructed at intervals of 1 m. Above NAP intervals of 2 m were maintained. The 5 m intervals which the map sheets of the Topographical Map adhere to were considered too rough for the present purpose. In principle, the present map should also lend itself to use for analyzing the elevation of prehistoric occupation traces.

Thus constructed, a number of characteristics can be read from the map. First, it is clear that the northern part of the plateau around the Bergumermeer and De Leijen is quite flat, with heights which barely come above 0 to 2 m NAP. However, this area exhibits rather steep slopes toward the coastal zone and is drained on all sides by a number of valley-like depressions. It can be assumed that in connection with the relatively deep position of the boulder clay, the steep slopes, and the reasonably good drainage, the development of the coastal peat there kept more or less in step with the rise in sea level.[11] Of course, this does not apply to the oligotrophic peat formation on the watershed in the middle of this area.

Further to the south, in the low central part of Friesland, this picture changes. Here the slopes along the coast are relatively steep, while the area between Drachten, Heerenveen, the lakes in the Zuidwesthoek, and the Boorne is quite flat and lies at an average depth of 2 to 3 m -NAP. Along the edge of this low-lying area, the relative position of the boulder clay is quite high. A direct connection between peat accumulation and sea

3 Van Giffen 1954.
4 Griede 1978; Roeleveld 1974.
5 Ter Wee 1976.
6 Contour maps were constructed from the spot height maps for the areas lying above 0 m NAP. These were reduced to a scale of 1:50 000, joined to pages having the same scale, then generalized for the final version at a scale of 1:100 000.
7 Specifically Dodewaard 1966; Dodewaard & Rutten 1977; Dontje & Rutten 1974; Van der Hurk & Kalkdijk 1963; Makken & Rutten 1971; Makken, Rutten & Bannink 1975; Veenenbos 1951.

8 Specifically Haans 1951; Heyink 1960; Van der Hurk & Makken 1964; Makken & Van der Hurk 1969; Veenenbos 1950; 1953.
9 The recording of the data for the Pleistocene contour map took place chiefly during the period 1981–82.
10 Veenenbos 1950.
11 However, in bowl-shaped areas old local peat nuclei can be present here too (Griede 1978).

level is not to be expected here; the peat belt was much broader than the coastal peat zone in the north and north-east. Moreover, peat did develop in places where drainage was poor – such is the case everywhere outside the direct drainage area of the Boorne.

The southern border of this basin is the ice-pushed boulder clay ridge, covered by Younger Coversand, which runs from Joure to Gaasterland and forms the transition to the boulder clay heights along the southern side of the Frisian-Drentian plateau. The lowest part lies near the Nannewijd, the zone where the northern and southern peat areas finally grew together, permanently isolating Gaasterland from the rest of the Frisian-Drentian plateau (see below). The boulder clay in this region lies for the most part right under the surface level and is pushed up in some places (up to 16 m NAP near Havelte). The landscape is transsected by a few deep stream valleys in which the boulder clay is absent or eroded to a great extent. The rivers Tjonger, Linde, Steenwijker Aa, and Oude Vaart empty out into the ice-marginal valley of the Vecht which on the Pleistocene contour map has the form of a basin averaging from 3 to 4 m -NAP. Eutrophic peat has grown continuously in these valleys in a relatively narrow strip along the rivers.[12] In the area where the Tjonger, Linde, Steenwijker Aa, and Oude Vaart come together, both eutrophic peat and, at a greater distance from the rivers, oligotrophic peat would have developed.[13] In its entirety, this area should be considered part of the peat zone of the coastal area of the Netherlands. Local peat formation on the higher grounds occurred only in flat and poorly-drained parts.

Finally, the eastern border area lies at a relatively high elevation and is relatively flat, with boulder clay just below the surface. It forms the watershed between the eastern (Drentian) and the western (Frisian) parts of the plateau. Data on the origins of peat formation in this region are scarce, but it can be assumed that during the Atlantic local peat development had already started. However, the maximum extension to the Bakkeveen–Fochteloo–Smilde line dates from the Early Middle Ages and later.

3.4 PEAT DEVELOPMENT RECONSTRUCTIONS

3.4.1 Introduction

The peat development reconstructions were based on a number of data which were either not previously available or, if available, were not previously used. Various authors have argued that the extension of the Frisian raised bogs cannot be verified any further because so much of it has been extracted. It is true that today almost all the raised bogs have been damaged or have completely disappeared.[14] However, excellent sources for the original extension are the maps made by Schotanus à Sterringa,[15] Huguenin,[16] and the first editions of the Topographical Map, which is based on surveys of the area carried out around 1850. The map of Schotanus in particular gives an enormous amount of detailed information (summarized in fig. 19). The extension of the then existing peat can be deduced by studying the map's legend, while the area in which the peat had already been extracted can be reconstructed in part from toponyms and parcelling patterns. This gives a much more detailed view of the maximum spread of the raised bog area in particular, than is possible from geological and pedological data alone. In this study, that picture is reproduced on the map which reflects the situation from around the year cal AD 400 (map VIII). It is assumed that at that time the lateral extension of the peat had reached its farthest borders. It should be noted here that the reconstructions of peat extension in the Late Iron Age and the Roman period, particularly in the northern sandy area and on the ridges between the Linde, the Steenwijker Aa, and the Oude Vaart, are almost certainly on the conservative side because of the lack of data on the oldest peat reclamations.

A reasonably trustworthy picture could be formed of the largest peat formation extension, but of course this reveals very little about when peat formation began. In order to obtain this information, the available geological and pedological data,[17] archaeological data, and [14]c dates were consulted. The archaeological data were used in such a way that settlements or graves form a *terminus post quem* for the start of peat formation. The absence of archaeological finds in a certain area is not used as an indication for peat accumulation in the reconstructions. The distortions in the distribution pattern of archaeolo-

12 De Groot *et al.* 1987.
13 Cf. Veenenbos 1950; Zagwijn 1986.
14 Cf. De Groot *et al.* 1987, fig. 1.
15 Schotanus à Sterringa 1718. Use has been made of a

reprint (1983) of the 1739 edition of the map.
16 Huguenin 1820–4, see Koeman 1963.
17 Especially the map sheets of the Geological Map and the accompanying sections and commentary.

Figure 19 The Province of Friesland: soil map, situation around AD 1700. After Schotanus à Sterringa 1739. Legend: 1 clay; 2 fen peat; 3 bog peat; 4 sand; 5 moor; 6 lake.

gical finds (chapters 5 and 6) show that this would be unwarranted.

18 Griede 1978; Van de Plassche 1982; Roeleveld 1974.

3.4.2 *The northern sandy area*

Griede, Roeleveld, and Van de Plassche[18] on the whole are in agreement that developments along the edges of the northern sandy area are closely related to the rise in sea level. In general, the inland limits of the fen peat are reconstructed at 0.5 to 1 m above mean sea level; in this study a consistent 0.5 m is maintained, based on the reported mean sea-level values from table 4. In a number of cases, this deviates somewhat from the depths employed by Griede and Roeleveld because use was made of Van de Plassche's investigation, which is more recent and specifically concentrated on the rise in sea level. In section 3.1 it has already been pointed out that bog peat developed only on the watershed in the area around Drachten, probably after 1250 cal BC. One indication of this is the fact that a number of barrows from the Middle Bronze Age or secondary interments from the same period in the already existing barrows have been found to the east and north-east of Drachten. It is assumed that in any case the peat that accumulated near De Leijen was oligotrophic in the beginning but developed rather quickly into eutrophic peat. This is clearly indicated by the absence of traces of bog peat in this area. Otherwise, it is not unthinkable that the Bergumermeer has always existed as a lake.[19] As shown by the palynological dating of the start of peat formation near Opende in the Sub-atlantic,[20] occupation was no longer possible here as from the Middle Iron Age. The beginning of peat development in the upper courses of the Boorne, the Tjonger, and the Oude Diep should be set somewhat later considering the relatively large number of Celtic field systems found in this area.

3.4.3 *The low central and south-western area*

The peat development in the low central and south-western area forms a rather unknown chapter in the geological history of Friesland. Except for Van Zeist's palynological investigation at Eernewoude,[21] no information about dating is known, only that in the Middle Ages the low central area, including the higher sandy area, must have been a large, continuous peat area. That peat has disappeared now for the most part because of peat reclamation, a fact that obviously does not make investigation any easier. The impressions derived from the contour map of the surface of the Pleistocene deposits (fig. 18)

and the relatively large distance from the coast, however, lead one to suspect that in this area peat formation and the rise of the sea level were not directly connected. The making of reliable reconstructions on the basis of available data was therefore almost impossible. This consideration led the author to conduct a brief drilling campaign in the Akmarijpsterpolder in 1987 aimed at taking ^{14}C samples which might provide insight into the beginning of the peat formation.[22] These were compared with the already existing radiocarbon datings from the archaeological investigations at Oldeboorn in 1981 and 1982. The results may be called striking (table 5). When the radiocarbon datings are plotted on a time-depth diagram, and the result is compared with the most reliable mean sea-level curve,[23] then only the Oldeboorn datings seem to fit into the picture in some degree. The Akmarijpsterpolder datings are all much too old, which should not be surprising for samples of oligotrophic peat. But the eutrophic peat is also shown to have lain roughly 2.5 m above the contemporaneous mean sea level.

The second series of radiocarbon datings from the Akmarijpsterpolder comes from one coring 1.5 km to the south-west of the first series. Here a flat area was chosen where the sandy subsoil lies at an average depth of 2.6 m -NAP. In some places the coversand layer is very thin. Allowing for a compaction of the peat of approximately 50% when plotted on a time-depth diagram, these datings show a rise which has the same gradient as that of the rise in sea level during the same period (1.7 m in 900 calendar years), though the level lay some 2.5 m higher. This seems to indicate that the water table in the low area to the south of the Boorne was linked to the mean sea level, but (via a gradient in the water table) with an appreciable rise which was undoubtedly related to the topography, the impermeability of the subsoil, and seepage. The topography in the whole area is quite flat; there

---

19 Pers. comm. M.W. Ter Wee. A reason for this supposition is the presence of a deep gulley filled with *pot* clay in the subsoil. The area in question has always constituted a depression and in fact still might be subject to settling.
20 Van Duinen & Van Zeist 1960.
21 Van Duinen & Van Zeist 1960; Van Zeist 1955.
22 In the planning stages of the drilling work, valuable advice was given by Dr W.A. Casparie (Biologisch-Archaeologisch Instituut), P. Cleveringa (Rijks Geologische Dienst), Dr O. van de Plassche (Dutch Organization for Scientific Research and the Vrije Universiteit at Amsterdam) and M.W. ter Wee (Rijks Geologische Dienst, Oosterwolde office). W.A. Casparie and

P. Cleveringa were also helpful in the field, identifying types of peat and taking samples. The material that was used for dating consisted of pure peat taken from a stretch of not more than 3–4 cm. In the field, the drillings were executed with the utmost care with a gouge measuring 4 cm in diameter. In the laboratory, samples were taken of the cores. The sample material was dried and checked for contamination with recent roots before it was handed in. The sampling points were first chosen after a preparatory drilling campaign. A special effort was made to choose places which were somewhat higher than the immediate surroundings to obtain a *terminus ante quem*.
23 Van de Plassche 1982.

are hardly any drainage depressions, and even today there is still some seepage.[24] Based on these observations, it is assumed that a raised water table throughout the entire area between the Boorne and the Tjonger, to the west of Gorredijk, was present in places with a relatively flat topography. The following discussion serves as support for this model.

In the Akmarijpsterpolder 2 series of corings, the transition from eutrophic to oligotrophic peat was dated at 4325 ± 50 b.p. This dating is indicative for the period in which the oligotrophic peat started to expand over a large area. A possible explanation for this process might be found in the course of the sea-level curve. Beginning at c. 4500 b.p. the curve flattens out. It is assumed that the peat continued to accumulate and became independent of groundwater influence in the course of time. At this point in time the process of oligotrophication began. This process probably occurred on a large scale, for in the sections accompanying map sheets 10 W and E and 11 W and E of the Geological Map it can be verified that at a certain moment the bog peat expanded from almost all of its nuclei over the surrounding fenlands, certainly in the south-west. In the Boorne and Drait deltas the process of oligotrophication began somewhat later, probably because the supply of nutrient-rich water there was relatively large.

This development occurred in the northern coastal area as well. In this case, the Hiaure pollen diagram is illustrative; in this diagram, according to Cleveringa, a slow development from eutrophic to oligotrophic peat formation can be observed, to be dated to the first half of the Sub-boreal.[25] It is plausible that this development can also be linked to the levelling-off of the sea-level curve,

and that this process led to the development of raised bogs on a large scale.

The Akmarijpsterpolder 1 series of corings shows that the nuclei of oligotrophic peat may have been very old. The samples come from three locations at various levels next to and on top of a local sand outcrop. To the west and south of the outcrop lies a rather flat area with depths at an average of 2.30 m -NAP. Oligotrophic peat developed here on the sandy surface; rushes and bits of heath were observed in almost the entire profile. Sphagnum was observed in a few of the corings.

The ^{14}C dates clearly show that the bog peat here came into existence at a very early stage. When the date 6480 ± 50 b.p. for the lower part of the oligotrophic peat, at a depth of 1.80 m -NAP, is applied as a *terminus ante quem* to the beginning of peat formation in the somewhat lower-lying surroundings, it suggests that the peat here must have started its development around 7000 b.p. Since the three dates are in agreement, their accuracy need not be doubted. The explanation for this early beginning of peat formation should be sought chiefly in the topography and possibly also in seepage. Early peat formation has also been acknowledged in other places in this area, among them those near Wartena[26] and Wijtgaard,[27] although here it is not as early as in the Akmarijpsterpolder. On the basis of these data and examination of the sections accompanying the geological maps, it is assumed that most of the nuclei of oligotrophic peat in evidence on map sheets 10 E and W and 11 E and W of the Geological Map[28] were of early origin. The radiocarbon dates of samples from Oldeboorn form better links with the contemporaneous mean sea level. The sampling points were located on sand ridges along

24 Uil (1987, 178 ff) shows that the whole low central area is a seepage area today. Here water from both the first water-carrying layer (especially the Eindhoven and Urk Formations) and the second water-carrying layer (under the Peelo Formation) plays a role. Seepage occurs wherever the Drente Formation is permeable. This is the case right in the area to the north of the Heerenveen–Joure line, where the boulder clay surface drops sharply and the pressure is proportionally greater.

25 Cleveringa, in: Griede 1978, 142.

26 The date which is accepted as *terminus ante quem* for the beginning of peat formation in this area, where the Pleistocene subsoil lies at 3.6 m -NAP, is GRO 2237: 4930 ± 70 b.p. (= GrN 2237: 5030 ± 70 b.p.), taken at a depth of 2.4 m -NAP (Van Duinen & Van Zeist 1960). Taking into account the compaction

factor and a formation rate of 10 cm per century at most, the peat here must have begun to accumulate at least 2000 years earlier, i.e. around 7000 b.p. The conclusion reached by Van Duinen and Van Zeist (1960, 129), that peat formation began during the Atlantic, meets with agreement here.

27 Dating the base of the peat layer resulted in 6100 b.p. at a depth of 4.50 m -NAP. Although De Groot et al. (1987, note 148) did not use this date because it does not agree with the pollen analysis, a date from a higher point in the section (Internal report of the Rijks Geologische Dienst 'Pollen 316') nevertheless does indicate early oligotrophic peat formation.

28 These are respectively, De Groot et al. 1987, inset map 5 and sections G to J; and Ter Wee 1976, inset map 1 and sections F to K.

Table 5 The central part of Friesland: radiocarbon dates for the beginning of peat formation.

coring	depth below NAP (in cm)	core number	dated material	lab. number	^{14}C date [cal BC]
Akmarijpsterpolder 1	178–180	core 22b	base oligotrophic peat	GrN 14906	6480±50 b.p. [5600]
	140–144	core 54b	base oligotrophic peat	GrN 14907	5255±40 b.p. [4000–4040]
	94–98	core 32b	base oligotrophic peat	GrN 14908	4520±80 b.p. [3220–3330]
Akmarijpsterpolder 2	260–264	core 1b	base eutrophic peat	GrN 14905	5035±40 b.p. [3790–3900]
	188–192	core 1b	base oligotrophic peat	GrN 14904	4325±50 b.p. [2920]
Oldeboorn 1	170–174	section A	base eutrophic peat	GrN 10343	3185±30 b.p. [1415–1520]
	151–155	section A	eutrophic peat on clay	GrN 10342	2975±30 b.p. [1180–1260]
Oldeboorn 2	168–172	section B	base eutrophic peat	GrN 11741	3400±25 b.p. [1680–1740]

the river Boorne. All of them come from sections of excavations of Neolithic and Bronze Age sites on sand ridges near the Boorne.[29] During the investigation it became clear that these sand ridges slowly had been covered over by phragmites peat after 3380±30 b.p. (charcoal from the Bronze Age occupation layer).[30] The moment of the appearance of the water table at the surface is probably best estimated by sample GrN 10343 (table 5).[31] As is to be expected, its ^{14}C dating of 3185±30 b.p. at 1.7 m -NAP easily coincides with the mean sea level: 1.7 to 2 m -NAP.[32]

In the area between the Tjonger and the Boorne to the east of Gorredijk, the situation is somewhat different. In the Middle Ages a bog peat area existed upon the broad watershed between the Tjonger and the Boorne and changed almost without interruption into the Fochtelooërveen. Only a narrow sand ridge, upon which is found the Zwartendijkster redoubt near Een, and a strip along both rivers remained free of peat. Despite an absence of datings, the maximum extension of this peat belt was probably reached after the Middle Bronze Age (after c. 1100 cal BC) since finds from the Middle Bronze Age have been discovered here. The pollen diagram from Allardsoog leads to the same conclusion.[33] It shows that peat formation began in the stream valley in the upper course of the Boorne during the Sub-boreal.

Oligotrophic peat developed at the earliest around the time of the transition from the Sub-boreal to the Sub-atlantic. It is not inconceivable that the exploitation of Celtic field systems, leading to increased run-off and, as a consequence, a deeper incision of the river, was an influence on this process of oligotrophication.

3.4.4 The south-eastern sandy area

The south-eastern part of the investigated area is formed by the drainage basin of the rivers Tjonger, Linde, Steenwijker Aa, and Oude Vaart (see fig. 17), all of which drained into the depression to the south of the ice-pushed ridge of boulder clay of Gaasterland, Steenwijk, and Havelte. These rivers must have emptied into the lower part of the Vecht drainage basin. The depression and the connected part of the Vecht basin remained a swampy region through all the periods, with eutrophic peat close to the rivers and oligotrophic peat at some distance.[34] The open water, in which the river Vecht discharged and which was connected with the western coastal area, was never far away during the periods under investigation.

The presence of the rivers kept the sandy grounds quite well drained. This explains the bog peat developing relatively late in the areas outside the actual river valleys. The formation of bog peat occurred especially in places

29 This investigation was carried out in 1980 and 1981 by J.N. Lanting and the author (Fokkens & Van Gijn in prep.).
30 Pers. Comm. Dr W.A. Casparie.
31 It is probable that with sample GrN 11741, taken at the same depth, somewhat older humus remains were also dated

because the top of the sand that had been turned over was included in the sample.
32 Van de Plassche 1982.
33 De Groot et al. 1987, 135, 136.
34 Cf. Veenenbos 1950.

with poorly-draining subsoil or a flat topography, such as to the north-east of the Paasberg near Steenwijk. The Eesveen, the Uffelterveen and the Vledderveen came into existence this way. The archaeological finds seem to indicate that these peat areas did not expand significantly until after 1500 cal BC.

3.4.5 *The eastern border area*

The eastern border area was occupied by the former Fochtelooër and Smildiger Venen, of which only a few remains still survive. There is only one absolute date for the beginning of peat formation here: 2520±55 b.p.[35] The sample for this dating comes from the nucleus of the original peat area. Other indications for dating are the archaeological data. The settlement excavated by Van Giffen near Fochteloo,[36] dated to the 2nd century BC, must have lain in rather damp terrain considering the presence of deep ditches, but there was as yet no peat formation. This indicates that the maximum extension of the peat first dates from after the beginning of the Christian era, and that during the Roman period the peat barely reached the eastern border area. This is corroborated by the presence of a number of Celtic field systems lying to the east of the settlement near Fochteloo.

3.5 OVERVIEW OF THE PALAEOGEOGRAPHIC DEVELOPMENTS

The following section will provide a short account and description for each palaeogeographic reconstruction (maps I–VIII). The archaeological data are used only insofar as they provide positive indications to supplement the geological data. The reconstructions of the salt-marsh areas are derived from map sheets 10 W and E and 11 W and E of the Geological Map. Those from the north are adopted from Griede and Roeleveld.[37] Zagwijn's study is used to fill in the gaps.[38]

For the peat formation in the low central area, the model developed in section 3.4.3 is employed. This means that eutrophic peat formation up to 2.5 m above mean sea level

is assumed. The transition to the area where the coastal peat zone is reconstructed up to 0.5 m above mean sea level is situated north of the raised bog area around Eernewoude because there the gradients are steeper and the breadth of the coastal peat zone is relatively small. In places in the low central area where there are also relatively steep gradients,[39] the reconstruction of the extension of the peat is restricted up to a contour lower than 2.5 m above mean sea level. This applies in particular to the northern border of the boulder clay heights in Gaasterland south of the Fluessen and the Slotermeer.

For the northern part of the area, the seaward boundaries of the coastal peat from the studies by Griede and Roeleveld were adopted. For the inland boundaries, however, a level of 0.5 m above mean sea level was adhered to.[40] In a number of cases this causes the reconstruction to deviate from those of Griede and Roeleveld.

The reconstruction of the stream valleys is based on the extension of the stream valley bogs as indicated on the map sheets of the *Bodemkaart van Nederland Schaal 1:50 000* (Soil Map of the Netherlands Scale 1:50 000, hereafter referred to as Soil Map) and the extension of the Singraven Formation as shown on the Geological Map.[41] These patterns have been maintained in the same form on the map until the period 1100–600 cal BC (2900–2600 b.p.), after which gradual changes occurred, as a process of oligotrophication began in the stream valley bogs between the upper courses and the higher-lying parts of the landscape. The stream beds which are indicated on maps I–VIII form a combination of present-day and reconstructed river courses.

3.5.1 *The palaeogeography around 4350 cal BC (5500 b.p.), Early Neolithic B (map I)*

For the period 4900–4200 cal BC, the Early Neolithic B, the palaeogeography is reconstructed for *c.* 5500 b.p. (table 4), the end of the Calais II transgressive interval. The mean sea level was around 5 m -NAP. Along the northern coastal and sandy area a relatively narrow coastal peat zone had formed, of which the upper limit was the 4.5 m -NAP contour.[42] The bog peat nucleus in the area

---

35 Klaver 1981, cited in: De Groot *et al.* 1987, 136.
36 Van Giffen 1954; 1958.
37 Griede 1978; Roeleveld 1974; Griede & Roeleveld 1982.
38 Zagwijn 1986.
39 By 'steep' is meant a drop of 2 m or more per km.
40 According to Van de Plassche 1982.

41 When these two patterns do not correspond, the more restricted extension of the peat of the Singraven Formation is adhered to in most cases because the soil section types vz and wp from the soil map often refer to more recently accumulated peat.
42 Cf. Roeleveld 1974, fig. 58.

surrounding Tergracht is taken from Griede.[43] In the low central and western areas, bog peat nuclei are reconstructed at places where oligotrophic peat accumulated continuously throughout the Holocene, according to subsidiary maps and sections, both accompanying the map sheets 10 W and E and 11 W and E of the Geological Map (see also section 3.4.3). Around the bog peat nuclei, in the low central and western areas, eutrophic peat is indicated up to the limit of the 3 m -NAP contour (see section 3.4.3). In the south, a rather extensive raised bog area is depicted north of the Heegermeer. The presence of this raised bog can be seen chiefly from section HH' accompanying map sheets 10 W and E. A few higher parts between 1 and 2 m -NAP have been left uncovered here.

In employing the model sketched above, it is assumed that the depression between Workum and Oudegaasterbrekken was already covered with eutrophic peat during this period and that oligotrophic peat probably accumulated on the higher parts. The depicted area of oligotrophic peat is consistently less extensive than the mapped maximum expansion.

According to Zagwijn's reconstruction,[44] the Pleistocene landscape during this period also comprised the northern part of the IJsselmeer up to Texel. The coastal peat zone of the western lagoon area reached Gaasterland and the Noordoostpolder, with an upper limit of 4.5 m -NAP. Based on Veenenbos's data, a raised bog zone was situated along the north-western border of the Noordoostpolder which continued to the Tjeukemeer. The extension of the raised bog is derived from map sheet 16 W of the Soil Map and Veenenbos.[45] On the basis of the same data, raised bog is also depicted in the area where the Tjonger and the Linde flow together. Considering the position of these peat areas in the stream delta, it is assumed that they were rather extensive from the beginning.

There are no indications of peat formation in the south and east during this period except in local depressions. The scarce geological data were used for reconstruction of the clayey border of the tidal flat area. In fact, only a small remainder of a Calais II channel near Jorwerd is known, 50 to 100 m broad and 4 m deep. It is assumed

that this indicates the former course of the Boorne.[46] The width of the Boorne estuary was made narrower than indicated on Zagwijn's map 3[47] as a result of discussions with M.W. ter Wee.

3.5.2 *The palaeogeography around 3050 cal BC (4400 b.p.), Middle Neolithic B (map II)*

Along the coast, this is the period of the Holland III regressive interval. The mean sea level was approximately 3.5 m -NAP. With the exception of the low central area, the coastal peat is reconstructed up to the 3 m -NAP contour. On the higher parts of the Frisian-Drentian plateau there was still no trace of oligotrophic peat formation except on a local scale. In the low central and western areas the bog peat nuclei are located at the same places as on the map of the Early Neolithic B, but are shown somewhat larger. Oligotrophication of the area as a whole started in this period, but sections accompanying the geological maps show that in the Boorne estuary this was not yet taking place on a large scale. This can be read from the sections which contain the Calais IV deposits. The sections also indicate a more large-scale extension of the oligotrophic peat area in the southwest. The upper limit of the eutrophic peat formation in the low central area is drawn at the 1.5 m -NAP contour.

The reconstruction of the estuary into which the rivers Boorne and Drait discharged has the same size as that of the previous period, although the eastern border is somewhat shifted following Griede and Roeleveld's reconstruction.[48] In the north, deposits from the Calais III transgressive interval are not found; consequently a reliable reconstruction of the clayey border of the tidal flat area is not possible.

3.5.3 *The palaeogeography around 2500 cal BC (4000 b.p.), Late Neolithic A (map III)*

Figures from publications by Griede and Roeleveld[49] form the references for the northern coastal area. The mean sea level was 3 to 3.2 m -NAP. Along the coast, the eutrophic peat made a strong seaward expansion over

43 Radiocarbon dating Tergracht III, Griede 1978, section XV, among others. Van de Plassche (1979) explains the position of this peat, the base of which lies at 3.40–3.45 m -NAP and which is dated at 5890±40 b.p. (GrN 7562), from the topography: a depression (of limited size) in which rainwater could stagnate.
44 Zagwijn 1986, map 3.

45 Veenenbos 1950.
46 Ter Wee 1976, 70.
47 Zagwijn 1986.
48 Griede & Roeleveld 1982, fig. 5.
49 Griede 1978, fig. 36; Griede & Roeleveld 1982, fig. 5c.

the Calais IVa deposits during the Holland IVa regressive interval.[50] A nuanced reconstruction for the western coastal zone is not possible because the Rijks Geologische Dienst makes no distinction between the Calais IVa and IVb deposits. On the basis of a few [14]c dates, however, it is clear that a number of channels were active during both intervals.[51] For this reason the extension shown on the geological maps has been taken as the basis for reconstructing the area covered with clastic deposits for this period. The extent of these deposits, however, has been kept to relatively narrow channels.

The northern limit for the inland expansion of the fenland zone has been kept at the 2.5 m -NAP contour; for the low central area this limit is the 1 m -NAP contour. The expanding peat formation threatened to make Gaasterland an 'island'. There are no indications that this actually occurred during this period, however. The presence of a number of findspots, among them a barrow near Sint Nicolaasga,[52] supports this observation.

This period saw the formation of bog peat on a broad scale. Concrete indications can be found in the radiocarbon datings from samples taken from the Akmarijpsterpolder (table 5), the Hiaure pollen diagram,[53] and sections belonging to the geological maps. It is assumed that oligotrophic peat formation also began near Rinsumageest and to the east of Leeuwarden during this period. This can be deduced from map sheets 6 W and E of the Soil Map. There is little to go on in establishing a date, but considering later developments the peat must have been formed before 2650 b.p.

3.5.4 The palaeogeography around 2100 cal BC (3700 b.p.), Late Neolithic B and Early Bronze Age (map IV)

The period from 2350 to 2750 cal BC was the end of the Calais IVb transgressive interval at the coast. The mean sea level was about 2.5 m -NAP. The coastal peat is reconstructed up to the 2 m -NAP contour. It is certain that the peat in the north had already advanced to this height, the evidence for this being a date obtained from eutrophic peat located near Bornwird which covered

Late Neolithic arable land at a depth of 1.6 m -NAP.[54] It should therefore be assumed, in contrast to what is shown in Griede's reconstructions,[55] that the sand outcrop near Bornwird during this period was covered by peat except for a small part.[56] The raised bog round Kubaard is still present in this period as well. Increasing wetness here is dated at 3830 b.p.[57]

It is assumed that bog peat formation in the low central area continued at the same rate as it had in the past,[58] while fen peat formation under the influence of groundwater came to a virtual standstill. According to the reconstruction, the upper limit of the bog peat layer coincided with the 0.5 m -NAP contour on the eastern side of this area. This indicates that the low flanged axe which was dredged up from the Van Harinxmakanaal near Garijp was deposited in or on the edge of the peat area.[59] Most of the existing fen peat became oligotrophic during this period.[60] This reconstruction also implies that the relatively low area near Nannewijd became covered with peat and that a connection was formed between the peat areas on the lower course of the Tjonger and the lower course of the Linde and that of the low central area. In this way Gaasterland and the higher area around Sint Nicolaasga became permanently isolated from the rest of the higher grounds. In practical terms this probably also put an end to the habitability of this region.

In the veenpolders (peat polders) to the north of Veenwouden and the low areas around the Bergumermeer and De Leijen bog peat developed on a limited scale. This peat lay on the edge of the raised bog which later developed on the watershed. Proof that this peat was still limited in range during this period is shown by numerous archaeological finds, among them settlements and graves from the late Beaker period.

3.5.5 The palaeogeography around 1500 cal BC (3200 b.p.), Middle Bronze Age A and B (map V)

The reconstruction of the area around 1500 cal BC coincides with the Dunkirk 0 transgressive interval as far as

50 Griede & Roeleveld 1982, 447.
51 Ter Wee 1976, 72.
52 This barrow has not been investigated and thus theoretically could be dated to the Bronze Age. However, the paleogeographic developments (see below) make this unlikely.
53 Griede 1978.
54 GrN 5295: 3930±50 b.p. (2425 cal BC); Fokkens 1982, 93, fig. 4.
55 Griede 1978, fig. 36.
56 An Early Bronze Age arrowhead from the Mellema terp near Oostrum must be regarded as, most probably, a find separated from its context, similar to many terpen finds.
57 Ter Wee 1976, 76, fig. 43.
58 In 900 years 70 to 80 cm.
59 Cat. no. 36.
60 Cf. Zagwijn 1986, map 5.

the coast is concerned.[61] During this period deep erosion channels formed, particularly in the west.[62] The palaeogeographic map shows no distinction between saltmarsh and clay-on-peat areas because this division could not be made with the available data. As a rule, the areas indicated as salt-marsh and clay-on-peat would have been more salt-marsh-like in character close to the tidal flat area; inland, basin areas occurred, as well as clay-filled drainage channels in the peat. The same applies to map VI.

The mean sea level was around the 1.7 m -NAP contour; the coastal peat zone is reconstructed up to the 1 m -NAP contour. Along the Boorne the sand ridges also disappeared under fen peat. In the low central area the raised bog is reconstructed up to the 0 m contour, which is probably on the cautious side.[63] The archaeological data from the areas between the Boorne and the Tjonger and between the Drait and the Oude Diep (north of Drachten) give no reason to suppose that on the higher grounds the bog peat formation had already been advancing on a large scale. In the east the raised bog zone probably already extended as far as the study area. There are no concrete data to back this up, however. This also applies to the presumed beginning peat formation north of Steenwijk. The ultimate extension which the peat had reached when extraction in this region began leads one to suspect that it must have been formed in this period.

3.5.6 *The palaeogeography around 800 cal BC (2600 b.p.), Late Bronze Age and Early Iron Age* (map VI)
By about 2650 b.p., the Dunkirk Ia transgressive interval had ended in the coastal area and the Holland VI regressive interval, with its expanded peat formation, began. It has turned out to be extremely difficult to make a reconstruction of the coastal area before 2650 b.p. because in the dating scheme used by the Rijks Geologische Dienst the Dunkirk 0 transgressive interval runs right up to 2650 b.p. with no distinction made between the Dunkirk 0 deposits and the Dunkirk Ia deposits.[64] Reconstructions of the north are available from Griede and Roeleveld.[65] For the first time, a salt-marsh zone can be seen to take shape above the average high tide level between the coastal peat and the tidal flats.[66] Peat formation came to an end due to good drainage, and from c. 2600 b.p. onwards the salt-marshes were suitable for human occupation. The mean sea level was around 1.3 m -NAP; inland the coastal peat zone is reconstructed up to the 0.5 m -NAP contour. A pollen diagram from Opende[67] indicates that the raised bog came into existence there during this period, while a diagram from Allardsoog also indicates oligotrophic peat formation taking place at this time. Dating derived from the Fochtelooërveen places the beginning of peat formation in this area in this period as well.[68] The extension of the raised bogs is still kept to a rather limited range on this map. The region between the upper course of the Tjonger and the upper course of the Peizerdiep must have been easily accessible and habitable, considering the large number of urnfields and Celtic field systems found there.

Incipient bog peat formation is indicated along the upper courses of the brooks and on the watershed. In doing this, the final extent of the bog peat layer – reached during the Roman period – is taken into consideration. It is assumed that the oligotrophic peat on the higher grounds originated predominantly between the beginning of the Early Iron Age and the end of the Roman period (2600–1650 b.p.), and that it also reached its maximum extent during this period.

3.5.7 *The palaeogeography around 400 cal BC (2300 b.p.), Middle and Late Iron Age* (map VII)
Around 2200 b.p. the Dunkirk Ib transgressive interval had just come to an end.[69] It is assumed that the mean sea level was approximately 1 m -NAP. Once more, the

61 Ter Wee maintained the period 3600–3000/2650 b.p. for the Dunkirk 0 transgression interval and did not distinguish a Dunkirk IA-interval (1976, 78). Griede (1978) and Roeleveld (1974) do make this distinction, however. A recent reanalysis of the ¹⁴c dates shows that the Dunkirk 0 transgressive interval probably lasted until 3400, perhaps locally until 3200 b.p. Just after 3200 b.p. the Dunkirk IA transgressive interval began, which reached its highest point around 2950 b.p. and ended around 2800 (Van de Plassche 1985). Van de Plassche's classification will be used from now on.

62 For the reconstruction of this channel system grateful use was made of a manuscript map prepared by Ter Wee (Ter Wee 1976, fig. 36 a.o.).

63 Cf. Zagwijn 1986, map 6.

64 This implies that the first *terpen*, which, according to Ter Wee (1976, 81) lie on top of the Dunkirk 0 deposits, were in fact built on Dunkirk IA sediments.

65 Griede 1978, fig. 39; Griede & Roeleveld 1982, fig. 5f.

66 Griede & Roeleveld 1982, 448.

67 Van Duinen & Van Zeist 1960.

68 De Groot *et al.* 1987, 135–6.

69 Van de Plassche 1985.

coastal peat zone is reconstructed up to the 0.5 m -NAP contour. The reconstruction of the salt-marsh area is based on the situation as it was sketched for the end of the Dunkirk ib transgressive interval[70] but is adapted to archaeological data: the distribution of *terpen* containing Ruinen-Wommels type pottery. In Barradeel in particular this means that a region which became or may have become habitable during the Roman period is retained as tidal flat area.

For the north-western part of the area of map sheet 11 W the data from the Geological Map were only partly used[71] because they were relatively too detailed and because comparable data for the area of map sheets 10 W and E are not available. Therefore the extension of the Dunkirk ib deposits is roughly shown as salt-marsh and clay-on-peat areas. The sections accompanying the map sheets to a scale of 1:50 000 give no indication that the tidal inlet which reached the Boorne valley had further penetrated the interior as a proto-Middelzee. The Marne inlet, however, had probably already been formed.[72]

3.5.8 *The palaeogeography around AD 400 (1650 b.p.), Roman period* (map VIII)

The Roman period reconstruction is set around 1650 b.p., the end of the Holland VII regressive interval. Reconstructions for this interval are difficult to make because vegetation horizons which separate the deposits of successive sedimentation phases are absent in many places. Only Griede indicates an area where vegetation horizons developed during this period.[73] The situation in the coastal area can be deduced from existing reconstructions for around 2000 b.p. The mean sea level was approximately 0.5 m -NAP. In the inland area, the maximum extension of peat formation is indicated. It is assumed that by 1650 b.p. the peat was already accumulating in all the places where it later would be dug away or still remains today. In the reconstruction the brook valleys are shown as eutrophic peat and the higher sandy grounds outside them as oligotrophic peat. Old maps were used to provide information about peat in places where it has disappeared completely due to exploitation.[74] The toponyms and parcelling patterns on

each of these maps show where peat was accumulating or had been exploited at the time the map was made. The heathlands were not mapped as peat, nor were the baselines of the villages in the south-west, from where the peat reclamation had started.

On the one hand, the map image produced in this way shows extremely extended peat surfaces, particularly in the centre and north, which probably is a much larger expanse than anyone had previously imagined. The old maps, however, leave little room for other interpretations: the extent of the peat has been reconstructed conservatively rather than that it has been overrated. On the other hand, it must be remembered that the oligotrophic peat was formed upon the higher parts relatively late. So when large-scale exploitation began the peat must have been no thicker than 1.5 m. This means that passing through the peat areas must have been much less difficult than in eastern Drenthe, for example. This also explains why the peat removal was so complete. The digging of peat could be done under dry conditions, and the digging of canals to nearby river valleys made drainage a relatively simple affair.

The archaeological distribution pattern seems to show that human occupation was able to sustain itself only around Oosterwolde and in the Steenwijker Aa and Oude Vaart drainage areas. On the other hand, coins found along the streams, even where they ran through the peat area, seem to indicate that intensive use was made of the streams as transport routes.

3.6 FINAL REMARKS

It will be clear that the developments sketched here give only a rough picture. But for the purpose of this study and as a palaeogeographical background for the archaeological distribution maps, these reconstructions must be considered adequate. It should be emphasized, however, that these maps are merely an approximation; they are not suited for a detailed locational analysis of individual sites because local factors can play an important role.

---

70 Griede 1978, fig. 40; De Groot *et al.* 1987, fig. 55c; Zagwijn 1986, map 7.
71 De Groot *et al.* 1987, fig. 55c.
72 Ter Wee 1976, 82.
73 Griede 1978, 93, fig. 41.

74 The *Chr. Schotanus Atlas* (1664), the *B. Schotanus à Sterringa* Map (1739), the Huguenin Map (1820–1824), the first military and topographical map of the Netherlands, scale 1:50 000 (1850–1862).

Chapter 4

Site and findspot formation processes: a discussion

4.1 INTRODUCTION

Site formation processes have been a well-known concept in the field of archaeology since the beginning of the 1970s. The American archaeologist M.B. Schiffer is generally acknowledged as the spiritual father of the current understanding of formation processes, certainly as far as the formulation of a coherent model is concerned.[1] Still it must be said that when Schiffer's first article appeared (1972), attention to this problem was already being shown in Europe as well.[2] Here, however, the concept was being described using the term *post-depositional change*.

Nevertheless, Schiffer's work is the most comprehensive, and he is the only author to treat this matter systematically, particularly in his book *Behavioral Archaeology*. In this work, Schiffer formulated a coherent conceptual framework within which the origin of the archaeological record can be explained. He did this as a reaction against the insufficiently critical use of sources by his fellow *New Archaeologists*. Typical of its positivistic scientific outlook, the *New Archaeology* expressed confidence that the theory of random sampling and investigative strategy produced data which were both objective and, for the archaeological record, representative. This idea, however, appears to have been incorrect. Although his model is only partially applied in the current study, it seems worthwhile to dwell briefly on the ideas employed by Schiffer.

4.2 'BEHAVIORAL ARCHAEOLOGY'

Schiffer first defined the central notions of his model, archaeological context and system context, in 1972. Sys-
tem context is, in principle, the context in which the archaeological materials, soil traces, etc., come into existence and are utilized. Thus the word 'system' here stands for the socio-cultural system such as that defined by Clarke.[3] Whenever those materials cease to participate in a system context they become part of the archaeological context, virtually synonymous with what is often called the archaeological record.

A number of processes which affect the archaeological materials have been distinguished in both the system context and the archaeological context. These are the so-called *site formation processes*. Here Schiffer distinguished two subgroups: the cultural and the non-cultural site formation processes. The principles of regularity which underlie these formation processes were called *transforms* by Schiffer. These patterns can be used to predict which materials have been deposited by a system (*c-transforms*) and what kind of interaction exists between these deposited materials and the environment in which they are found (*n-transforms*).[4]

Schiffer distinguished four kinds of cultural formation processes: S-A, A-S, A-A, and S-S processes, in which the S stands for system context and the A for archaeological context. S-A processes are the most important. They explain which activities have repercussions in the archaeological context and how that takes place (*cultural deposition*). In A-S processes the reverse of S-A processes takes place, in that pieces of the archaeological record are restored to the system context by way of such processes as the plundering of abandoned sites, treasure hunting, collecting, and excavating. A-A processes transform materials from one state into another within the archaeological context. Examples of this are ploughing, earth levelling, and other activities which disturb the

1 Schiffer 1976.
2 Ascher 1968; Clarke 1972; 1973; Daniels 1972.

3 Clarke 1978.
4 Schiffer 1976, 15–6.

archaeological record.[5] Finally, s-s processes are linked to the movements of cultural materials within the system context. They appear, for example, when there is a change in the consumer group (*lateral cycling*) or in the activity for which an object is used (*recycling*).

4.2.1 *Points of criticism*

Schiffer's approach emphasizes the development of *transforms*, particularly the cultural formation processes, since up until then these had been the least elucidated. He was able to do this because, in his interpretation, the cultural formation processes comprise a vast area. This is made possible through the way in which he defines the notion of system context in *Behavioral Archaeology*. Schiffer even regards such activities as excavations and surveying operations as A-S processes whereby the objects from the archaeological record reappear in the system context, implying a non-exclusive definition of system context. In this vision, everything involving human interference belongs to cultural formation processes. In my opinion this is an incorrect approach which developed because Schiffer made no distinction between site and findspot.

The above-mentioned definition stands in contrast to the one Schiffer formulated in his 1972 article: '*Systemic context* labels the condition of an element which is participating in a behavioral system. *Archaeological context* describes materials which have passed through a cultural system, and are now objects of investigation of archaeologists.'[6] Clearly Schiffer here regards as system context only the historic and prehistoric cultural systems which are being studied. That is indeed a sensible and very useful definition. By regarding all systems in which human interference is present (therefore the present system as well) as system context, which Schiffer has done since 1976, an unambiguous use of this notion is no longer

feasible. Site disturbing processes are suddenly ranked in the same class as site forming processes. Binford's criticism of Schiffer is closely linked with this problem.[7] Although these points of criticism do not reduce the value of Schiffer's approach in itself, I believe they make it necessary to adapt the synthetic model of 'behavioral archaeology'. In particular the definition of system context and archaeological context has to be reinstated as Schiffer's 1972 definition (see above quotation). That makes it possible, following Butzer, to speak of site formation and site deformation processes,[8] or perhaps rather of site formation and findspot formation processes in which the first always has bearing on the system context, the last on the archaeological context.[9]

4.3 MAP FORMATION PROCESSES

Most studies of site formation processes are involved with the investigation at the level of the site. Attention is focused on the excavation of findspots and the interpretation of resulting data. For an investigation such as this one, however, which relies chiefly on data from museums and private collections, a completely different category of formation processes is relevant: those which have influenced the origin of distribution patterns.

To a certain extent, the processes which are operative on a regional level are the same as those which hold for the findspot level, but there are also specific regional processes which must be distinguished. This does not so much involve those processes which influence the distributions of finds within findspots as it involves factors which have influence on the discernibility of sites as a whole. It might therefore be possible to speak of *map formation factors*, since these influence the establishment of finds distribution patterns. Because only a small

---

5 Schiffer 1976, 29.

6 Schiffer 1972, 157.

7 Binford (1981) points out that Schiffer regards even s-s processes as a disturbance of the archaeological record. Schiffer would be endlessly searching for a Pompeii where nothing has disturbed the solidified picture of the cultural system, including processes of site abandonment, etc. Although this is an example of Binford's typically exaggerated characterization of the problem, I agree with the thrust of the criticism.

8 However, Butzer's concepts of *site formation* and *site modification* have a completely different meaning than that proposed here (1982, table 3.1, among others). My definition of site is 'a place where human activities occurred in the past'.

This is in contrast to the definition 'A site is any place, large or small, where there are to be found traces of ancient occupation or activity.' (Hole & Heizer 1973, 111), a definition employed by Schiffer.

9 When flint from a Paleolithic site is reused by a group of Late Neolithic farmers, the notion of site deformation processes is applicable (when the Paleolithic site is being studied). The flint does not once again enter the Paleolithic cultural system. It is taken by the Neolithic inhabitants from its original context, which is thereby distorted. However, when the Neolithic site is studied it is indeed a matter of the admission into the system context; after all, the flint is reused and reappears in the archaeological context.

amount of work has been conducted in this area and no coherent approach has been devised, the following section will discuss the concept in more detail.

The first point of discussion is the framework in which the processes are classified in this study. The above discussion clearly indicates which meaning is intended here by the notions of system context and archaeological context. Various formation processes are distinguished within this which, in order to avoid confusion with the concepts used by Schiffer, are not being addressed here as cultural and non-cultural processes. First I would like to emphasize the moment of definitive abandonment, that is the moment when an object becomes a part of the archaeological context (*deposition*). In particular, Schiffer dwelt on the processes taking place before the deposition, in other words on site formation, while in this study most of the attention will be paid to processes which take place after the deposition. This can be referred to by the term findspot formation or by the old term *post-depositional processes*. Following Daniels's practice, those processes can be grouped into two categories: processes taking place before the archaeologist arrives on the scene, which Daniels calls distorting processes, arising after deposition (i.e. *post-depositional processes*) and distortions which come about through investigation (*research processes*).[10]

4.3.1 *Post-depositional processes*

Post-depositional processes comprise all post-depositional changes which affect the archaeological record before the archaeologist becomes engaged at the site. These factors may be of either natural or human origin.

Natural changes
Post-depositional changes brought about by natural causes have been described by, among others, Butzer, Gifford, and Schiffer.[11] Gifford distinguishes in particular animal activities, roots, climatic aspects, geological aspects, and soil conditions as non-cultural formation processes. With her scheme as a basis, these processes might be grouped in the following manner: a. biotic processes: plant and animal activity; b. geological processes: sedimentation and erosion; c. geochemical processes: weathering, soil processes.
Of these three, the biotic processes are especially im-

Table 6 Preservation conditions for various archaeological materials in different matrices. Legend: + good, ± fair, − poor.

matrix	archaeological material			
	pottery	flint	other types of stone	bone (not burnt)
clay	+	+	+	+
peat	−	+	±	−
sand	±	+	+	−

portant for the site-level of analysis. In the Netherlands, for instance, every archaeologist is familiar with the disturbing effects of animal tunnels. Through the tunnels that they dig animals can make soil traces difficult to interpret and can move finds either horizontally or vertically.[12] However, these processes exert little influence on the distribution pattern of findspots within a region. At this level, it is rather the chemical and especially the geological processes that are of the most importance. In particular, erosion and sedimentation can be responsible for huge distortions in the archaeological distribution patterns because these processes cause old surfaces to disappear or fall out of reach. This is certainly the case on the western side of the Frisian-Drentian plateau.

The geochemical qualities of site-covering sediments can have a large influence on the preservation of archaeological materials. In addition, chemical reactions in the soil within findspots (oxidation in particular) can also be an indication of the original presence of already decayed materials.[13] Verdigris, specks of phosphate, etc., are well-known examples. It is, however, the preserving qualities, in particular, which play a role at the regional level (table 6). In the study area, these processes have been most influential in the preservation of bone and pottery.

Anthropogenetic changes
The post-depositional changes brought about through human activities are practically all linked to land use.[14] It is a well-known fact that archaeological materials are more easily discernible in freshly-ploughed arable land than in forested areas, for instance, or grassland. Archaeological activities therefore are often focused on

10 Daniels 1972, 202.
11 Butzer 1982; Gifford 1978; Schiffer 1983.
12 A.o. Stein 1983.

13 Schiffer 1983.
14 Schiffer calls these A-A processes.

ploughed land. However, it is not only current land use which affects the distribution pattern. For an investigation such as the present one, which is based on an inventory of finds over a long period, it is also past agricultural methods and reclamation history which are of great importance.[15] So in the Netherlands, the old arable lands (called *essen* in the northern Netherlands) must be counted as an important findspot formation factor. It has indeed already been recognized as such.[16] The old arable lands were created by the practice of sod-manuring (until the early 20th century). Heath sods or forest humus were brought into the *potstal*, i.e. a byre which is adapted to the sod manuring process, in which the manure from the animals being kept there was collected during the winter. In the spring these enriched sods were transferred to the fields, in the course of many centuries resulting in the heightening of the arable to sometimes more than 75 cm. Considering the extensiveness of some *es* complexes, this type of land use could explain large blind spots in the distribution maps.

Reclamation history can also be an important factor. This is especially the case in the northern Netherlands (see section 6.2.2), where large reclamation projects were carried out by the government during the Great Depression before the Second World War. Thus arable was reclaimed from heath with the spade. Occasionally archaeologists and amateur archaeologists were notified when some artifact was found, but more often the archaeological materials were lost, because they were either not seen or not recognized.[17] At best, familiar monuments (especially barrows) were investigated beforehand. In addition to the heath reclamation efforts, the large-scale peat excavations are a strong distortion factor for the archaeological distribution pattern.

Another factor not to be underestimated is erosion brought on by human activity. Agricultural activities in particular, also known as socio-economic factors, can lead to severe distortions.[18] Barrows can be levelled or ploughed out and other types of findspots can equally be destroyed. Even *hunebedden* (megalithic monuments) have not remained untouched, like the *hunebedden* in

Drenthe, destroyed to supply stones for the paving of roads or construction work. The history of land use in particular plays a role in this respect. In regions which were reclaimed early in the Middle Ages these effects can be quite considerable,[19] while in those districts reclaimed later – for barrows, at any rate – they can be nil.[20]

Finally, later (prehistoric) occupation is also one of the activities which lead to distortion. Thus an Iron Age farm built over a Mesolithic encampment generally constitutes a radical distortion of the Mesolithic site. Even re-use of materials can occur, but nevertheless (when we study the Mesolithic cultural system) this is not a cultural process in the sense of Schiffer's *Behavioral Archaeology*. It is, after all, a process which takes place centuries after the abandonment of the investigated site! The result of all these processes is that certain sites are easily discernible as findspots while others are barely discernible or have even completely disappeared. That does not mean, however, that every findspot which still exists will also be discovered; this depends on the archaeologists' investigation strategy.

4.3.2 *Research processes*

Through the choice of research area, excavation methods, surveying methods, etc., sources of error are introduced which result in a completely distorted distribution pattern of archaeologically demonstrable remains. One of the few authors who has paid extensive attention to these factors is F.W. Hamond.[21] He derived his data from research on Linearbandkeramik (LBK) culture settlements on the Aldenhovener Platte, an investigation area of 6132 km^2.[22] After analysis of the post-depositional processes he came to the conclusion that 'The nature of LBK sites makes it unlikely, though, that a significant number will have been totally destroyed by post-depositional decay processes. Paradoxically it is the nature of the data-recovery process itself which may contribute most spatial bias to the known distribution of sites.'[23]

The research factors which, according to Hamond, de-

---

15 See Baudou 1985.

16 Brongers 1976; Kooi 1979.

17 Occasionally reclamation operations have also caused large distortions at the site level, see for example Kooi 1979, fig. 73.

18 Kristiansen 1985.

19 Baudou 1985.

20 Hansen 1985.

21 Hamond 1978; 1980.

22 Hamond 1978.

23 Hamond 1978, 128.

termine the distribution pattern on the Aldenhovener Platte are:[24] '1. The location of archaeologists active in the area. 2. The extent of their fieldwork, this attenuating with distance. 3. The nature of this fieldwork, systematic fieldwalking being more efficient and effective in the discovery of sites. 4. The rate of development of archaeological investigation in different areas.' One more category can be added here: 5. the specific period(s) that the local archaeologist is interested in.

Considering the present state of the archaeological investigation on the western part of the Frisian-Drentian plateau, factors 3 and 4 can be ignored. Whether points 1, 2, and 5 are of importance remains to be seen (see Chapter 6).

In addition, regarding point 5 there are the following remarks. Most archaeologists specialize in certain areas and, within these areas, in certain periods or even specific cultures. This applies to both professional and amateur, or rather local, archaeologists. As a consequence, a field-survey which is carried out without a systematic plan will lead to a distorted image of the archaeological record because materials which are indeed visible go un-

observed or are even ignored. In both the northern Netherlands and the Netherlands as a whole, this factor has caused an overrepresentation of moraine flint finds, although its extent is difficult to assess.[25]

4.4 TOWARDS A METHOD OF ANALYSIS

The preceding discussion gives a general overview of various distorting factors. Now the question is how these data can be further processed in the interpretation and description of the find materials. In other words, is it possible to determine what percentage of the materials are sifted out through a specific filter of transforming processes? If that could be done, then one might be able to reason backwards from the present distribution pattern of finds to the original situation before distortion took place. This procedure would enable a more reliable analysis of the distribution maps. In the following chapters an attempt will be made to design such a method so that the data from the Frisian-Drentian plateau can be properly evaluated.

---

24 Hamond 1980, 215.

25 An illustrative anecdote that can be mentioned here concerns one of the local archaeologists whose collection consisted almost exclusively of moraine flint. When asked, 'Do you sometimes find pottery, too?' he answered, 'Certainly, but it doesn't interest me. I always ignore it. If you'd like to have it I'll bring some along sometime.'

Chapter 5

Map formation analysis: designing a method

5.1 INTRODUCTION

Although practically everyone today is aware that map formation processes have influenced the distribution pattern of archaeological finds on a regional scale, hardly any attempts have been made to estimate the effect of those processes. To the extent that any explicit attention is paid at all, it is usually confined to a summary of possible disturbing factors which 'should be kept in mind' in interpreting the data; that is to say, a qualitative rather than a quantitative approach. Only in exceptional cases are the disturbing factors provided on distribution maps. Brongers, for instance, indicated the *essen* on his map of Celtic field systems, and Kooi did the same on his map of urnfields.[1] Besides the *essen*, which can conceal urnfields, Kooi indicated the arable as it was in 1853 as well as the coversands; Brongers did this on a separate map. Both the *essen* and the coversands can make urnfields indiscernible, or during their formation can be the cause of their destruction, making them 'blind spots' on the map. In the final interpretation of site patterns, however, in both studies the data have scarcely been processed. They never went beyond the identification of sources of distortion. The same is true for the work of most authors who report on regional investigations.

The reason that the distorting factors are merely indicated and are hardly considered in the interpretation of distribution maps is that no methods have yet been developed. When it is a question of one or two variables, it is still possible to represent them on a distribution map. But when more map formation processes are involved in the study, the picture becomes cluttered and meaningless. The alternative, to summarize all relevant variables on separate maps, is certainly useful but is an even less satisfactory solution because it is not possible to

combine the map images. It should be possible to summarize the various map images in one overall picture. One problem in attempting this is that not all factors produce disturbing effects in the same way. Moreover, while the possibility that a site will be encountered within the archaeological context is positively influenced by some factors, it is negatively influenced by others. In other words, the combining of map formation factors is not simply a question of counting and subtracting.

5.2 QUANTIFICATION OF MAP FORMATION PROCESSES

What should be included in a method for quantifying the effects of map formation processes? First, it should be established which factors have been at work. Next, the geographic extension of each factor must be mapped. Finally, an assessment must be made to determine which distorting effect a particular factor has produced. If these data are known, then the materials needed for quantifying map formation processes are present. The problem, however, is that the question centres on spatial distributions.

For a number of years, the quantification of spatial information has formed part of an approach in geography called *Geographical Information Systems* (GIS).[2] A geographical information system is a computer program combined with a database of spatial information. The database contains information about grid cells of equal size. Each legend unit (the category of grid-cell values) is given a unique numeric code with which arithmetic and logical manipulations can be executed. The result is a coded map in the form of a database of grid-cell values.[3] In this way all sorts of maps can be quantified. If the same grid is used and the position of the grid remains

1 Brongers 1976; Kooi 1979.
2 Burrough 1987.

3 Van den Berg *et al.* 1985.

the same, then the grid-cell values of different maps can be combined and arithmetically manipulated. GIS are increasingly being used in urban and rural planning and physical geography. An existing situation can be quantified and, by use of computer simulation, the effect of various measures or changing situations can be predicted.

It is not difficult to imagine the usefulness of this method for archaeology; the list of new users is quickly increasing. With help from GIS it is possible, for example, to analyse location-choice factors or distribution patterns in a way that is much faster and more accurate than with the help of previous methods.[4] One of the problems of the present study, i.e. the representativeness of distribution maps, can also be approached with GIS. This might be called map formation analysis. GIS provide the methodical framework for the quantification of spatial data, but the actual procedures are determined by the aims of this study.[5] The method which was followed will be dealt with more closely in the following section.

5.3 MAP FORMATION ANALYSIS

In the analysis of map formation it must first be established which distorting factors are present in the study area. This is strongly dependent on the area's geology, reclamation history, etc. The second step is the mapping and quantifying of these factors. Each factor is reproduced on a separate map. These maps can be digitized by placing a grid over them and defining the surface areas of each of the units that are distinguished per grid cell. Next the effect of these factors is evaluated and translated into formulas. This makes it possible to combine the maps arithmetically. By combining several maps and formulas, new maps can be produced which might be called archaeological visibility maps. These maps show how large the chance is (per grid cell) that findspots are still present and that they can be detected.

The last step involves a confrontation of the visibility maps with the actual distribution maps. Several possibilities for further analysis are present, provided that the distribution maps are also digitized or at least that the

number of findspots is known per grid cell. One of the simplest applications is the selection of areas where, based on the analysis, the data which have already been collected can be considered representative of the archaeological record. In those areas the settlement patterns can be analysed and interpreted. Another application is to make a simulation of the original archaeological distribution map by correcting the present map for the effects of various formation processes. Of course here the underlying map should be a digitized palaeo-geographic map.

In Chapter 6 the elaboration of each of the above-mentioned steps will be dealt with in more detail. The rest of this chapter will present a number of methodical aspects of a more general nature.

5.4 SOME METHODICAL ASPECTS OF THE QUANTIFICATION OF SPATIAL INFORMATION

5.4.1 *Grid size*
In order to represent spatial information numerically a grid has to be laid over the map so that one or more values can be fixed per grid cell (fig. 20). This value can simply be the presence or absence of a certain factor, expressed as 1 or 0, for instance. It can also be an estimate of the surface area within the grid cell of the factor in question.

The mesh width of the grid being laid over the map is important; it determines the resolution of the final analysis. A cell of 500 × 500 m, for instance, should produce a high resolution. In the present study area, however, such a degree of detail is impossible. In the first place, the information regarding map formation factors is not available in such detail. Most maps from which this information is taken are generalizations of a limited number of observations.[6] It would be incorrect to base detailed analyses on these maps. Secondly, the quality of the find recovery data does not allow for this degree of resolution either. Finally, the extent of the study area, 70 × 70 km, is a limiting factor. The number of grid cells to be quantified would be 19 600, a hopeless task applying the method used below. For this reason, a cell

---

4 Wansleeben 1988.
5 The GIS packages which now exist were not used in this investigation since they were not yet available when the method was designed (1985). The same effect is reached by linking a database and a drawing program.

6 An average of nine cores per km² is customary for the survey for geological and soil maps at a scale of 1:50 000; this is supplemented by the survey of landscape and terrain conditions.

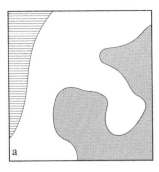 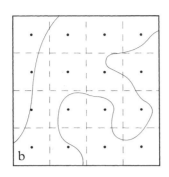 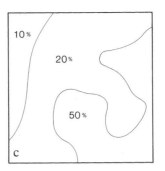 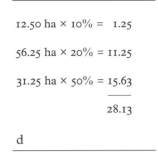

Figure 20a–d Model to show the method used to establish surface area estimates and index figures with the help of a dot planimeter:
Figure 20a A cell measuring 1 km² with three land use units;
Figure 20b The same cell with an estimate of the surface area of the map units using a dot planimeter; each dot represents 6.25 ha;
Figure 20c The same cell showing the permeability values per map unit;
Figure 20d Calculation of the index figure for the archaeological visibility.

size of 1 × 1 km was chosen for this study. At this level practically all information is available, including that from the Soil Maps and Geological Maps. Moreover, the advantage of the square kilometre cell is that the existing co-ordinate system of the Topographical Map of the Netherlands on the scales of 1:25 000 and 1:50 000 can be used to identify the squares.

5.4.2 Surface area measurement

In addition to the size of the grid cell, the way in which the surface areas are measured significantly influences the accuracy of the analysis. In the current investigation it was decided to determine the surface area of each unit discerned within each grid cell. The *presence-absence* method is perhaps suitable for analysis of location choice factors with the help of GIS,[7] but for map formation analysis a more accurate form of surface area measurement was deemed necessary.[8] Otherwise it would be imposs-

ible, for example, to apply different values to the various forms of land use within a grid cell in terms of distorting effects. Consequently, it was necessary to look for a reliable and, most importantly, efficient form of surface area measurement. In applying GIS, frequent use is made of a digitizer linked to a computer. Although the use of a digitizer is one of the most accurate methods for measuring surface areas, this technique is primarily suitable for the graphic reproduction of spatial information. When used for surface area measurement it means that in each grid cell the perimeter of each unit to be measured must be digitized individually. The computer then very accurately calculates the surface area of the plane within the contour. This is a manageable method for a few grid cells but not for the amount of cells which had to be analysed for the current investigation. The other methods have the same disadvantage,[9] not to mention the fact that they are too precise for the intended purpose.[10]

More suitable for determining the surface areas within a spatial unit is the dot planimeter. This is a simple, easy-to-make instrument. It is a transparent overlay, on which a number of dots are printed in a regular cell pattern (fig. 20). Each dot represents a square area with an outer measurement that is related to the distance between the dots. Planimeters with a high density of dots make more precise measurements than planimeters on which the dots are further apart. The planimeter is laid over a plane and the number of dots that fall within the borders of each unit inside that plane is counted. The

7 Wansleeben 1988.
8 With the *presence-absence* method, only the presence or absence per grid cell of a certain factor is coded, so measuring takes place only on a nominal scale level. Such values cannot be manipulated with formulas, such as those necessary for the proposed method. For this purpose at least an interval scale is needed.
9 See Monkhouse & Wilkinson (1977) for a survey. A number

of other methods mentioned by Monkhouse and Wilkinson, such as the square method, the strip method, and the geometric method are not suitable, primarily because they were developed for the calculation of one or a few surface areas.
10 The conclusions that are based upon these analyses can only be of a general nature. Basing them on extremely precise observations would not result in additional information or greater accuracy. See further section 4.4.

number of dots, multiplied by the surface area that each dot represents, determines the surface area of the measured plane.

Monkhouse and Wilkinson[11] regard the Blakeridge grid, a dot planimeter with 100 dots per 4 × 4 cm, as the most reliable tool for estimating surface areas. The greatest precision, however, is not always necessary, and for this reason a test was made to determine how many dots per grid cell would be sufficient in our case in order to obtain a reliable result. This was done by first measuring ten representative sections of 1 × 1 km with a grid of 400 dots per 4 × 4 cm. Then the same sections were measured with grids containing 36, 64, and 100 dots per 4 × 4 cm. Comparison of the results of the measurements using a Chi-square test[12] showed that measurements with the 64-dot planimeter still lay within the 95% reliability range. A number of 36 dots per 4 × 4 cm no longer seemed to produce a sound estimate. Thus it was decided to carry out all surface area measuring with the help of a dot-grid of 64 dots per 4 × 4 cm, that is 16 dots per square of 1 km^2 at a scale of 1:50 000, the scale at which all measurements were made. Each dot therefore represents 6.25 ha.

5.5 INDEXING DISTORTION FACTORS

Another important part of map formation analysis is the composing of formulas to describe the effects of distorting factors. These formulas will be reproduced here as index ciphers. In the calculations in which the formulas are used, the concept of *archaeological visibility* (AV) is an important element. Archaeological visibility is described here as the chance that archaeological findspots in a map unit will be discovered despite the presence of distorting factors. The visibility is expressed in percentages; the maximum is 100%, that is to say that the number of finds gives an optimal representation of the original distribution. Two distinct indexes are distinguished, both the result of a number of distorting factors:

1. The index of distortion by post-depositional factors (post-depositional index: PDI). The formula used to calculate this index is composed of different elements linked with various involved factors, that is distortions of a natural character (PDI$_N$) and distortions brought

about by human activity (soil use: PDI$_S$; reclamation history: PDI$_R$). The PDI is calculated per cell with the formula

$$PDI = (AV_1 \times A_1) + (AV_2 \times A_2) + (AV_3 \times A_3) + \ldots + (AV_n \times A_n)$$

in which AV is the archaeological visibility in each map unit and A the unit's area. The final formula for the combination of the parts reads[13]

$$PDI_T = ((PDI_N + PDI_S) \times PDI_R) / 150.$$

2. The index of distortion by research factors (research index: RI). The RI determines the chance that a site, if archaeologically visible, will also indeed be discovered. The formula for calculation reads

$$RI = (AV \times I_1) + (AV \times I_2) + (AV \times I_3) + \ldots + (AV \times I_n)$$

in which AV is the visibility in a grid cell and I represents the research intensity.

3. Combining the two indexes PDI and RI produces a total picture of the measure of representativeness of the finds distribution pattern per grid cell. This is a new index cipher: the index of archaeological visibility (VI). The VI is rendered as the product of PDI and RI

$$VI = PDI \times RI.$$

An example serves to illustrate the establishment of index ciphers and AV values (fig. 20). Suppose that the effect of land use on the distribution of findspots is being estimated. First a grid is laid over a topographical map. For each grid-cell calculations are made to determine the size of the surface area covered by different forms of land use: in this example 12.5 ha is covered by forest; 56.25 ha by heathland; 31.25 ha by grassland ($A_1 = 12.5$, $A_2 = 56.25$, $A_3 = 31.25$). The visibility of findspots in each of these forms of land use is estimated at: 10% in forest, 20% in heathland, and 50% in grassland that is occasionally ploughed ($AV_1 = 10\%$, $AV_2 = 20\%$, $AV_3 = 50\%$).

Applied to these figures, the formula produces a result of PDI$_S$ = 28.13 for distortions by land use (($12.5 \times .10$) + ($56.25 \times .20$) + ($31.25 \times .50$)). That means that in this grid cell 28.13% of the findspots are archaeologically visible, at least if land use is the only factor determining the PDI.

However, this conclusion does not mean that the findspots will also be discovered. In the end it is the research factors that make that determination. So it may be that the grid cell in the example lies in an area where there

---

11 Monkhouse & Wilkinson 1977.
12 See also Burrough 1987, 112–6, for a method to test the

reliability of surface area measurement.
13 For a more detailed computation see section 6.4.

has never been any activity carried out by local or professional archaeologists (R_1), but only chance finds have been reported (R_2). If it is supposed that we estimate the AV of these reports at 10% and that of archaeological activity at 50%, then the formula for RI $((0 \times .50) + (100 \times .10))$ produces a result of RI = 10%. In this grid cell, therefore, VI is equal to 2.81% ($28.13 \times 10\%$). In other words, of the number of visible findspots only 10% will be discovered, and the result is that the number of findspots confirmed in this grid cell cannot be more than 2.81% of the actual number present. Conclusion: the distribution of findspots in this grid cell is not representative of the original site pattern.

This schematized example shows how the index ciphers can be determined. Just one more remark should still be made concerning the concept of archaeological visibility. In the example above, the different types of findspots are not differentiated. Even so, it should be obvious that the AV is not the same for all varieties of findspots. Physical characteristics play an important role. Some findspots manifest themselves as scattered concentrations of flint, others as mounds clearly observable in the landscape. The appearance is first determined by historical site formation factors. It is exceptionally difficult to build this aspect systematically into a regional analysis such as the present one. In principle each period has its own AV values, and a generally applicable formula is impossible to produce. Nevertheless, in the interpretation of the distribution pattern it is necessary to take into account the differences in the visibility of site-types, which are influenced by site forming as well as site distorting factors. Therefore, this aspect has been accounted for in the final analysis in Chapter 8, but not in the general layout of map formation analysis as presented in Chapter 6.

It is assumed that the AV should never be zero. Even in areas where a 1 m-thick clay cover conceals the prehistoric surface, a findspot can be discovered by chance. Table 9, for example, shows that 2% of the finds are discovered during building activities. In this study it is assumed that, except in lakes, visibility is always at least 1% because of chance factors.

Finally it should be mentioned that since few studies of map formation processes have been carried out, the establishment of AV ciphers is fairly arbitrary. For this reason the ciphers used in this study cannot be adopted indiscriminately for other investigations without subjecting the hypotheses to critical analysis. As has been suggested earlier, it will turn out, moreover, that conditions differ from region to region.

5.6 CONFRONTATION WITH THE DISTRIBUTION MAPS

What happens after the distorting factors have been analysed? Is it possible to correct the distribution maps for distortions? Theoretically speaking, this should be the case, because the distorting factors are estimated and quantified per grid cell. It is possible, for example, to multiply the number of findspots indicated in a grid cell by the VI for that cell to reach an estimate of the number of non-visible findspots. This method can be satisfactory in areas where the density of the finds is quite high and the distorting factors relatively few.

Another situation is created when the finds density is low and no findspots are to be found over large areas because the distorting factors make discovery impossible. Considering that multiplication by zero is always zero, no correction takes place in empty grid cells; they remain empty. Therefore, for areas without finds another method must be followed to simulate the occupation pattern. One of the possible ways to create a reconstruction in such a situation is to use as a point of departure the premise that the principle of uniformity is applicable. That is to say, an analysis is made of occupation density and occupation pattern in regions where the distribution map presents a representative image. These regions serve in turn as a model for the entire area.

The methods, roughly presented here to use map formation analysis data for the simulation of occupation patterns, are of course not a guarantee for producing accurate occupation reconstructions. Clearly a large number of other factors related to the social and physical environment must still be involved in the investigation. The result must be regarded as a model that can be used as a guide in continued archaeological field research. It can also serve as a basis for regional issues such as those which are central to this study. Although it would be an interesting exercise in itself to draw up such simulation models, it has not been done in this study. The computer work required for such a task is too complex and the extent of the study area and the number of periods being studied also make this too difficult. The results would be trivial. It makes more sense to develop such a simulation model for an area of more limited size and chronological range so that the relevant variables can be better controlled.

Chapter 6

Map formation analysis: an application

6.1 INTRODUCTION

In Chapter 5 the basic principles of map formation analysis were expounded. In this chapter the method will be developed in more detail using the western part of the Frisian-Drentian plateau as an example. First it will be determined which factors have distorted the findspot distribution pattern. The measure of distortion caused by these factors is called archaeological visibility (AV). These factors can be described as filters which reveal as findspots only a portion of the originally existing sites. The AV can assume values between 1% and 100%. These should not be accepted as exact measurable values, however. If it is supposed that the AV for the land use factor is 100% for arable and 50% for forest, it should be understood that these are relative values expressed in absolute numbers so that they can be used in arithmetic calculations. The distribution of each distorting factor is reproduced on separate maps (figs. 21–34). Finally, all factors are weighed and arithmetically combined to produce new maps, specifically the maps of post-depositional factors (figs. 36–38) and the map of research factors (fig. 35). The last step is to make a combination resulting in the representation of the archaeological visibility of findspots in the area (fig. 40).

In mapping the various factors the Soil Map and the Topographical Map at a scale of 1:50 000 were used. Whenever the Soil Map was not available, the Geological Map[1] was used. Only the sandy grounds have been mapped. The clay regions of Westergo and Oostergo were not included because the sediment cover there is more than 1 m thick and these areas have been covered by clastic sediments since the Early Neolithic.

6.2 POST-DEPOSITIONAL PROCESSES OF NATURAL ORIGIN

It has already been stated in section 4.3.1 that the geological and geochemical processes in particular have a significant influence on the archaeological visibility of sites on a regional scale. Biotic factors are important at the site level but can be ignored in a regional investigation.

In the northern Netherlands in particular geological and geochemical processes are connected with the sediments which cover prehistoric surfaces, namely clay and peat deposits. The Soil Map was therefore chosen as the basis for the mapping of post-depositional processes of natural origin. This map is based on a pedogenetic classification system and has a profile-type legend, by which it is possible, in principle, to separate the different sediment covers from each other.[2]

In assessing the chemical processes the nature of the deposits in particular was held to be of importance. In assessing the geological processes the thickness of the deposits was taken into account. Other aspects such as soil hydrology, soil productivity, clay content, etc., can be ignored as map formation factors, at least on a macro-regional scale.[3] In this way the following units remain:
1. peat and clay covers more than 40 cm thick;
2. peat and clay covers less than 40 cm thick;
3. *vaaggronden*, i.e. soils with little soil formation (only driftsand areas);
4. water.

1 In 1987, when the map formation analysis was carried out, the relevant map sheets 12 W and 16 W and E of the Soil Map were not yet finished. The Geological Map was therefore used in their place.
2 De Bakker & Schelling 1966.

3 With micro-regional investigations and possibly location analysis (Bakker 1982) these aspects can indeed be of interest. By micro-regional scale is meant the site and its immediate surroundings (site territory). The macro-regional scale comprises many such micro-regions.

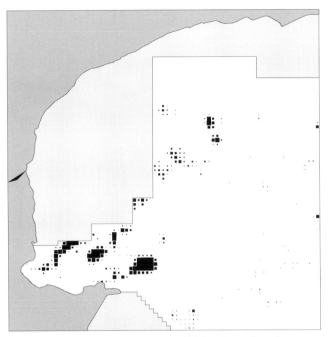

Figure 21 The western part of the Frisian-Drentian plateau: the estimated surface area of water in the mapped area.

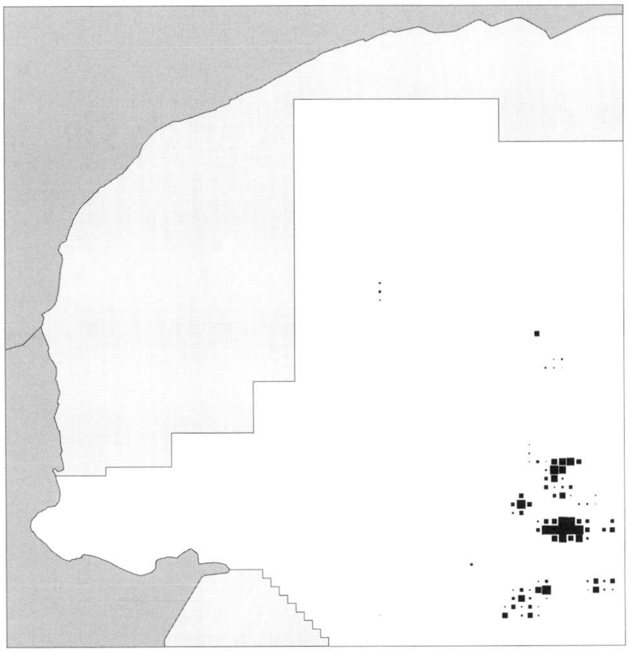

Figure 22 The western part of the Frisian-Drentian plateau: the estimated surface area of vague soils in the mapped area.

6.2.1 *Geological processes*

The geological processes which concern us here in the Netherlands are aeolian, marine, and fluvial erosion and sedimentation. In the flat northern Netherlands, solifluction is of marginal importance, even in the areas where the coversand topography shows a relatively pronounced relief.

Erosion

Almost all the stream valleys in the western part of the plateau have courses that run north-east–south-west. These are not very wide, and the rather slight fall has kept them from cutting down deeply (see fig. 17). Only in the lower reaches of the Linde as well as the Tjonger valleys are wide and filled with peat. Therefore the lateral erosive activity is also slight. Marine erosion has been much more drastic, but it is difficult to localize (see Chapter 1). It is true that the continuous rise of the sea level during the Holocene drowned a large part of the prehistoric landscape, but this has only been accompanied with a lot of erosion in the actual tidal-flat area and in the area of the Middelzee. Further inland, the marine sediments were deposited under much calmer conditions and have had more of a conserving than an

eroding effect. To summarize, the erosive influence of running water on the finds distribution pattern since the Neolithic must be regarded as quite small. Considering that the Middelzee area during the Neolithic for the most part lay too low for occupation to have been possible, no extensive habitable area will since have disappeared there either (see Chapter 3).

The above comments also apply to the lakes to a certain extent (fig. 21). The lakes for the most part formed in depressions which had already been filled with peat, partly since the Late Atlantic and Sub-boreal.[4] For this reason the lakes can indeed be regarded as blind spots in the distribution maps (AV = 0), but the question remains as to what extent occupation took place in those regions since the Neolithic.

Aeolian erosion can constitute a much greater influence. It is known that arable land, barrows and even entire settlements can disappear in driftsand areas, either through deflation or dune formation.[5] It is difficult to estimate the distorting effect of driftsands. They are certainly not impermeable to finds, seeing that driftsand areas are often

---

4 Ter Wee 1976; Zagwijn 1986; Van Zeist 1955.
5 See Van Gijn & Waterbolk 1984; Popping n.d.

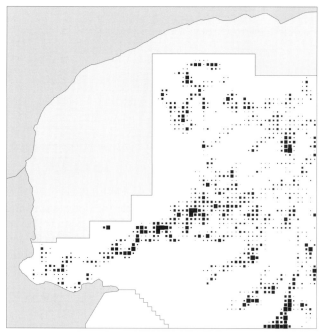

Figure 23 The western part of the Frisian-Drentian plateau: the estimated surface area covered by peat and clay horizons with a thickness less than 40 cm in the mapped area.

Figure 24 The western part of the Frisian-Drentian plateau: the estimated surface area covered by peat and clay horizons with a thickness greater than 40 cm in the mapped area.

just the places where artifacts, exposed by the wind, have been found.[6] For lack of better data, therefore, the visibility has been set at 50% (AV = 50). In figure 22 the units are mapped which are indicated on the Soil Map as *duinvaaggronden*, i.e. dune soils with little soil formation. Sometimes *vlakvaaggronden*, i.e. level soils with little soil formation, can also be included here on the basis of the explanation given with the relevant soil map.

Sedimentation
Sedimentation processes are undoubtedly the most important geological map formation factors on the Frisian-Drentian plateau. Large parts of the area have gradually become covered with clay and peat deposits. As soon as these sediments reach a greater thickness than the average plough zone (*c.* 20–40 cm),[7] the archaeological visibility is practically nil: only by such activities as deep ploughing,

ditch digging, road construction, etc., will more findspots be discovered. In this connection, the concept of 'cover' on the Soil Map is important. The Soil Map speaks of a cover whenever less than half (<40 cm) of the top 80 cm of the ground is covered by another material.[8] So a distinction is made between soils without cover (sandy grounds), soils with a clay or peat cover up to 40 cm thick, and clay and peat soils in which a thicker sediment layer lies on top of the sandy subsoil (see introduction section 6.2).
In this study it is assumed that findspots lying under a cover more than 40 cm thick (fig. 24) are invisible. In these cases the AV is therefore practically nil regardless of the composition of the cover. If the cover is thinner than 40 cm (fig. 23), findspots can be discerned through ploughing. Land use and research factors are in this case of primary importance.
Particularly when in an area covered with a thin peat

6 Foley (1981, 170), for example, showed how wind action over a period of time can create horizons in which artifacts from different periods are concentrated. Naturally such horizons form attractive survey locations.

7 See the profile descriptions by De Bakker & Schelling (1966), among others, which show that the ploughed layer is seldom deeper than 20 cm in both the peat soils as well as the mineral soils.
8 De Bakker & Schelling 1966.

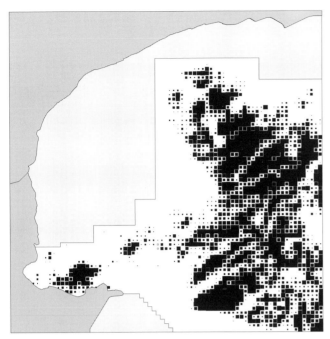

Figure 25 The western part of the Frisian-Drentian plateau: the estimated surface area not covered by peat or clay horizons in the mapped area.

Table 7 Archaeological visibility (AV) of different geological map formation factors.

geological map formation factor	AV
peat and clay > 40 cm	1%
peat and clay < 40 cm	60%
no sediment cover	100%
driftsand	50%
water	0%

organic materials are prevalent because of the anaerobic conditions there, at least insofar as these materials are imbedded in the clay itself.

On the other hand, peat deposits have specific chemical properties which are not favourable for bone, stone and pottery preservation. Prehistoric pottery, which is generally porous, can disintegrate completely when it gets into contact with peat, with root activity as a contributing factor. Porous stone such as granite can also fall apart completely under these conditions. In general, bone is no more likely to remain preserved in acidic peat. Metal objects do remain well preserved, although they acquire a brown 'peat' patina. Leather and skins, and of course wooden implements, also remain preserved. The last categories are generally found only during excavations, particularly during the investigation of trackways and the like. These statements apply chiefly to the preservation of materials which are imbedded in the above-mentioned deposits or come in direct contact with them. Of course, the time which has elapsed between the covering and the abandoning of a site is also of importance in determining the degree of preservation.

Reclamation history is another important factor in the weathering of archaeological materials. So pottery, for example, in particular prehistoric material which is not hard-fired, is generally no match for changing moisture and temperature conditions. In other words, pottery that has been removed from its context by ploughing and has come to rest in the ploughed layer continues to fragment and disappears after a number of years.[9] So without going into the question of whether historic and prehistoric pottery was deposited in pits and wells or was left lying on the ground, it is not likely that very much pottery will be found in areas long under cultivation. In the case of pottery left on the surface, the chance of coming across finds is even smaller because disintegration had already begun before the material arrived in the subsoil. These considerations lead to the conclusion that sites

layer a sand hillock is exposed as a result of ploughing, this often arouses the interest of archaeologists. Nevertheless, it must be stated that a thin cover is in general a distorting factor, not least because these areas are usually low-lying or wet (groundwater level III is the rule) and are often used as pasture land. The visibility is therefore certainly lower than in grounds without a cover. For this reason I would like to set the AV for a cover up to 40 cm at 60%. Whenever a cover is completely absent (fig. 25), all findspots have the same measure of visibility in principle (leaving aside differences in site-type); the AV is therefore 100%. The visibility figures used for the various units are summarized in table 7.

6.2.2 Geochemical processes

On a regional level, in particular the properties of soils which influence preservation are of importance. So in the poor, water-permeable sandy soils of the northern Netherlands, adverse preservation conditions for organic material are prevalent. Wood, plant remains (including seeds), and bone material are therefore seldom found in a non-carbonized state in sandy soils. In the clay area however, excellent preservation conditions for

9 See Thrane 1985.

Table 8 Archaeological visibility resulting from post-depositional processes of human origin.

land use	AV
pasture land	10%
arable land	100%
heath land	5%
forest	5%
driftsand	50%
built-up area	1%
es cover	1%
raised area	1%

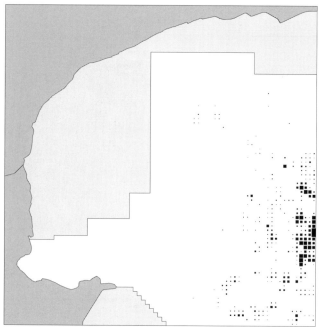

Figure 26 The western part of the Frisian-Drentian plateau: the estimated surface area of arable land in the mapped area.

characterized by finds categories of predominantly organic materials and pottery (see table 6) are virtually invisible on the Frisian-Drentian plateau.

Depending on the intensity of research (see section 6.5), flat graves and settlement areas with little or no durable materials fall in this category. It has also been stated elsewhere that Bronze Age settlements and flat graves in particular became invisible in this way.[10] This fact must be given thorough consideration in interpreting the distribution maps.

Geochemical disintegration has therefore had a significant distorting effect on a number of materials. However, vastly varying agricultural activities and the excavation of the peat have made it almost impossible to represent this factor on a map. We must assume that any possible preserving action of the peat on organic materials was annulled by reclamation, the net effect being the same everywhere: the organic materials have decayed unless they were imbedded in airless deposits or filled-in pits. Pottery lying in arable similarly undergoes deterioration in quality and visibility after a number of years.

6.3 POST-DEPOSITIONAL PROCESSES OF HUMAN ORIGIN

Strictly speaking, post-depositional processes of human origin can be divided into land (or soil) use and the raising of land. Land use includes present-day classification of the landscape into land-use classes which are understood as indicated on the Topographical Map. There seems to be an overlap here with units which have already been designated as post-depositional processes of natural origin, namely water and driftsands. On soil maps and topographical maps lakes have the same sur-

face area and the same value (AV = 0%), so there is no apparent difference. However, the units which apply to driftsands on the Soil Map are not the same as the driftsands indicated on the Topographical Map. Besides the driftsands, various forms of land use are shown on the Topographical Map (forestation most especially) for the areas depicted as *vaaggronden* on the Soil Map. It was therefore necessary to re-assess the distribution of the driftsands on the Topographical Map. Deposits of human origin comprise in particular *plaggen* soils (see section 6.3.2) and raised terrains.

6.3.1 *Land use*
As has already been indicated in section 4.3.2, land use and reclamation history are the most important post-depositional factors of human origin in the current study area. Because the data are based only on the investigation of existing collections, it is especially important to map land use which may have had influence on recovery conditions over an extended period.[11] In other words, pres-

10 Thrane 1985; Vasbinder & Fokkens 1987.
11 In any case these are the landscape elements which have remained more or less constant since people began to be

interested in prehistoric finds, that is since the middle of the last century.

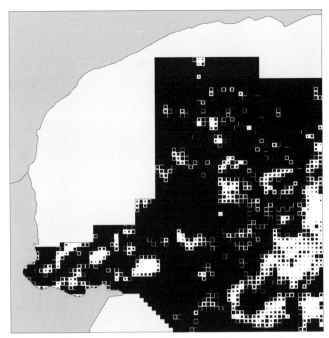

Figure 27 The western part of the Frisian-Drentian plateau: the estimated surface area of pasture land in the mapped area.

ent-day land use, particularly the specific location of arable and pasture lands, has more significance for further research (surveys, etc.) than for the evaluation of the origin of the finds distribution pattern.

The distinction between arable and pasture plays a large part in the visibility of findspots. In pasture lands, for example, only animal and human digging activities lead to discovery, one reason why on the pasture lands of the island of Texel – where the mole has no habitat – almost no finds have been unearthed.[12] Because of this, no more than 10% of the findspots are visible there. On the other hand, visibility is optimal in areas where agriculture predominates; recently-ploughed, rain-soaked fields are an El Dorado for archaeologists.

One of the biggest problems in mapping arable and pasture as land use categories in a region like the northern

Netherlands is that the units are generally small in surface area and occur highly fragmented across the landscape. This makes mapping almost an impossible task in the method used for area measurement, but for the sake of completeness it was nevertheless carried out. Only the agricultural land was mapped (fig. 26). It is assumed that the sum of the areas of all other classes per km section, subtracted from the total, reflects the pasture area (fig. 27).

Another aspect of agricultural land that has a distorting effect is the erosion of findspots through reclamation and ploughing. The extent of the distortion changes from place to place. It varies according to the moment in time of reclamation, the period in time that the land is cultivated, and the intensity and type of farming methods.[13] Although erosion can be considerable, it has probably not led to the complete obliteration or corruption of sites. On the contrary, ploughing brings finds to light and is therefore a positive influence on archaeological visibility. Specific types of sites, however, are indeed made indiscernible through agricultural activities, barrows being one example. For instance, approximately twenty Late Neolithic barrows of the Single Grave culture have been identified in the study area. Together they span a period of *c.* 650 calendar years. This means that a maximum of one barrow was built in each generation. The entire area was inhabited during this period, however, so there would have been many more barrows constructed.[14]

Apart from the fact that ploughed-out remains of barrows are occasionally found, another indication of destroyed barrows is the distribution of hammer axes. This category of artifacts occurs almost only in graves. As grave goods they form a characteristic element of the Single Grave Culture.[15] Thirteen such hammer axes have been found as stray finds in the study area. If we begin with the assumption that all these were grave goods and that the proportion of graves with hammer to graves without hammer is approximately 1:4,[16] then the thirteen separately found hammer axes should correlate with *c.* 52 barrows or surface graves. It can therefore be assumed that the number of barrows now known represents considerably less than 28% of the original

12 Woltering 1979.
13 Baudou 1985; Hansen 1985.
14 It is also assumed that this was not a period of strong social stratification, which offers the possible explanation that only the tribal leader from each generation (or another similarly

important person) would have been buried in a barrow (Fokkens 1986; Lohof 1991).
15 Lanting & Van der Waals 1976.
16 This figure is based on written information from A.E. Lanting (1988).

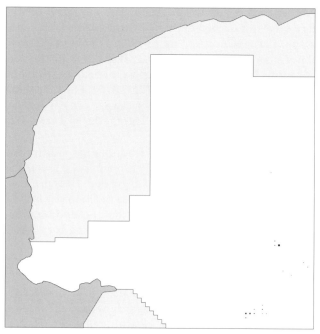

Figure 28 The western part of the Frisian-Drentian plateau: the estimated surface area of drift sands in the mapped area.

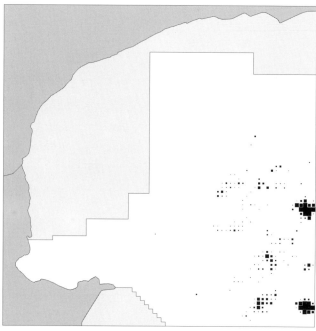

Figure 29 The western part of the Frisian-Drentian plateau: the estimated surface area of heathland in the mapped area.

number.[17] For Bronze Age barrows, which are without finds for the most part, the visibility is probably significantly lower still.

Heath and forest areas form a more constant element in the landscape of the Frisian-Drentian plateau. Parts of the forest areas are remains of older forests, but most were planted before and just after the Second World War as part of relief work projects for the unemployed. The forests often lie in former drift sand areas and initially were planted to prevent further sand drift. Considering the extent of the forested areas on the Frisian-Drentian plateau (especially in the south-west and south-east), this factor must be understood as having a great influence on the archaeological finds distribution pattern (fig. 30).

The heath areas are but small remnants of the once extensive heathlands. The massive reclamation activities which took place during the 1930s eliminated most of these heathlands. The parts that remain are scrupu-

lously preserved as natural monuments. This factor is particularly influential in the south-eastern part of the study area (fig. 29).

Since heath and forest areas are rarely or never ploughed and the nature of the overgrowth gives little insight into the subsoil, they are seen to have great influence on archaeological visibility. Only by animal activities (moles, rabbits, foxes, etc.) and digging activities do finds come to light. Further, ruptures in heath vegetation regularly lead to sand drift, which leaves the subsoil exposed. However, the visibility in forest and heath areas must be roughly estimated to be practically nil ($AV = 5\%$).

Driftsand areas also form a fairly constant factor in the landscape, at least in proportion to arable and pasture areas (fig. 28). When they are not covered by other forms of land use, they maintain the same value for archaeological visibility as is shown on the map of natural factors ($AV = 50\%$).

17 This brings the minimum number of barrows and surface graves from the period of the Single Grave culture to 72, divided over 650 years. That means that per thirty-year generation three barrows were built up for as many lineage

elders. Even this number is still far too small. In other words, there must be considerably more graves which have disappeared or remain undiscovered.

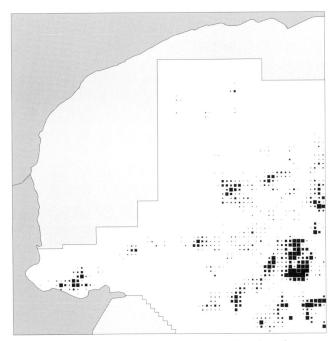

Figure 30 The western part of the Frisian-Drentian plateau: the estimated surface area of woodland in the mapped area.

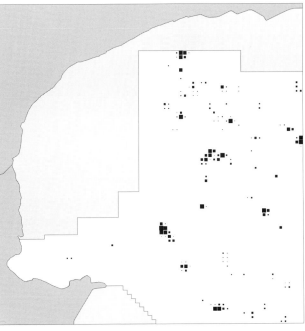

Figure 31 The western part of the Frisian-Drentian plateau: the estimated surface area built over in the mapped area.

Built-up areas (fig. 31) and roadways form a land use category which occupy increasingly more surface area, particularly since the Second World War. The built-up areas around places such as Heerenveen, Joure, Drachten, and Bergum, still hamlets at the beginning of this century, have experienced a growth explosion since the 1950's. On a present-day map of archaeologically accessible areas these areas form extensively disturbed units (AV = 1%). It is possible, however, that the finds density in these areas is quite high due to increased digging activities and construction. This aspect will reappear in the survey of the research history (section 6.3.2).

Roadways are not included as a post-depositional factor in this study because the surface area of roads within a km-cell is difficult to determine. This factor is probably easier to map in microregional investigations with smaller observation cells. Roads which have covered the same area for a long time can be regarded as distorting factors. Recent road construction is increasingly accompanied by archaeological investigation. For this reason it can even have a positively distorting effect on finds density.

6.3.2 Covers of human origin

On a regional level, *plaggen* soils are an important post-depositional factor for archaeological visibility (see also section 4.3.2). A *plaggen* soil comes into existence through centuries of fertilizing with sods which were brought into the byres during the winter and spread out over the fields in the spring when they had become dung impregnated.[18]

The Soil Map speaks of black and brown *enkeerdgronden*. In the northern Netherlands, black *enkeerdgronden* are most prevalent, occurring in regions where the only available material was heather sods. When forest litter is used the result is brown *enkeerdgronden*, richer in humus and

18 It may be confusing that in terms of human geography (Bouwer 1970) the word *es* is applied to cultivated grounds belonging to *es*-villages. From a pedological point of view this does not necessarily mean a thick, raised, fertilized surface layer, which is also commonly called an *es*. For the sake of differentiation in this study the term '*es* cover' is used whenever the intended meaning of *es* follows the definitions of the Soil Map (De Bakker & Schelling 1966). In all other cases the term '*es*' is used.

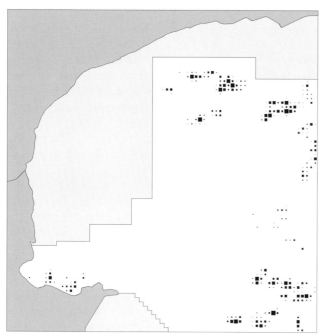

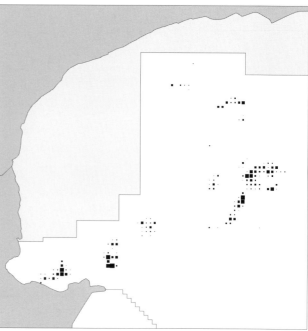

Figure 32 The western part of the Frisian-Drentian plateau: the estimated surface area covered by *plaggen* soils in the mapped area.

Figure 33 The western part of the Frisian-Drentian plateau: the estimated surface area of reworked topsoil in the mapped area.

more acidic.[19] According to the pedological definition, *enkeerdgronden* have darker topsoil which is thicker than 50 cm.[20] This indicates that the thickness is greater than the average plough zone, therefore *plaggen* soils in fact are completely impermeable ($AV = 1\%$).[21] The *plaggen* soils lie scattered over the whole sandy area of the Frisian-Drentian plateau, but there are concentrations in Gaasterland, on the north-eastern sand ridges, on the ridge between the Tjonger and the Linde, the area around Oosterwolde, and in south-western Drenthe (fig. 32).

Raised areas are usually low-lying areas in which the texture of the soil was improved, or industrial zones near larger places such as Heerenveen and Drachten (fig. 34). Generally speaking, no archaeological observations were made when these areas were raised. The visibility therefore has been set at 1%.

6.3.3 *Reclamation history*

Reclamation history is a difficult factor to map. Many areas were exploited very early on and are barely recognizable in today's land parcelling patterns. Probably many findspots were lost during reclamation activities from before 1900. Although there were many people interested in antiquities at that time, collections were not put together systematically and only a few finds ended up in museums. It is quite possible that the scarcity of finds in the area between the Boorne and the Tjonger, for instance, is partly a result of this early practice of reclamation, but there is no proof for this.

The situation was different during reclamation activities that took place in the 1930s. At that time archaeological investigations by museums and other institutions were made. In addition, the northern Netherlands had a number of local archaeologists who were actively involved in collecting finds and offering archaeological as-

19 Kuiper 1977.
20 De Bakker & Schelling 1966.
21 Although it is true that the *es* cover was not applied all at once, and as a consequence finds were ploughed up into the *es*

cover as well, there is a good chance that these finds have been lost due to disintegration. Therefore investigations which do not make use of coring equipment rarely recover artifacts as a general rule.

Figure 34 The western part of the Frisian-Drentian plateau: the estimated surface area of raised land in the mapped area.

sistance to reclamation efforts. It was this local activity which produced a great many finds and in a number of cases led to excavations by the Rijksmuseum van Oudheden or the Biologisch-Archaeologisch Instituut.

For the actual mapping of areas of early reclamation

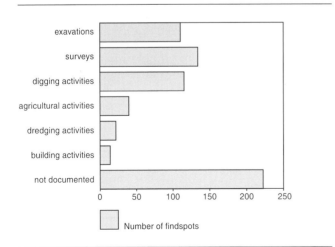

Figure 35 Overview of the circumstances pertaining to find-recovery.

activity there are but a few points to go on, unless an analysis is made of the parcelling patterns or comparisons conducted between successive versions of topographical or cadastral maps. The Soil Map, however, also provides some insight. The excavated terrains indicated for the western part of the Frisian-Drentian plateau are mostly related to peat reclamation, heath reclamation or forestation (in Gaasterland, for example). These are mapped in figure 33. On the Soil Map, however, these units are much smaller in surface area than the areas which were actually reworked.

The overview of the circumstances pertaining to find-recovery (fig. 35) shows that a proportionately high number of finds were uncovered during excavation and reclamation activities, which were generally carried out manually. Fewer finds were unearthed during construction activities, but that is partially a result of the fact that in urban expansion zones many finds have already been discovered before building begins. Nevertheless, practice teaches that during present-day construction activities many finds simply go unrecognized or are suppressed out of fear of holding up building progress. In spite of this, the distorting effect on finds distribution here is not as great as the effect of manual reclamation during the 1930s.

Because the distorting influence of these factors in certain areas could have resulted in a relative increase in the number of finds (if the non-measurable reclamation activities from before 1900 are left aside), the archaeological visibility in reclaimed areas is greater than in the areas where this factor has not had any influence. The increase in the number of finds is set at 50% for reclaimed areas; for cultivated areas the figure is 20%.

6.4 THE POST-DEPOSITIONAL FACTOR INDEX (PDI)

In order to determine the combined effect of all post-depositional factors on archaeological visibility, the filtering effect per km-section is calculated. This is done by multiplying the surface area of each mapped factor by its AV-value. The principles involved in this calculation have been given in section 5.5 but were then not yet worked out. This will be done in the following material. The formula for PDI is composed of a number of sub-formulas which are connected to the maps from which they are derived. These are the Soil Map, or the map for soil covers (PDI_{cover}), the map for soil use (PDI_{soil}), and the map for reclamation factors (PDI_{recl}).

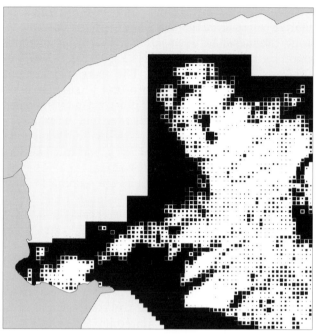

Figure 36 The western part of the Frisian-Drentian plateau: distortion of the map due to soil covers in the mapped area.

Figure 37 The western part of the Frisian-Drentian plateau: distortion of the map due to pedological factors in the mapped area.

Each of the subformulas is calculated with the formula (section 5.5)

$$PDI = (AV_1 \times A_1) + (AV_2 \times A_2) + \ldots + (AV_n \times A_n)$$

and these are combined in the final formula[22]

$$PDI_{total} = ((PDI_{cover} + PDI_{soil}) \times PDI_{recl}) / divisor.$$

The formulas can now be filled in as follows:

– PDI from areas with a cover

$$PDI_{cover} = (.60 \times A[_{cover<40}]) + (.01 \times A[_{cover>40}]) + (.50 \times A[_{driftsand}]) + (.0 \times A[_{water + built-up area}]) + (1.0 \times A[_{uncovered}]).$$

The sum of these surface areas is 100 ha (1 km^2). Figure 36 shows what the distorting consequences of this factor are.

22 The divisor is the factor by which the figure must be divided in order to keep the index figures within the 1–100 range, since the maximum archaeological visibility is 100%. In this investigation the highest number that the final formula can produce is 15 000 for a km-section without distorting cover, completely under cultivation and completely reclaimed $\{(PDI_{cover} + PDI_{soil}) \times PDI_{recl} = (100 + 50) \times 100 = 15\ 000\}$. Therefore the divisor must be 150 to reduce the figure to the 1–100 scale.

– PDI from pedological factors

$$PDI_{soil} = (.10 \times A[_{pasture}]) + (1.00 \times A[_{arable}]) + (.05 \times A[_{heath}]) + (.05 \times A[_{forest}]) + (.50 \times A[_{driftsand}]) + (.01 \times A[_{built-up area}]) + (.0 \times A[_{water}]).$$

The sum of these surface areas is 100 ha (1 km^2). Figure 37 shows the distortion for pedological factors.

– PDI from reclamation and town-building

$$PDI_{recl} = (.50 \times A[_{reclaimed}]) + (.20 \times A[_{town-building}]).$$

The sum of these surface areas is less than 100 ha. Figure 38 shows the areas in which this factor could have led to a higher representativeness of finds distribution.

6.5 DISTORTION BROUGHT ABOUT BY RESEARCH PROCESSES

A number of processes have been discussed above which influence archaeological visibility. One important distorting filter, however, has not yet been looked at, namely that of the nature and intensity of research (see also section 4.3.2). The following sections will therefore trace which differences exist between the finds distribu-

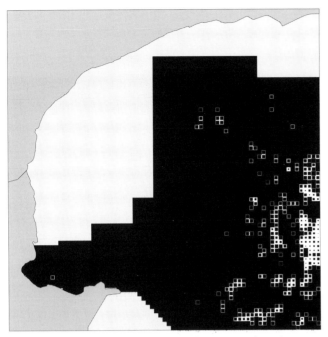

Figure 38 The western part of the Frisian-Drentian plateau: distortion of the map due to anthropogenic factors in the mapped area.

Table 9 The western part of the Frisian-Drentian plateau: the number of findspots divided according to the discoverer's archaeological knowledge. In this diagram the Celtic field systems, coins, and finds about which little is known have been left aside.

finds category	found by		total
	archaeologists	laymen	
clearly recognizable artifacts			
axe of flint or other type of stone	53	130	183
hammer axe	13	30	43
chisel	2	4	6
dagger, sickle	9	13	22
Geröllkeule	7	11	18
bone, antler	1	6	7
bronze artifact, coin	0	24	24
grinding stone	6	8	14
large pottery fragment	8	12	20
hunebed	0	1	1
total	99 (29%)	239 (71%)	338
poorly recognizable artifacts			
flint assemblage	23	4	27
flint arrowhead	17	11	28
hammer stone, etc.	3	2	5
small pottery fragment	16	6	22
quern	13	7	20
grave	29	6	35
settlement traces	5	1	6
total	106 (74%)	37 (26%)	143
sum total	205 (43%)	276 (57%)	481

tion patterns of laymen and professional archaeologists. In this way it will be determined to what extent the presence or absence of archaeological activities distorted the finds distribution pattern. Attention will also be paid to the possible effects of differences in working methods and interest among archaeologists.

6.5.1 Presence and absence of archaeological activities

The well-known Frisian amateur archaeologist H.J. Popping once described the differences between the observations of laymen and professional archaeologists: 'It is striking that so many urnfields have been found, so many burial sites such as *tumuli* and *hunebedden* have been investigated, and still there is so little written about settlements from those periods in the Netherlands. There continues to be an ignorance of these matters among the people of this country. An urnfield with an abundance of pots arouses the attention, the other mentioned objects betray themselves by their above-ground construction. A settlement like this one[23] cannot be re-

cognized on the surface; it is the finds in the ground which must be the proof. As far as the finds themselves are concerned: in general, an attractive stone axe or hammer is carried off, but a grinding stone, a quern often goes unrecognized, not to mention the smaller flint tools.'[24]

A survey of the findspots on the Frisian-Drentian plateau, with emphasis on the recognizability of the finds

23 Here is meant the settlement in the '150-*bunder*' (150 ha), about which this article was written.

24 Popping 1933c, 1–2.

and the status of the finders (table 9), shows that a number of the statements reported by Popping are indeed true. From table 9 it appears that artifacts which can be classified as 'clearly recognizable', such as stone and flint axes and bronze objects, are observed most often.

The basis for the distinction between good and poor recognizability is that with clearly recognizable artifacts the form simply indicates that this is 'something' man-made. This is not the case with querns, for instance, especially when weathering is involved. With grinding stones and whetstones, however, it does hold. Flint arrowheads are regarded as poorly recognizable because they often lie amidst other flint material and therefore go unobserved by laymen. Another member of this category is the group of findspots characterized by pottery sherds. Even whole pots have often gone missing. Although they are highly recognizable, the chance that whole pots will be preserved intact is quite small, mostly because of their fragility or the finder's lack of familiarity with their archaeological value. One regularly hears stories of reclamation activities in which numerous pots were found 'that just shattered so nicely when you had them thrown to you and you knocked them back with the shovel'; it's not for nothing that there are two known 'paper' urnfields in Friesland.[25] In my opinion, Popping's observation applies only to reclamations and other digging activities assisted by archaeologists (active as well as passive).[26]

In this regard the role which people such as Popping, Siebinga, and others play in reclamation activities should not be underestimated. In the introduction to the above-mentioned article on the '150-bunder', Popping says that he gave 'instructions' to peat labourers, telling them what they could expect and explaining how to recognize finds. He also made it clear that he would make it worth their while to recover finds, thereby stimulating the labourers to report finds. The result was that he built up a vast collection. To a certain extent Siebinga followed the same working methods. We have him to thank for the many finds from the Vossehoogten (Beaker burials) to the south-west of Marum. These large collections cannot in fact be seen separately from reclamation activities. The finds recovered by Van Vliet around Wijnjeterp and Barendse in the same region are also connected with reclamation or forestation.

Burial grounds or individual graves are almost never recognized by laymen. In only a few cases have complete or almost complete pots or an axe been found, but not the grave monument itself. At the very most they managed to remember that the finds came 'from an elevated area'. Popping was incorrect in this respect. In areas where there has been no archaeological activity, grave monuments are hardly ever recognized, apart from *hunebedden* and urnfields to a certain extent.

On the basis of these considerations, the rather unspectacular conclusion must be drawn that the presence or absence of archaeological activities has particular consequences for the visibility of findspots which are difficult for laymen to recognize. On the other hand, it is clear that the groups of finds which can be described as clearly recognizable (table 9) can in many cases be regarded as the tip of the iceberg. Thus, when a layman finds a stone axe at a construction site in an area that is covered by a peat layer more than 1 m thick, this must be regarded as an extremely valuable find. In the past, however, such finds were often dismissed as meaningless exceptions.

The above data can give an impression of the extent to which the number of established findspots in the areas where archaeologists have been active is greater than in the surrounding areas. The figures in table 9 indicate that a total of 205 out of 481 findspots were discovered by archaeologists, that is *c.* 43% of the total number of findspots.[27] In other words, approximately two times as many findspots have been discovered in areas where archaeological activities have taken place as outside these areas. That means that in areas where archaeologists were active the archaeological visibility was optimal (AV = 100%); in other areas it has been set at 50%.

Archaeological activities have been recorded by mapping the finds recovered by a number of prominent local archaeologists, i.e. Popping, Siebinga, and Voerman (fig. 39). They were chosen because they were active right at the time of the important reclamation period during the

---

25 That is, finds that have only been reported via oral tradition (Elzinga 1973, 29).

26 Passive assistance here means that someone lives in a particular region who is known for his or her interest in antiquities and is ready to serve as a gathering point. When such a person purchases artifacts, the willingness to report or to safeguard finds usually greatly increases. Many museums have experienced this, sometimes to their detriment.

27 The difference between clearly and poorly recognizable findspots is not further dealt with in the analysis here because the visibility is also strongly determined by historic factors which are not in order at this stage.

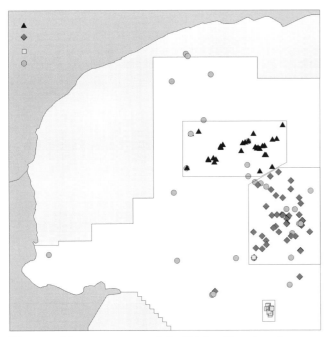

Figure 39 The western part of the Frisian-Drentian plateau: the territories, indicated by outlines, covered by the most important local archaeologists in the mapped area.
Legend: triangles found by J. Siebinga; lozenges found by H.J. Popping; squares found by H. Voerman; circles found by J.K. Boschker.

1930s. The finds gathered by Van Vliet, Tj. Vermaning and a number of other local archaeologists fall within the borders of this area and are not shown separately in figure 39. Also not indicated are the finds of J.K. Boschker or of the Biologisch-Archaeologisch Instituut and the Rijksmuseum van Oudheden because these are not spatially concentrated and do not reflect any particular area of lengthy investigation, such as is the case with Popping, Siebinga, and Voerman.

6.5.2 *The nature of the archaeological activities*

Hamond[28] makes clear that the way in which a particular collection comes about is determined by a large number of factors, among them the location of the archaeologist's residence, mode of transportation, char-

acter of the fieldwork, etc. In section 4.3 it has been pointed out that the specific period that the archaeologist is interested in also plays an important role.

On the Frisian-Drentian plateau, the latter is particularly important. In many collections, for example, pottery is poorly represented, which is not only due to the fact that sherd material is not easily recognizable. Only all-round archaeologists such as Siebinga and Popping collected pottery on a regular basis; Voerman did so to a lesser degree. It is clear that such factors are of great importance to the way in which the finds distribution pattern takes shape. It is also apparent from figure 39 that the activity radius of the archaeologist plays a role. Popping had a motorcycle at his disposal, while Voerman recovered most of his finds while walking with his dog in the driftsands.

Nevertheless, a detailed analysis such as the one carried out by Hamond is not appropriate here. The reason that Hamond delved so deeply into this category of map formation factors was that he believed that the post-depositional processes of natural origin on the Aldenhovener Platte were of minor importance and came to the conclusion that research factors would determine the final picture.[29] On the western part of the Frisian-Drentian plateau the situation differs considerably. The post-depositional factors have had a great influence in most of the study area, therefore the nature of the archaeological activities there is of proportionally minor significance. Consequently, the idea of a detailed analysis of this factor has been abandoned.

6.6 COMBINING THE MAP FORMATION FACTORS

We have now come to the point in the analysis where all the different map formation factors can be combined to what is called the archaeological visibility index (AVI). The formula for this is (section 5.5)[30]

$$AVI = (PDI_{total} \times RI)/divisor.$$

The combined map is reproduced in figure 40. Since the original map is difficult to read because the image is determined by the low values for AVI, the contrast is heightened by showing the areas with a visibility index

28 Hamond 1978; 1980.
29 Hamond 1978.
30 In this case the research index is equal to the visibility of archaeological activities. The formula then becomes $AVI = (PDI_{total} \times AV_{research})/divisor$. In this case the divisor is

50 because the maximum value resulting from the first part of the formula is 5 000 (PDI = 100, Research activities = 50). If we want to set the maximum AVI value at 100, then it must be divided by 50.

of more than 50% in white. In doing so the area in which local archaeologists have been active is made visible. This shows how very important the research factors have been. This map is the end point of map formation analysis in this study. It simply shows that no representative finds distribution pattern exists for a large part of the western Frisian-Drentian plateau. The archaeological visibility is very low over almost the entire region, even for monumental findspots such as barrows. Only on the highest parts of the plateau can a few areas be distinguished which have some measure of representativeness. This includes in particular the regions which drew the attention of local archaeologists during the period of reclamation activity. Professional archaeological practice had proportionately little influence on the finds distribution pattern because of the absence of specifically targeted research projects.

6.7 CONCLUSION AND CONTINUED RESEARCH

From the previous discussion it has become clear that distribution maps of the western part of the Frisian-Drentian plateau must be approached with great care. For large parts of the study area it would be irresponsible to draw any conclusions without taking map formation factors into consideration. That means, among other things, that developments sketched by Waterbolk in 1966 (section 1.5) must be revised at the very least.

A more general question which this research gives rise to is how map formation analysis can be used. One possible application is the setting up of simulation models. Attempts to do this within the framework of this investigation have been made, but the extensive spatial and chronological scales appeared not to be suitable for such models. Therefore, the potentials for answering research questions were too low to warrant paying much attention to. In an investigation of a smaller area with a less expansive time frame however, the designing of computer simulations does make sense.

As a suggestion for a possible simulation application, it might be possible to correct the existing finds distribution pattern for the calculated filters, the index ciphers. A few tests in this area clearly show that the problems that appear in such a simulation lie with empty cells in particular. Indeed, if a cell is empty it remains empty even after correction because it is being multiplied by

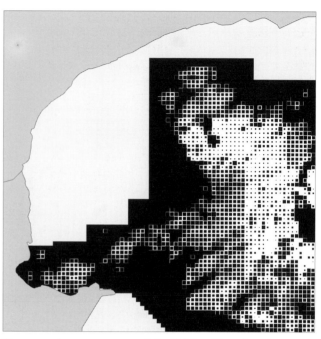

Figure 40 the western part of the Frisian-Drentian plateau: archaeological visibility in the mapped area.

zero. Solutions will have to be found for this, with the help of trend surfaces or similar procedures for averaging finds distribution patterns. However, such a solution should be re-established for each chronological period because the finds distribution patterns always differ.

The use of GIS is of great value in such simulation models. This method can also be helpful in determining those factors which were important in prehistoric location choices. But it is also true here that GIS is especially useful in micro-regional studies which relate to one or two archaeological periods.

An alternative for this study, chosen out of sheer necessity, is the traditional 'eye-ball' method. That means nothing more than a visual analysis of available data. This is reached by projecting the finds distribution patterns for the various periods onto the archaeological visibility map (fig. 40 and maps I'–VIII'). In the analysis of the finds distribution patterns, map formation will therefore assume an important place. This also puts us in a position, as far as is possible, to make sounder judgements about the areas in which the visibility can be deemed fair or good (the white areas in fig. 40).

Chapter 7

Occupation history: a few theoretical principles

7.1 INTRODUCTION

In the previous chapter an analysis was carried out to determine which factors have distorted the archaeological record in the northern Netherlands, so in principle a reliable discussion of the occupation history in the investigated area should now be possible. The concept of 'occupation history' has a negative connotation today because in the past it was one of the cornerstones of the cultural-historical approach so vilified by *New Archaeology*. Occupation history can be structured in a different way, however, a process which in the Netherlands has been chiefly theoretically articulated by Slofstra.[1] Without calling myself a disciple of Slofstra's historical-anthropological approach, I want to express agreement with the idea that each problem and period has its own significant issues which should be approached from various relevant models. These models can derive from various scientific disciplines (anthropology, history, sociology) and do not necessarily have to be adopted in their entirety. Although this may evoke the appearance of eclecticism, it can be avoided by clearly showing the extent to which the applied models are relevant to the formulated problem. The following is a justification for a significant number of the principles chosen to describe the occupation history and to explain the cultural processes contained within it.

A few words shall be devoted to my personal background and scientific interests. I believe that it is important to be explicit in describing these kinds of backgrounds because it is clear that they are decisive in the choice of research themes and interpretations.[2]

An explanation for much of the form and contents of this dissertation can be found in the relation of how it originated. It was started in 1981 as a research project for the Dutch Organization for Scientific Research (NWO), for which aims were formulated to a large extent by the applicants, i.e. professors J.D. van der Waals and H.T. Waterbolk of the Rijksuniversiteit at Groningen. From 1982 to 1985 little work was done on the dissertation itself, but many hours were spent teaching and setting up a lecture series on theory and methodology, among other activities. These activities led to an entirely different way of viewing the object of research and phrasing the appropriate questions. The result was a new scheme with different accents and aims. The work which had already commenced, however, formed a restrictive framework. Chiefly because the quality of the data was too poor and did not lend itself to the testing of inspired theories, I looked for ways to impart more expressiveness to the known data. That resulted in the map formation analysis, initially intended to be accompanied by a number of simulation models which might be able to describe the occupation history. This undertaking was abandoned for two reasons: the realization that this work would produce few meaningful results when carried out on the scale at which I executed the research and that too much time would be necessary to draw up and test the computer models. Finally I decided to present the study as an exploratory one and to give extra attention to the question as to how the inhabitants reacted to their drowning habitat, a question that was already central to the original grant proposal.

The choice of explanatory models and themes must be seen in the light of my course of study. After receiving a bachelor's degree in social geography at the Vrije Universiteit at Amsterdam, I studied cultural prehistory at the Rijksuniversiteit at Groningen. During that period I spent many months assisting in the excavations at Swifterbant, which is noticeable from the rather extensive

---

1 Amongst others Slofstra 1982.

2 For a discussion of this issue see amongst others Bourdieu 1989.

treatment of that group of findspots in Chapter 8. By way of a graduate project,[3] following the excavations at Oostwoud and later at Kolhorn and Oldeboorn, under the direction of J.N. Lanting, and barrow investigations in Maarn, under the direction of J.N. Lanting and J.D. van der Waals, a great deal of my archaeological interest turned to the Beaker period. This is also noticeable in Chapter 8 and in other publications.[4] In 1985 I began leading a research project in the Maas valley which up until now has focused on Bronze Age and Iron Age settlements. This work, and the lecture series at the Rijksuniversiteit at Leiden on the Bronze Age which I conducted, account for my interest in this period and the problems connected with it.

The choice of explanatory models has been further determined by articles which I have read more or less coincidentally over the years in the context of the preparation for one of the lecture series and for this dissertation. Although I realize that I am often drawn to political-economic models, I make no choice for any particular trend in theoretical thought. I do, however, distance myself from the logical-positivistic variation of 'New Archaeology' and assume an increasingly critical attitude towards the use of neo-evolutionistic models by archaeologists (see section 7.3). Neither does the system-theoretical approach have many concrete application possibilities as an explanatory model, in my opinion. Here I agree with much of structural archaeology's criticism of what it calls functionalistic archaeology.[5] Finally, the writing of this paragraph is a result of discussions on 'value-free science'. Value-free science does not exist, not even in excavations and surveys. Even the choice of research object and of research location and methods of documentation involves a number of values and presuppositions which result in certain things being found or recognized and others not being recognized.

7.2 THE SPATIAL FRAMEWORK OF THIS STUDY

Although the Frisian-Drentian plateau may have been in an isolated position as a physical-geographic unit, it appears from the character of the finds and findspots there that the inhabitants were always part of larger social groups. A separate Frisian-Drentian culture in fact can-

not be distinguished. Even the *terp* culture has a much broader distribution.

Figure 1 shows which area around the northern Netherlands has been taken into consideration. It is striking that when similarities and differences between archaeological cultural areas are being examined for any period, the river area appears as a sort of border zone. When the contacts maintained by the northern Netherlands are traced by way of the material culture, the main activity always seems to gravitate round relations with Denmark, Schleswig-Holstein, North-western Germany, and the mid-Rhine area. The contacts with regions to the south of the Rhine appear to have been of less importance but were not entirely absent. It creates the impression that the river area always played an important role in this connection as a dividing zone between two large 'cultural provinces'. It is not correct to speak of a sharp borderline; what is being discussed here, rather, is a transition area, a diffuse border having the character of a language or dialect border.

In Chapter 8, insofar as is possible, the above-mentioned similarities and differences will be substantiated by discussing spatial relations at the north-west European level. Naturally, such an approach can only be sketchy. This applies to the treatment of subjects such as social stratification, exchange networks, settlement patterns, etc.

7.3 SOCIAL ORGANIZATION

Since the 1960s, the social organization of pre- and protohistoric societies has been given systematic attention. This is not to say that the subject was ignored before this time, but that it did not belong to the standard procedure. The main cause of the change in emphasis was the influence of the *New Archaeology* movement which was based in particular on the work of Sahlins,[6] Service,[7] and Fried.[8] Archaeologists adopted their neo-evolutionistic models with almost complete and uncritical acceptance. Various reasons can be advanced to explain this. In the first place, the lucid descriptions by Sahlins of the 'Big Man' and 'Chief' ideal types and the clear definitions by Service and Fried of various levels of integration and differentiation made it possible for archaeologists to put these concepts into operation. In the second place, the

---

3 Bornwird, Fokkens 1982.
4 Fokkens 1984; 1986.
5 See for example Hodder 1986.

6 Sahlins 1963; 1968.
7 Service 1971.
8 Amongst others Fried 1967.

propositions for putting the concepts into operation as they were introduced by Binford and Saxe in particular were profoundly influential.[9] Stimulated by their work, archaeologists interpreted the most divergent elements of burial ritual or settlement patterns in terms of status differences.

The criticism which can be brought to bear can be summarized as follows. First, most archaeologists took no notice of the discussion which took place in anthropological circles on the models constructed by Sahlins, Service, and Fried. According to the criticism, Service's inductively reasoned levels of social integration are too strictly modelled on ethnographic stereotypes.[10] This means that one must be careful of being too quick to 'recognize' one of the ideal types. Moreover, much archaeological research hardly goes any further than labelling the investigated community in terms of social stratification while paying little attention to associated social structures.

In this regard, the amount of attention given to the differences between attributed and achieved status positions is often exaggerated. A child's grave with an axe or hammer axe in it is seen as a sign of attributed status, corresponding to a stratified or even a class society; that is an oversimplified way of reasoning. Moreover, few people seem to realize that Fried's model of state formation is mainly deductively reasoned and that his 'stratified society' is hypothetical. It is a missing link which in any case has not made an appearance in the last 2000 years and was necessary as a transition stage between the 'ranked society' and the state.[11]

Finally, the notion of status is often applied much too easily. A decorated Bell Beaker, a slightly larger byre part of a farm, a house without a byre part in a peasant village, a barrow that is a bit larger than most, and numerous other things have already led to speculations about differences in status. In speculating thus, in many cases the social structure of the society in question is often ignored. There is also a lack of integrated analyses of different aspects of the archaeological record. One investigator bases his work on hoards, another on burial customs, and still another on settlement structures, while it is clear that none of these components on its own is representative of the society as a whole.

Of course by the above remarks I do not contend that the investigation of social organization is pointless; on the contrary. However, it is necessary to approach the work more critically and in describing the social organization not to restrict oneself to criteria that make determination possible within an evolutionary framework. In addition, there should be an integrated approach based on different aspects (hoards, burial fields, settlements).

A few general remarks should be made here on the social organization of prehistoric societies in the northern Netherlands beginning with the Neolithic to serve as a framework for what will be dealt with in Chapter 8. In my opinion, the whole period beginning with the Early Neolithic is one of segmented tribal communities. In such a society, the segments are formed by local groups which are politically and economically independent of each other.[12] Kinship is generally an important integrating element and exchange networks play an important role in the integration process. The degree of stratification was low up to the Late Bronze Age. This is not to say that everyone was equal, or that there were no persons of higher social status. It does mean that there was little centralized authority. The first signs of greater complexity can be seen in the Late Bronze Age and the Early Iron Age. From that moment on there is a systematic appearance of archaeologically identifiable persons who, we can suppose, had united larger groups beneath them. Roymans sketches the socio-political organization in northern Gaul as '... a less complex chiefdom organization, in which a great number of chiefs occupied rather autonomous positions and recognized a supreme authority only in specific situations, mainly during external warfare.'[13] This picture may apply to the situation in the northern Netherlands as well, certainly from the Middle Iron Age onwards.

7.4 EXCHANGE NETWORKS

The Netherlands, and certainly the northern Netherlands, is an area with few natural minerals. Almost all the materials used for making stone or metal objects had to be brought in from elsewhere. Small axes of flint or other types of stone could perhaps be fashioned from stones carried along as moraine material, but the making of larger flint axes required a dependence on sources

9 Binford 1972; Saxe 1970.
10 A recent survey of this issue can be found in Van Bakel, Hagesteijn & Van de Velde 1986.

11 Fried 1967, 224.
12 Sahlins 1968, 21.
13 Roymans 1990, 261.

further away. Importing was a necessary activity that is demonstrable throughout prehistory. The question is, how did it work? Is the trader-blacksmith a real figure in a tribal society? Were there markets? What commodities were offered in exchange? These questions are occasionally posed in the margins but are seldom given systematic treatment in Dutch archaeological literature.[14] For a good understanding of the functioning of social structures, however, it is important that such questions be answered.

Trade and exchange are a pair of concepts that are often presented in opposition to each other. Trade is seen by some as a relatively recent development, whereas exchange and a sort of diffusion of artifacts should be understood as the normal prehistoric situation. The actual situation, however, is more complex; there are primitive societies existing today in which exchange networks are the most important, but mechanisms that look very much like trade also exist. These are often sustained by 'entrepreneurs': people who take it upon themselves to engage in trade. Sometimes an entire community is involved in manipulating trade, such as the Siassi in New Guinea. The term 'middlemen' can be applied here.[15] But this, according to Sahlins, is still not an open market economy. That is to say, there is no competition comparable to that in our Western market economy. That is why authors such as Sahlins emphasize the political aspects of reciprocal trade and exchange, a point of departure that in my opinion is the only correct one for primitive societies.

Notions about reciprocal exchange[16] have been determined in particular in the work of Mauss.[17] Mauss talks about gift exchange, and the essence of this idea is that the giver obliges the receiver to offer a gift in exchange. By giving gifts, the giver places himself in a superior position and stays there until the gift is reciprocated. The first giver then becomes the receiver, thus beginning a new relationship. Characteristic of this form of

exchange is that the gift is unalienable, that is to say it cannot be exchanged for other goods so it has no intrinsic value.[18]

In contrast to gift exchange Gregory poses commodity exchange, a notion described by Marx as the exchange of alienable goods between traders who are in a position of mutual independence to each other.[19] Alienation in this connection means passing on or dealing in private property. An important question is how the two elements within a society relate to each other: how do goods become gifts and how do gifts become goods? That these transfers took place in the Bronze Age, for instance, is apparent from the fact that certain hoards[20] which are considered to be hoards of scrap metal are composed of objects which in their original context probably circulated at different levels: prestige objects and foundry refuse deposited together. That means that a transformation took place from the level of gift exchange to the level of commodity exchange.[21]

Gregory studied how such processes take place by looking at different exchange systems in Papua New Guinea. A typical characteristic, as both Marx and Sahlins emphasized, is that commodity exchange begins at the social borders of clan-based communities.[22] When someone obtains an item from outside his community he can do with it as he wishes; it is alienable. However, should he give the item to one of the members of his tribe or clan, a relationship of dependence is created that belongs to gift exchange.

This still does not explain why exchange networks existed in prehistoric times, but it does make the functioning of such networks more understandable. The exchange of articles between communities can be referred to as commodity exchange or as trade, if you like. Hoards of ingots or of larger numbers of end products can probably be interpreted in this sense. This can be the work of middlemen or entrepreneurs, but it is also feasible, as happens in the Kula, that annual visits are made by a

14 Among the exceptions are Van den Broeke 1986; Lohof 1991; Roymans 1990; Van de Velde 1979.
15 In the case of the Siassi, a map (Sahlins 1972, 283) clearly shows how the middlemen position came into being. The Siassi inhabit a group of islands between New Guinea and New England and handle the overseas transport of the merchandise. The inhabitants of New England and New Guinea have no contact with each other apart from this trade relationship.
16 Sahlins 1972.
17 Mauss 1923.

18 Gregory 1982, 18.
19 Gregory 1982, 12.
20 E.g. the Drouwenerveld hoard of 1984 (Butler 1986).
21 Of course it can also be assumed that such hoards were the 'possessions' of grave and sanctuary plunderers. To judge by the number of hoards containing scrap metal, however, this occupation would have to have been practised too widely to serve as an acceptable explanation.
22 Gregory 1982, 168.

group to a friendly tribe (or a neighbouring island) in order to exchange goods.[23] It is plausible that different levels existed within the exchange networks, particularly as from the Bronze Age. That implies that not all gifts are exchangeable with each other; certain gifts have more status than others. Gregory reports, for instance, that in the Kula at least five levels exist, with shells and bracelets belonging to the highest level and certain items of food to the lowest. It is quite possible that different levels like these existed during prehistoric times as well. The highest might be called the prestige goods network. Social status may have played a role in this regard, a role that in turn was connected with the organization of the exchange between communities.

7.5 HOARDS

In my opinion, hoards cannot be viewed apart from their role in the exchange networks. Certain hoards can be interpreted as hidden merchandise, judging from their context and composition; others can be understood as hidden treasures, and an important category as votive gifts. In the northern Netherlands most hoards are classified as votive deposits, especially the hoards from the Bronze Age and the Iron Age. Some large Iron Age hoards deposited in moors are interpreted (with reference to such historical sources as Caesar and Tacitus) as offerings to the gods in thanksgiving for victory in battle.[24] For votive hoards from the Bronze Age such an explanation is less obvious. Current interpretation of the moor deposits often sees them in connection with the destruction of wealth by the elite. This could have served different purposes. On the one hand, the giver satisfies both ancestors and gods with his offering and at the same time he thereby receives prestige in the world of the living.[25] On the other hand, the practice of deposition might serve to break down the cumulative effect of the reciprocal gift cycle. In a system of competitive gift-exchange, the limits of what can be produced are

reached at a certain point and the circulating supply must be reduced. For example, in some areas of Papua New Guinea this situation leads to an enormous pig-slaughtering feast every few years. Suppose that the cumulative effect of exchange leads to a gift that ought to consist of at least 1000 pigs; at the exchange feast 500 pigs can be slaughtered, thereby reducing the debt to 500 pigs.[26] A similar destruction of a part of the debt sometimes takes place at the level of individual exchange. Then the hoards or feasts are small. But it can also occur at the level of villages or larger social units. In the last case, the organizer of the ritual (the tribal chief among the Kwakiutl, the village head in New Guinea) is the one who can earn status. Presumably it is such people and their kin whom we know as the Drouwen 'chief' and the Drouwen 'princess'.[27]

7.6 KINSHIP STRUCTURE

The concept of kinship was mentioned several times in the above. Although this anthropological concept has long been a part of the English language literature, it is hardly ever used by Dutch archaeologists. It is considered one of those things that one cannot dig up. This is perhaps correct in a literal sense, but digging it up is unnecessary. Kinship and similar concepts are preferably used to serve as a framework for interpretation.

The study of kinship, marriage regulations, etc. has been dominated since the 1950s by the fundamental work of Lévi-Strauss.[28] Lévi-Strauss gives central position in his work to marriage as the binding agent in primitive societies. Marriage is understood as a form of 'exchange' in which reciprocity and mutual trust are of great importance. A woman can be seen here as the 'ultimate gift' in which the giving party asks the receiving party for a reciprocal gift in kind; through kinship, economic and political ties are also forged (compare section 7.3). The fact that marriage is given significance in this way does not mean that every marriage must be seen as a result of

23 In the Kula these exchange journeys are made reciprocally in a sort of exchange system at a higher level: one year group A visits group B, using canoes intended only for this purpose, the next year the voyage is made by group B (Gregory 1982, 198). Naturally, such a journey can be coupled with feasts, etc., and has as its purpose to keep up the stock of exchangeable gifts. Apart from this, gifts are exchanged principally at special occasions: marriage, funerals, or other events in which the

exchange of gifts would be appropriate and solemn.
24 Levy 1982.
25 Gregory 1980; 1982.
26 Among the Kwakiutl (American west coast), a similar system of destroying gifts is called *potlatch* (Gregory 1982, 60 ff).
27 Butler 1969.
28 Lévi-Strauss 1949.

cool calculation, such as marriages within the nobility in the Middle Ages. Often marriages involve rules and taboos whose meanings have almost entirely been lost. Nevertheless, they are upheld as part of the tradition, and in this way they fulfill their role.[29] Kinship thus plays a very important role in the development of social structures and should be involved in archaeological discourse.

7.7 SETTLEMENT STRUCTURE, SETTLEMENT PATTERN, AND SETTLEMENT SYSTEM

The concepts of settlement structure, settlement pattern, and settlement system are quite often used interchangeably in archaeological usage, and the reader has to find out for himself from the context exactly which meaning is intended. To avoid this kind of confusion I am following the definitions which Flannery provides through the 'Skeptical Graduate Student' in one of his discussions with the 'Real Mesoamerican Archeologist'.[30]

The 'settlement structure' is to be understood as the internal organization of a settlement (social as well as spatial). In the study area, up to the Late Iron Age, this can be characterized as open settlements consisting of a small number of dispersed farmsteads located some distance from each other. Clusters of houses which might be called villages only appear as late as the Roman period, in particular in the 2nd century AD (Chapter 8). The farmstead consists of a main building and several barns and sometimes a second residence. Judging by the average size of the living parts of the houses, it can be determined that the standard household during the Iron Age and the Roman period consisted of a nuclear family (6–10 persons). During the Middle Bronze Age and the beginning of the Late Bronze Age, the large byre houses perhaps accommodated an extended family (10–15 persons; see Chapter 8).

The 'settlement pattern' is described as the distribution of settlements, cemeteries, sanctuaries, arable land, etc. in a particular region. Included here are the differences between various types of settlements, the location in the landscape, etc. In the framework of this study, the possibilities for drawing conclusions about the settlement pattern are restricted, because the available data are too fragmentary.

Finally, the 'settlement system' is the compilation of rules which governed the establishment of the pattern. According to the Skeptical Graduate Student this is the ultimate goal of the archaeologist's search.[31] The settlement system explains how the relationships between settlements, cemeteries, ceremonial sites, etc., came into being. Again, the fragmentary nature of the data from the study area prevents the drawing of significant conclusions. Therefore, when remarks are made in Chapter 8 about the settlement system, these will usually have been based on data taken from a broader context.

7.8 TERRITORIALITY

The concept of territoriality is frequently used in relation to the Frisian-Drentian plateau. A territorial division of the Frisian and Drentian landscape is taken for granted by most writers. The landscape has always been strictly compartmentalized by its natural borders, and the historical *marken* (see section 7.8.1) correlate with this division. It is evident that the *marke* has also served as a model for ideas about the prehistoric territorial structure of the Frisian-Drentian plateau.

This line of reasoning is also followed by Waterbolk, who has used his adaptation group model as a means to prove continuity of occupation on the Frisian-Drentian plateau. As territorial communities, *marke* and *dingspel* (former judicial district in Drenthe) form an integrated part of that model and, also seen in that light, an evaluation of territoriality on the Frisian-Drentian plateau is necessary.

7.8.1 *'Buurschap' and 'marke': a historical perspective*
The uncultivated territories in the middle, eastern, and northern Netherlands have been called *marken* as far back as human memory. The first mention of this concept dates from AD 792[32] and signifies a *buurschap* (neighbourhood) with a surrounding area. 'The *buur-*

29 Goody, for example, makes a reasonable case for the possibility that there is a connection between the rules for the giving of a dowry and for inheritability on the one hand and a society's economic basis on the other (Goody 1976). Thus in a community which is engaged in intensive cultivation, where land is an important factor, the rules of inheritance are aimed at keeping landholdings within the kin-group.
30 Flannery 1976, 161–2.
31 Flannery 1976, 162.
32 Slicher van Bath 1978, 238.

schap or the *buur* is the community of those who share rights and duties based on the possession of houses of the settlement recognized as *"buurhuizen"* (neighbourhood houses).'[33] The *buurschap* is therefore a 'small local nucleus of the population living in the countryside'.[34] The territory of the *buurschap* as well as its border is indicated by the notion of *marke*.[35] The *marke* is therefore the area that is held in common and where no private claims were possible.

Slicher van Bath describes the development of the *marke* as a territory with rights and duties as a logical consequence of the agricultural system. He envisages a balance being struck between arable land and wasteland. 'The size of the livestock was determined by the number of animals that was able to find sufficient food on the swampy ground overgrown with wild shoots.' Further, the extent of arable land was dependent on the amount of manure that could be produced. In addition, the practice of sod manuring created a tight connection between wasteland areas, regeneration time, and arable areas.[36] The wastelands were consequently of great importance in the agricultural system, and their use had to be regulated.

The *buurschap* had a great deal of autonomy in this regard, and the system was very flexible in principle. The image of the rigid *marke* organization that many derive from the situation which has existed since the last century does not apply to the older periods.[37] It is certainly not the case that the *buurschappen* should be seen as closed communities with little 'give' left in them. Within the *buurschappen*, divisions of yards, exchanges of ownership, etc. continued to occur. Even divisions of *buurschappen* and their *marken* were not uncommon and probably sprang from the need to cultivate new arable land.[38] According to Slicher van Bath, it was the population increase that accounted for the increasing isolation of the *marken* since the 13th century,[39] but Heringa does not agree with this notion. In his point of view it is rather a gradual process, a consequence of the lack of pasture and meadow areas, among other things. Heringa sees the closing of the *marke* as a process that is characteristic for farming communities, '... no more than the

practice of refusing non-local farmers access to the *marke*, probably nothing new and, in a world of farmers, nothing peculiar.'[40]

The division of the *marken* as we know them today did not occur until the 19th century. Demoed makes clear that the drawing of boundaries was a more or less arbitrary matter. The government had wanted to break down the *marke* societies since the end of the 18th century in the hope that by making private initiative possible agrarian production would rise.[41] In 1810 a law was passed to promote the cultivation of wasteland, but in Drenthe it was viewed as absolutely useless. Moreover, the wastelands were indispensable in the agricultural system. Finally, after pressure was exerted by the authorities division ditches were dug or ploughed, but at first they remained unheeded. The common ground continued to be used jointly.[42]

There is much more to be said about *marken*, *marke* rights (*waardelen*), and *marke* partners, but most is related to developments which took place at a later time and bear little relevance in this context. We must adhere to the picture sketched by Heringa for the original situation: autonomous *buurschappen* with a flexible structure, each having its own *marke* with no hint of an overall *marke* organization.

7.8.2 *Territorial communities and adaptation groups*

Since 1974 Waterbolk has been trying to describe and account for Drenthe's territorial structure with the help of his adaptation group model. This model describes the territorial structure of agrarian communities in homogeneous, isolated areas. The smallest unit in the model is the territorial community, the occupational unit. Each of these communities has a occupational area whose dimensions are adapted to the size of the occupational group, the social structure, the function of the site, etc.[43] In this we recognize the *buurschap* and its *marke*. According to Waterbolk the average size of the territorial community is 10–20 persons, a number which has repeatedly come forward as a settlement unit in investigations in the northern Netherlands.[44] Such a group cannot live in complete isolation. Variation in available

33 Heringa 1985, 69.
34 Slicher van Bath's wording, cited by Heringa (1985, 69).
35 Heringa 1985, 70.
36 Slicher van Bath 1978, 237.
37 Heringa 1985, 70.
38 Heringa 1985, 72.

39 Slicher van Bath 1978, 237, 241.
40 Heringa 1985, 80.
41 Demoed 1989, 60.
42 Demoed 1989, 65 ff.
43 Waterbolk 1974, 155.
44 Waterbolk 1965, Kooi 1979.

food, mortality resulting from epidemics, the danger of endogeny, etc., form a biological necessity for maintaining contact with other groups.[45] In isolated areas, therefore, a number of such communities should be present in order to reproduce themselves. Waterbolk sets the minimum number of people for such an adaptation group at 200–300 persons.[46] Such a group thus consists of a number of territorial units which live in a 'group territory' that is preferably homogeneous in ecological potential and bordered by rivers, peatlands, open water, etc. In other words: isolated from other territories in which similar units live.[47]

Waterbolk uses this model in connection with the model of the historical *marke* in order to show that the territorial structure in Drenthe goes back at least to the Late Iron Age, possibly even to the Middle Bronze Age.[48] To do this, he combines topographical, historical, and archaeological data. Agrarian societies, according to Waterbolk, are always structured following the principles described above, and if occupational continuity is demonstrable, then continuity of this structure is plausible.[49] In this vision it is obvious that the prehistoric adaptation group would have acted as a unit as well. Applied to the problem of a 'drowning' landscape (see Chapter 9), it could be expected that when a specific group territory becomes too small to maintain an adaptation group, the group as a whole would decide to leave. Indeed, their sense of mutual connection, communal dialect, politics, religious traditions, etc., would ensure that such a decision would be made *en bloc*.

The archaeological consequence of this theory is that, if one settlement or cemetery is discovered from a certain period in a part of a particular territory, there would have been at least 10 to 20 others in the same area.[50] Conversely, if no trace of occupation has been encountered for a certain period in a part of such a territory, then it would not be necessary to look any further: the area would have been too small for an adaptation group and therefore would have remained empty.

A problem with this model is that it combines biological patterns with the historical *marke*, so that the model acquires socio-political content. This content, however, is determined to a great extent by the historical model, giving rise to a sort of static whole in which the spatial as well as the social organization remains the same. In this way the social organization of the communities of Medieval Drenthe becomes the model for the entire prehistoric period. In the context of investigation into the prehistoric past, however, the appropriate model should be based on tribal organization, and that cannot be linked directly with what was socially and politically customary during the protohistorical and historical periods. There are also methodological objections to Waterbolk's working method. He analyses the distribution of barrows, urnfields, and Celtic field systems in the light of the clearly defined *marke* areas. The hypothesis is that there was no more than one territorial community within the boundaries of every historical *marke*, and Waterbolk also thinks that this is demonstrable.[51] In the early periods (the Late Bronze Age and the Early Iron Age) the structure may have been more fine-meshed, but it did exist.[52] In his opinion it does seem to be possible, therefore, to demonstrate continuity of territorial structure. Waterbolk even suggests that the tripartite division of Drenthe into Westenveld, Zuidenveld, and Noordenveld goes back to prehistoric times on the basis of the fact that in two of these *dingspelen* one rich cemetery was found which may indicate a central location.[53]

The most important argument refuting this method of reasoning is that it is based on the comparison of spatial distributions. A similar distribution is thus deemed synonymous with a similar structure and organization. Even apart from the fragmentary character of the archaeological distribution patterns, especially on the western part of the Frisian-Drentian plateau (see Chapters 5 and 6), this is methodologically incorrect. First it should be demonstrated that both distribution patterns are connected and that they were created by the same processes.

45 Waterbolk 1974, 155.
46 Heidinga (1987) uses the notion of *kerngewest* (nuclear region), referring both to the area and to the population living in it (numbering from 250–500 persons). In the historical period Drenthe had three such nuclear regions which all represented political entitites as well (Waterbolk 1987b, 12, 13).
47 In German the term is *Siedlungskammer*, but this does not convey the idea of a territory with a minimum size.
48 Waterbolk 1987a, 214.

49 Waterbolk 1987a, 215.
50 If a habitational unit consisted of 10–20 persons and the minimal size of the adaptation group was 200 persons, then the entire adaptation group consisted of at least 10 to 20 habitational units.
51 Waterbolk 1982; 1987a, 183.
52 Waterbolk 1987a, 206.
53 Waterbolk 1987a, 207.

In addition, the use of polygonal structures for the identification of spatial patterns is a precarious business, as was shown in a striking way by Hodder and Orton.[54] Whether one's assumptions are based on an artificial polygonal structure or on the *marke* division makes no difference.

The above criticism certainly does not mean that there was no territoriality on the Frisian-Drentian plateau. However, the existence of a territorial structure must be derived from the archaeological data, without help from the *marke* structure model. The problem here is that it is difficult to get an impression of the representativeness of the database and that one arrives at conclusions that are unjustified (see Chapters 5, 6, and 8). The use of a spatial framework (such as the *marke* division or Thyssen polygons) as an analysis method thus gives an illusory certitude. In addition, the spatial structure should not be seen apart from the social organization which likewise, as far as possible, must be derived from the archaeological data. For this purpose the settlement structure, the coherent whole of settlements, cemeteries, and ritual places can be used. It will be clear that during the 4000 years before the beginning of the Christian era, which are discussed in this study, dynamic developments in settlement structure took place. There have been indications of a certain territorial structure in all periods, which however have become more archaeologically recognizable only after the Late Bronze Age, with the appearance of cemeteries and Celtic field systems. The fact that such cemeteries were probably used by the same kin group over long periods indicates the presence of a territorial structure. However, it is equally apparent from regular transfers of burial locations, archaeologically perceived as discontinuity in cemeteries of a specific period, that the structure was flexible and offered space for the relocation of farms and for the incorporation of new units in a particular area. The territorial structure was therefore constantly in motion. The *marke* division is the end of this development, its specific form could be maintained because the system had ultimately been politically and juridically underpinned.

54 Hodder & Orton 1976.

Chapter 8

The occupation history beginning with the Neolithic

8.1 INTRODUCTION

The goal of this chapter is not to use empirical data to reconstruct the occupation history but to place these data within a broader spatial and social framework. Topics concerning archaeological cultural connections, economics, continuity of occupation, and social organization will be treated for each period separately. In addition, the settlement pattern which has been recognized or can be expected in the Netherlands and adjoining regions will be described in rough outline. Finally, the distribution of findspots in the study area will be analysed.

8.2 EARLY NEOLITHIC

8.2.1 *General framework*

The Neolithic in the Netherlands begins with the arrival of Bandkeramik farmers in the southern Netherlands. This does not mean, however, that agricultural practices were immediately adopted everywhere. For a long time afterward, groups of hunter-gatherers who made little or no use of agricultural products continued to live in our regions. The Bandkeramik farmers can indeed be regarded as full-time farmers who employed a mixed economy to adapt themselves specifically to loess plateaus.[1] Although the *Wanderbauerntum* (shifting cultivation) no longer serves as a model, the fact remains that the Bandkeramik culture quickly spread over the European temperate zone.[2] The first Bandkeramik farmers in southern Limburg can be viewed as colonists who came from neighbouring regions to establish themselves with a completely developed system of agrarian exploitation. To what extent this caused conflicts with the groups of hunter-gatherers already living in the area is not known;

it is not even clear whether such groups were still living in southern Limburg at that time.

The material culture of the Bandkeramik farmers remained quite homogeneous until *c.*4900 cal BC, although there was some regionalization. Afterwards a shift took place in the Netherlands to various other cultural units: the Limburg culture and the Rössen culture, passing into the Michelsberg culture. These groups also exploited the areas outside the loess zones and, with the exception of the Rössen culture, covered an area that reached the rivers Rhine and Maas. It is also clear that contacts existed between the Rössen communities and other groups in the northern European lowlands, among them the Ertebølle and related culture groups.

To turn to the hunter-gatherers, an incorporation of agrarian elements was taking place in the economies of those groups maintaining themselves in river valleys, delta regions, and territories further removed from the loess areas. Grain cultivation, cattle-breeding, and pottery production were gradually taken up, but were adapted in scale and form to the existing way of life. Examples of this taking place can be found within the Swifterbant, the Hazendonk, and the Vlaardingen/Stein culture groups. Although these groups did either cultivate or import grain and keep some cattle, they were predominantly dependant on hunting and gathering, activities which also determined their settlement pattern and social organization.

When considering the situation in the northern Netherlands, it is clear that the first completely agrarian communities in that area belonged to the Funnel Beaker culture groups. Because there is no loess in the north, Bandkeramik and Rössen farmers did not settle there. Neither are there indications of Michelsberg-related groups establishing themselves north of the river Rhine. Artifacts which in the southern Netherlands are associ-

1 Bakels 1978; Barker 1985.

2 Barker 1985, 147.

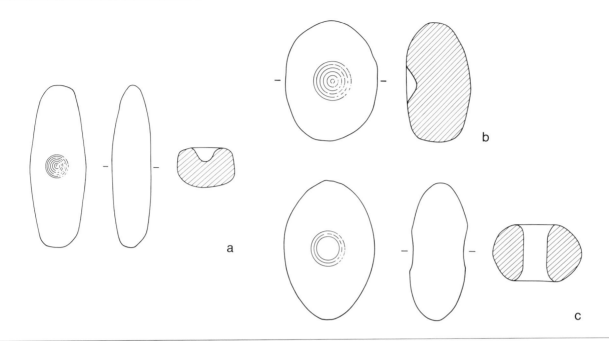

Figure 41 *Geröllkeule* from the western part of the Frisian-Drentian plateau. Legend: a FM 1973-III-3; b FM 1969-III-1; c FM 4:5. Scale 1:3.

ated with the Rössen culture have been found in the north, but these can be interpreted as imported elements used by local groups living a predominantly Mesolithic existence, especially the Swifterbant group and their predecessors.

There is no evidence for Late Mesolithic occupation in the higher regions of the Frisian-Drentian plateau. The latest date for the De Leien-Wartena phase is around 5700 cal BC.[3] Later dates are attributable to the Swifterbant group. Neither can Late Mesolithic 'survival' be demonstrated on the higher grounds of the northern Netherlands; the youngest date for Late Mesolithic 'survival' is around 5100 cal BC.[4] Based on the available data, the only possible conclusion to be reached is that after *c.* 6700 cal BC, Mesolithic occupation on the higher grounds of the Frisian-Drentian plateau was very sparse or per-

haps even non-existent.[5] However, stream valleys and perhaps lake shores and similar locations probably were exploited, as they were by the Swifterbant group. Indeed, Waterbolk sees in the ^{14}C dates indications for continuity between Late Mesolithic groups and the Swifterbant group.[6] It is likely that the higher grounds were densely forested, suitable for hunting certain types of animals but probably less attractive as an occupation area than the transition zone between stream valleys and forested areas where both environments could be exploited.

Apart from the find assemblages belonging to the Swifterbant group, there remain a number of finds categories which are often attributed to the Early Neolithic A and, as such, are therefore interesting in this context. They will be the first to be discussed in the following section.

8.2.2 *Early Neolithic A: find assemblages not related to the Swifterbant group (5300–4900 cal BC; 6400–6000 b.p.)*
Regarding those finds not associated with the Swifterbant group, there are a number of artifact categories (mostly found in isolation) whose chronological alloca-

3 Lanting & Mook 1977, 39–40.
4 Lanting & Mook 1977, 40.
5 The Swifterbant moraine flint industry gives reason to believe that these Late Mesolithic assemblages can be very

difficult to recognize both typologically and technologically (Deckers 1986). So Late Mesolithic findspots might still be hidden between the many undated assemblages.
6 Waterbolk 1985a, 279.

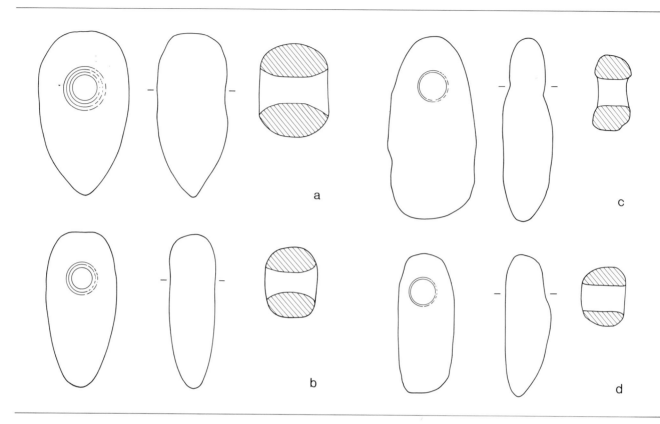

Figure 42 *Spitzhauen* (a, b) and *Plattbolzen* (c, d) from the western part of the Frisian-Drentian plateau. Legend: a FM 218-109; b FM Wijkel collection no. 8; c. FM 1969-III-33 (cat. no. 35); d G 693 (cat. no. 186). Scale 1:3.

tion is uncertain. First are the so-called *Geröllkeulen*: perforated or unperforated pebbles (fig. 41). The Dutch specimens have been discussed by Hulst and Verlinde who finally reached a vague definition of their function at the end of an extensive typological treatise.[7] Their work passes over the fact that *Geröllkeulen* with one or two recesses probably had a different function than that of the completely perforated specimens. This latter group is interpreted by various authors as having served as weights on digging sticks. This type of implement is typical of hunter-gatherer economies on higher ground and is most probably Mesolithic in date.[8] Indeed, *Geröllkeulen*

are regularly found in Ertebølle and Maglemose contexts.[9] The artifacts with recesses can possibly be interpreted as stoneworking implements (for pecking) or as fire drill stones.[10] This group is also difficult to date; it is usually placed in the Mesolithic or Early Neolithic. One of the arguments for this is that the pecking technique is used in modelling the artifacts.

Seven specimens have been found in the study area of which one is found in clear association with Funnel Beaker pottery and flint (fig. 41: a). However, this need not mean that this group of artifacts was still in regular use until the Middle Neolithic B, any more than the completely perforated specimen found in *hunebed* D53.[11] On the basis of the above considerations, the decision has been made to regard the *Geröllkeulen* as predominantly Late Mesolithic elements and not to include them in the distribution maps.

7 A striking implement in which the thumb (and index finger) can be inserted in the recesses (Hulst & Verlinde 1976; 1979).
8 Broadbent 1975–77; Vynsrygg 1987.
9 Hulst & Verlinde 1976, 110.

10 Shaw 1944. Apart from the examples which clearly exhibit an incomplete two-sided perforation.
11 Van Giffen 1951, 104; but see Bakker 1979, 110.

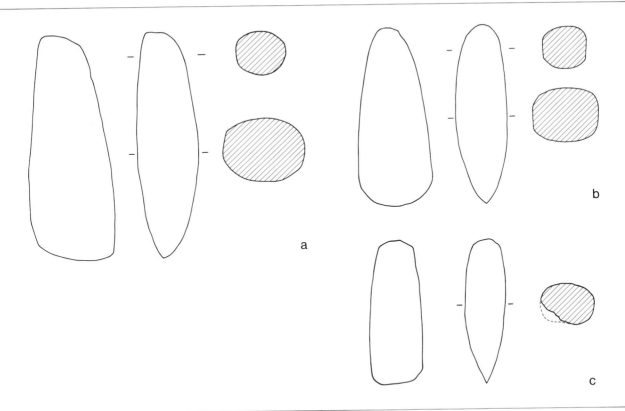

Figure 43 Stone axes with a round cross-section from the western part of the Frisian-Drentian plateau. Legend: a FM 1975-IX-54; b GD 114; c Vermaning collection 1966-VIII-1. Scale 1:3.

The so-called *Spitzhauen* also belong to the early dated finds. These are hammer axes with one end blunt and the other pointed which are understood to have functioned as picks or pickaxes (fig. 42: a, b). They frequently show pecking marks and have hourglass-shaped perforations.[12] Three specimens are known from the study area, all without context. As with the *Geröllkeulen*, dating is difficult because of the absence of clear associations. *Spitzhauen* occur in Mesolithic as well as Early Neolithic contexts, but contexts more recent than the Early Neolithic A are not known. Neither have been found in Swifterbant findspots. For this reason this group of artifacts has not been included in the distribution maps.

The so-called *Plattbolzen* found in the northern Netherlands form another category of artifacts that is difficult to date (fig. 42: c, d). Elsewhere they were found in the context of late Bandkeramik and Rössen culture. In the northern Netherlands there is a possible connection with activities of Early Neolithic groups, the latest being the Swifterbant group.[13] Therefore this artifact group is included in the distribution map of the Early Neolithic B. In general *Plattbolzen* are found on the higher sandy grounds and in my opinion they reflect special activities (possibly connected with woodworking), perhaps temporary encampments, but no permanent occupation in that area (see section 8.2.3).

Finally, a group of stone axes is considered to be of Early Neolithic date: the stone axes with a round cross-section (fig. 43). Brandt distinguishes two variations: axes with a pointed butt and axes with a blunt butt. There are also

12 Brandt has rather impressionistically split the group into two typological parts, with the A group being regarded as the oldest. There is also absolutely no basis, from a statistical point of view, for the typological subdivision made by Hulst and

Verlinde, nor does it have any datable value, any more than Brandt's subdivision. It is therefore pointless to use these subdivisions (Brandt 1976; Hulst & Verlinde 1979, 186).

13 Jager 1981, 244.

variations possible in the cross-sections: circularly rounded (variant a) to flattened sides (variant b).[14] It is often difficult to know where to draw the line between these and axes with a rectangular cross-section, a problem which is also apparent in the type plates.[15] Brandt has found no stone axes with a round cross-section in a clearly datable context in his study area. Most of them are stray finds. The stone axe with a round cross-section is a type which rarely occurs in Schleswig-Holstein, in contrast with Denmark, where it is regularly found in Ertebølle contexts.[16] Brandt regards it as the oldest type of stone axe; this opinion is corroborated by the fact that it is unknown within Funnel Beaker contexts.[17] Like the *Plattbolzen*, the specimens from the northern Netherlands, in my opinion, can be associated with special activities of the Swifterbant group or associated groups on the higher sandy grounds.

It is difficult to assign the above-mentioned artifact types to a particular period as long as no clear associations exist which make better dating possible. In fact, there is a whole range of possible interpretations, with the above argument as an example. Anyone who wants to demonstrate occupation traces in the period in question can make use of the same artifacts in his argument. However, no matter how one looks at the evidence, these finds do not fill in the hiatus between the Late Mesolithic and the Funnel Beaker culture on the higher grounds. The scarcity of finds indicates that the plateau was probably used for short hunting expeditions. In my opinion, there is no indication of permanent or even seasonal exploitation of the higher grounds.

8.2.3 *Early Neolithic* B: *the Swifterbant group (4400–4000 cal* BC; *5550–5200 b.p.)*

General framework
The Swifterbant group is defined by evidence found during excavations at the type site at Swifterbant.[18]

The Swifterbant sites on natural levees are dated between 4400 and 4000 cal BC.[19] Characteristic artifacts include T-shaped antler axes and pottery with pointed bases, impressions under the rims and fingertip decoration.[20] In addition *hohe durchlochte Schuhleistenkeile* and *durchlochte Breitkeile* occur. At Swifterbant the findspots are very clearly identifiable as dark-coloured cultural layers of variable thickness in the clay subsoil.[21] In addition to Swifterbant and its surroundings, settlement traces have been found at a small number of places along the river IJssel in Gelderland and the river Vecht in Overijssel.[22] Outside this area the only possible indications of occupation are stray finds consisting of *Breitkeile*, T-shaped antler axes, and probably also *Plattbolzen* and stone axes with a round cross-section.

The distribution area of the *durchlochte Breitkeile* is very extensive, but this category of artifacts appears to have been used by various Early Neolithic cultural groups, among them the Swifterbant group.[23] In his survey, Van der Waals notes that the *durchlochte Breitkeile* findspots are located predominantly in the river valleys. He accounts for this by connecting the findspots with the users' preference for settling in wet areas.[24] The distribution of T-shaped antler axes does not contradict this conclusion, but of course this is also related to preservation conditions.[25]

Settlement pattern
The only Swifterbant group settlements which have been investigated in detail up to now are a few findspots near the type site. The question is whether these findspots are representative as site-types for the Swifterbant group. There are a number of arguments supporting an affirmative answer to this question. In the first place, the sites near Swifterbant span a period of at least two hundred years during which the locational preferences and the economic basis appear hardly to have changed at all. In the second place, there are significant similarities with

---

14 Brandt 1967, 167.
15 Compare Brandt 1967, *Tafel* 23.7, a *Felsrundbeil* whose cross-section is almost rectangular. Although Brandt does not mention it, the pointed neck in this specimen and others like it, which is not found on rectangular axes, has been decisive in identifying round axes. In doubtful cases, this criterium is also used in the present study.
16 Brandt 1967, 130.
17 Bakker 1979, 86.
18 Deckers *et al.* 1980; Van der Waals & Waterbolk 1976.

19 Lanting & Mook 1977, 48–50.
20 Deckers *et al.* 1980; De Roever 1979.
21 Fokkens 1978.
22 De Gaste, Groenlo, Heemse, Spoolde; Clason 1983; Lanting 1986; Lanting & Mook 1977, 57.
23 Lanting & Mook 1977, 56; Van der Waals 1972.
24 It should be observed that artifact findspots are not necessarily connected with the place of settlement (Van der Waals 1972, 161).
25 Van der Waals 1972, fig. 61.

the closely-related Ertebølle culture, of which many findspots in Denmark in particular have been investigated. These similarities include the nature of the site location and, partly, the economic basis. The members of the Ertebølle cultural group set up their semi-permanent settlements predominantly in wet environments and coastal areas which they exploited as hunter-gatherer fishermen.[26] The findspots along the coast are characterized by thick cultural layers with shell refuse, or middens, the so-called *Køkkenmøddinger*. The inland sites, such as Ringkloster, were also located in a wet environment but had no shell middens.

The question of the representativeness of the Swifterbant findspots on natural levees is related to the interpretation of the duration of the settlement: should these findspots be seen as seasonal encampments or as permanently inhabited settlements? Clason interprets the bone spectrum, including bones of the aurochs and the wild horse, as indications of a stable environment in which the natural levees did not flood each year, making possible occupation which lasted longer than one season.[27] The palaeobotanical investigation and pollen analysis seem to point in that direction as well. For instance, Casparie *et al.* see in the presence of spikelets of naked barley – refuse which is normally left behind after threshing – an indication of grain cultivation and processing on the site.[28] Arable farming would have been quite possible (though on a moderate scale) on the higher parts of the natural levees, where a mixed forest of oak, beech, elm, wild apple, lime, and alder grew.[29] Despite these derivative indications of permanent occupation, the stratigraphy at various investigated sites clearly shows that the natural levees flooded regularly.[30] Site S3 in particular showed successive occupation layers and hearth levels, divided by clay layers (some of them very thin). It is also clear that parts of the sites have disappeared because of shifting stream channels.[31] In addition, there are the botanical remains in the form of stinging nettle seeds, among others, showing that the sites were sometimes abandoned.[32] These arguments, however, do not

necessarily contradict a model of permanent occupation on the fresh water tidal delta. It is possible that people regularly chose to move to another dwelling site within the same ecological zone, thereby frequently returning to the same place. In this connection, the continuity in hearth locations and the presence of a cemetery at site S2 are indications of repeated occupation.

In addition to the above considerations, one should keep in mind that the river dunes, lying somewhat higher than sea level and certainly suitable for arable farming, were 'enclaves' of higher grounds in the delta area situated within a kilometre of the findspots on natural levees. They could have formed an integrated part of the settlement system. It seems possible to work from a model in which the sites on natural levees were permanently inhabited during a certain period of time. In times of extremely high water, the population could seek refuge on the higher river dunes. The dunes could also have been the location of the fields, while the grain could have been threshed on the levee sites, if need be. The most important means of subsistence, however, would have been hunting, fishing, and the gathering of hazelnuts, wild apples, etc. The environment was perfectly suited to these activities. There is no reason to suppose that the findspots in the Vecht valley or further upstream in the IJssel valley were characterized by a different exploitation practice than those in the delta region.

The above discussion leads to the conclusion that the Swifterbant group had an essentially 'Mesolithic' economy aimed at the exploitation of the river and delta region, where the sources of food already present were supplemented by grain products. It is my opinion, therefore, that future investigation on the higher grounds of the Frisian-Drentian plateau, or outside it, will uncover few if any traces of permanent occupation by the Swifterbant group. The settlements can be seen as semi-permanent, that is to say inhabited for more than one year. The southern border of the Swifterbant group distribution area is the river Rhine. Its equivalent south of this border, in the Rhine and Maas delta, is the Hazendonk

26 Andersen 1975.
27 Clason & Brinkhuizen 1978; Zeiler 1986.
28 The argument followed by Casparie *et al.* (1977, 51) is that finding threshing refuse means that threshing took place at the site because transporting unthreshed grain would not have been economical. It makes for a heavier load. This argument, however, does not necessarily fit with prehistoric reality. It is possible that spikelets remained in the grain storage facility after winnowing. Bakels postulates a comparable situation for

the transport of unthreshed grain at Hekelingen (Bakels 1986).
29 The varieties of grain indicated are naked barley (*Hordeum vulgare* var. *nudum*) and then cultivated emmer wheat (*Triticum dicoccum*). Naked barley has been demonstrated in the Rössen context, among others (Casparie *et al.* 1977, 51).
30 Deckers *et al.* 1980, 132.
31 Deckers *et al.* 1980; Fokkens 1978.
32 Casparie *et al.* 1977.

Table 10 The western part of the Frisian-Drentian plateau: determination of site-type on the basis of individual specimens of different finds categories for the Early Neolithic B. The columns and rows represent finds categories and site-types respectively.

site-type	finds category			total
	axe	perforated adze	antler axe	
settlement	0	3	0	3
grave	4	0	0	4
hoard	1	0	1	2
unknown	4	3	2	9
total	9	6	3	18

group.[33] Considering the fact that the latest date for the material in Spoolde is around 3900 cal BC,[34] it does not appear unreasonable to assume that both groups existed, for the most part, at the same time and that the end of the Swifterbant group coincided with the end of Hazendonk-3, around 3900 cal BC.[35]

Findspots in the study area (maps 1 and 1')
Only eighteen findspots are known in the study area which can be attributed to the Swifterbant group or its contemporaries (table 10). These concern stray finds of *durchlochte Breitkeile*, *Plattbolzen*, stone axes with a round cross-section, and antler axes.
For example, numerous antler artifacts were found when a swimming pool was built near Donkerbroek.[36] Judging from descriptions and photographs, the assemblage appears to be comparable to that found at Spoolde.[37] The finds were uncovered in deep peat layers in the Tjonger valley and possibly date from different periods. A few typical T-shaped antler axes indicate that the Swifterbant group is represented in any case. At a further distance from the valleys, five axes with a round cross-

section and four *Plattbolzen* were found. The *Breitkeil* from Oostrum probably represents activities along the coast, just as the specimens from Marum and Diever represent activities in the river valleys.
An ever-returning question is whether these finds are only the tip of the iceberg or whether they indeed suggest very sparse occupation during this period. The present study tends to support the latter conclusion. This support can be gained from the ascertainment that the artifacts attributable to this period belong to the category 'highly recognizable'. Nevertheless, only a small number of these artifacts have been found in the study area. The palaeogeography gives no reason to assume that between the Early and Middle Neolithic large parts of the higher grounds were lost. Large parts of the coastal zone from the Early Neolithic A, however, did disappear under clastic sediments because of the rising sea level. The sites in the river valleys could also have systematically disappeared through peat accumulation and the deposit of clastic sediments.[38] The distribution as it is now known appears to be underrepresented as far as the stream valleys and coastal areas are concerned. It should be considered representative for the higher grounds, in any case for the areas with a sufficient measure of archaeological visibility.

8.3 MIDDLE NEOLITHIC A: AFTER THE SWIFTERBANT GROUP (4000–3400 CAL BC; 5200–4700 BP)

In section 8.2 it was argued that the higher grounds of the Frisian-Drentian plateau were probably uninhabited during the Early Neolithic B: the Swifterbant groups mainly exploited the stream valleys and delta regions. This situation probably continued throughout the Middle Neolithic A. Although Voss, in his analysis of the Funnel Beaker culture using the hypothetico-deductive method, attempts to show that the West Group developed from local Mesolithic populations,[39] indications of occupation in the northern Netherlands in the

33 Louwe Kooijmans 1974; 1976b, figs. 9 and 10.
34 Clason 1983.
35 Louwe Kooijmans 1976a, fig. 4.
36 The artifacts were found thanks to the attentiveness of H.J. Popping, who knew that the site was of archaeological interest.
37 Clason 1983; Lanting 1986.
38 The sites near Swifterbant owe their visibility to the fact that they are located in a polder in which the surface lies at a depth of 5 to 6 m -NAP.

39 Voss (1982) assumed that a sedentary population has thinner and therefore more breakable pottery because they didn't have to carry it around. He therefore expected that as a population grows more sedentary the thickness of its pottery would be reduced. According to Voss, such a reduction is indeed identifiable: 4 mm, sufficient for him to support his arguments. He does not mention the fact, however, that in his analysis mainly grave pottery was used.

Middle Neolithic A have been scanty up until now.[40] No traces of the Michelsberg culture have been found north of the river Rhine; indications of successors to the Swifterbant group are also absent, at least on the higher sandy grounds. Just as rare are ^{14}C dates for the period 4000–3400 cal BC, with the exception of a few chance dates from the period 3650–3400 cal BC which are difficult to explain.[41]

Just as scarce are elements which in Scandinavia would be considered Early Neolithic. It is true that a few flat hammer axes have been found in our regions, but not in the study area. An early Funnel Beaker occupation, dating to the Middle Neolithic A (the Scandinavian Early Neolithic C), could be concluded from this. Finds have been unearthed very recently in the Noordoostpolder (site P 14) which point to early Funnel Beaker occupation,[42] but their context is not yet clear. Concrete indications of similar traces on the higher sandy grounds have been absent up to now.

Likewise absent are any other elements which could prove to be concrete indications of occupation during the Middle Neolithic A. Thin-butted axes have not been found in the study area. Although various Early Neolithic artifact groups might continue on into the Middle Neolithic A, positive associations for them are not known. With these considerations in mind, the decision has been made not to include a map from this period in the series. The Frisian-Drentian plateau may have been inhabited during this period, but concrete evidence for this has not been forthcoming so far. If there was occupation at that time it would in any case have been limited to settlements of small groups which stayed along the edges of the plateau and in the stream valleys. An early Funnel Beaker phase, with long barrows and the characteristic Fuchsberg phase pottery, appears to be absent from the Frisian-Drentian plateau, site P 14 notwithstanding.

8.4 MIDDLE NEOLITHIC B (3400–2900 CAL BC; 4700–4300 BP)

8.4.1 General framework

In the northern Netherlands the Middle Neolithic B is synonymous with the phases A–E of the Funnel Beaker culture.[43] The Dutch Funnel Beaker culture is part of the West Group of similar megalithic cultures. The West Group covers north-western Germany and the Netherlands north of the river Rhine. The core of the Funnel Beaker culture is formed by the North Group, which covers Denmark, parts of Norway and Sweden, and northern Germany.

The first, Early Neolithic phase of the Funnel Beaker culture in Scandinavia begins around 4000 cal BC (5300 b.p.) and is essentially non-megalithic. The Middle Neolithic begins around 4700 b.p. with a second Funnel Beaker phase which is characterized by a greatly expanded number of findspots, the building of passage graves, and an abrupt change in pottery style.[44] This development coincides with the rise of the West Group, which in many aspects is a direct derivative of the North Group.

Madsen, one of the few authors who has explicitly addressed these issues, sees the growing scarcity of natural resources, particularly of suitable settlement sites, as the cause of these developments.[45] Madsen emphasizes that this scarcity should not be seen as absolute but as relative to the accessibility of various exploited environments. He connects the building of megalithic burial monuments, while referring to corporate groups, with the symbolic expression of land rights; he connects the rapid expansion of the inhabited area with a slash-and-burn economy which is extensive in land use.[46]

The period during which hunebedden, the megalithic graves of the Funnel Beaker culture in the Netherlands, were built is relatively short. In the North Group as well as the West Group this phase lasted until c. 3000 cal BC (4450 b.p.), after which yet another change in pottery style appeared.[47] During this phase the transition to the Single Grave culture took place, which in this study is included in the first part of the Late Neolithic (Late Neolithic A).

The developments which take place in the northern Netherlands to a large extent run parallel with developments occurring during the Middle Neolithic in Denmark and north-western Germany; they should be analysed in that regard. This cultural unit is probably closely connected to the economic basis, which can be

---

40 See also Bakker 1979, 115 ff.
41 Waterbolk 1985a, 280.
42 Pers. comm. J.A. Bakker.
43 Bakker 1979, 137; Brindley 1986: horizons 1–5.
44 Madsen 1982, 201.

45 Madsen 1982, 221.
46 Elsewhere I have already explained that this model can also be applied to the situation in the northern Netherlands (Fokkens 1986).
47 Bakker 1979; Madsen 1982, 201.

characterized as slash-and-burn agriculture in forest clearings on the sandy grounds.[48] From the settlement traces as well as the locational preferences, it appears, however, that hunting and gathering still played an important part in the economy.[49] Not surprisingly, in Denmark there is a clear economic and spatial continuity in the transition from the Ertebølle to the early Funnel Beaker culture. During the Middle Neolithic the agrarian aspect of the economy was prominent, but hunting and gathering remained a clearly recognizable component.[50]

8.4.2 Settlement system

The settlement pattern of the Funnel Beaker culture in the Netherlands is still not well known, despite the work of J.A. Bakker. Reasons for this include the fact that so few findspots have been excavated; most are only flint scatters. The investigations of Madsen and Skaarup,[51] among others, have made this picture much clearer for the Danish situation. In Jutland both hunting as well as settlement sites from the middle phase of the Funnel Beaker culture are known, both of them showing specific locational preferences. House plans are still not well known, although in the past various claims have been made. On the basis of three concrete examples, Madsen concludes that these must have been predominantly light structures, probably huts.[52] Even the settlement sites themselves were probably not inhabited for longer than ten consecutive years, a picture that fits the model of the slash-and-burn economy. Zimmerman, however, has discovered rectangular dwellings with a central row of posts in Flögeln, while rectangular house plans were also exposed at excavations in Westphalia near Heek.[53] These indicate that the tradition of rectangular dwellings, which in our area only become clearly visible in the Middle Bronze Age, had its origin in the Middle Neolithic.

In recent years, sites have been discovered at a number of places in Denmark which have been compared with the British causewayed enclosures. Madsen ascribes to them the same purpose: that of central (perhaps ceremonial) places which functioned at a tribe or sub-tribe level within the tribal society.[54] In his opinion, megalithic graves and settlements cluster round these central places, a situation which Renfrew postulated earlier for Neolithic Wessex.[55] Madsen finally supposes that there is a correlation between the distribution of settlements and megalithic graves, in the sense that the last can be used to indicate the location of the first.

It is not possible to propose a similarly nuanced picture for the situation in the Netherlands. Only very few settlements have been investigated with the spade, and even fewer have been published.[56] The concise material gives no reason to suppose that the situation for hunting and habitation sites in the Netherlands differs significantly from that in Denmark, even though the settlement pattern in our area is much less obvious than the Danish pattern appears to be.

A great deal has already been written about the relationship between hunebedden and settlements in particular. Bakker, following Renfrew's example, has tried to distinguish territories in the area in which hunebedden are found with the aid of Thiessen polygons.[57] The results plainly show that it is dangerous to work with Thiessen polygons on the Frisian-Drentian plateau: naturally, the largest territories are to be found in the areas poor in finds. Bakker did not, therefore, elaborate this picture any further.

Harsema has adapted Madsen's Danish model to fit the situation in Drenthe.[58] Harsema distinguishes clusters of hunebedden, especially along the eastern edge of the plateau, which he describes as territorial communities in which one hunebed is attributed to each settlement as the symbol of the mutual solidarity existing within the village community.[59] This point of view sees the groups of hunebedden as fairly concentrated within the territory of small groups of settlements.[60] The question is to what extent this model, which is es-

---

48 Bakker 1982, 88; Fokkens 1986, 14.
49 Madsen 1982; Skaarup 1973.
50 Madsen 1982, 204 ff.
51 Madsen 1982; Madsen & Juel Jensen 1982; Skaarup 1973; 1975.
52 Madsen 1982.
53 Flögeln: Zimmerman 1980; Heek: investigation of W. Finke and Chr. Kahn; Trier 1989, 22.
54 Madsen 1982.

55 Renfrew 1973.
56 Bakker 1979, Appendix B.
57 Bakker 1982, fig. 7; Renfrew 1973; 1976.
58 Harsema 1988; Madsen 1982; 1988.
59 From Harsema's publication it becomes clear that he is working from the model of the Drenthe marke organization, which regulated rights and duties within the territorial community (Harsema 1988, 19).
60 Harsema 1988, 14.

sentially identical to Renfrew's original Wessex model,[61] can be maintained when it is confronted with all the finds from the Funnel Beaker culture. Especially when the western part of the Frisian-Drentian plateau is taken into account, the distribution area appears to be much more extensive than that of the megalithic monuments. Obviously, this situation is partly related to the absence of concentrations of suitable building materials: large boulders can be found outside Drenthe as well, but only incidentally and not in concentrations near the surface such as on the boulder clay heights along the edges of the Frisian-Drentian plateau. Although map formation processes could have led to the disappearance of *hunebedden*, they do not adequately explain the almost total absence of these burial monuments in central Friesland and on the Veluwe.

In my opinion, the distribution of the *hunebedden* can be explained only if a distinction is made between a colonization phase and a developed phase of the Funnel Beaker culture. Although nothing is known of the colonization process, the Danish situation can be helpful in making it understandable. There a megalithic tradition developed around 3400 cal BC and a rather abrupt change in the pottery style occurred. The number of sites also increased greatly.[62] The birth of the West Group and the colonization of new areas can be regarded in the light of these events. It is difficult to say how these changes should be explained. Possibly they are connected with a successful agricultural innovation which made it possible and attractive to exploit the dense mixed deciduous forests. Madsen connects the rapid expansion of the West Group and associated groups with the extensive land use involved in the slash-and-burn economy.[63] The colonization stage must have been a rather quick development, possibly comprising not more than two or three generations; *hunebedden* which were built during phase A of the Funnel Beaker culture can be found as far as Gaasterland.[64] After this initial phase of expansion, the occupation condensed within the colonized areas. It is likely that during the first phase the *hunebedden* can be seen as ceremonial centres of groups of people

living in the vicinity, and the building of the *hunebedden* can be seen as associated with the reclamation of the surrounding area by a clan or kin group. In my opinion, we should be thinking here of groups of 50–100 persons maximum[65] who felt connected through kinship ties, whether in a directly traceable line or not.

For the more developed phases of the Funnel Beaker culture, however, one can no longer assume a direct relationship between the location of a *hunebed* and a claim on the land in the immediate vicinity. New *hunebedden* continued to be built at the edges of the Frisian-Drentian plateau, but it is conceivable that their location had less and less to do with the actual spatial distribution of their builders. In order to understand this situation, one might refer to Bloch's research on Madagascar, where large collective graves are still in use.[66] Bloch aimed his investigation primarily at the social organization which underlies the use of collective graves. He describes how the Merina are organized in tomb groups. Membership in such a group is based on kinship relations. The communal tombs are not neatly placed in the centre of a territory, but nevertheless they are the symbol of rights on particular areas of land which do not necessarily form a continuous territory. The explanation of this discrepancy lies in the fact that the tombs are seen as the remains of tribal capital cities of a mythical realm whose layout and history are known to everyone through folklore.[67] Burials in the tombs take place with a great deal of ceremony and are attended by all members of the tomb group. These burial rituals do not always take place directly after death, however. Especially in the case of more distant groups the dead are buried temporarily, to be interred in the tomb with the proper honours at a later point in time.

When the Malagasy example is applied to the Funnel Beaker megalithic graves, a number of aspects of the expansion of the *hunebedden* can be explained which do not find expression in the models of Harsema, Madsen, and Renfrew. The assumption is that the *hunebedden* gradually lost their initial significance as territorial markers, but in the symbolic sense they did continue as unifying ele-

61 Renfrew 1976.
62 Madsen 1982, 201.
63 Madsen 1982, 221.
64 Rijs: Bakker 1979, 154.
65 Müller figures that in order to build the *hunebed* known as the Kleinenkneten in Oldenburg, 109 500 man hours were necessary, or 100 persons working for 3.5 months at ten hours a

day (1990, 215). That probably means that the work of erecting a *hunebed* involved not only its 'users' but others as well.
66 Bloch 1971; 1975.
67 Chatwin shows the perception of such a mythical landscape and its practical sides in his fascinating story of the 'songlines' in Australia (Chatwin 1987).

ments in the social organization and in this capacity constituted ceremonial centres. The erection of a *hunebed* during the developed phase of the Funnel Beaker culture can be seen as a symbol of the establishment of a new clan, split off from an existing group.[68] This new clan could also have functioned as a corporation even if it were far away from the location of the *hunebed*. Burial in the collective grave could have taken place after temporary burial near the dwelling place and could have been accompanied by ceremonies in which the entire clan was involved.[69] The location of the *hunebed* in this model is also significant in relation to the location of other *hunebedden* as centres of other clans. In this way, the *hunebedden* landscape in its developed phase should be seen as a reflection of the social organization of the Funnel Beaker community and not so much of its spatial organization.

Hoards
An important group of finds, the hoards, has not been discussed so far. This is a category of finds which is relatively well known because the limited size and the spectacular character invite rapid publication. Indeed, a number of papers have been written about Funnel Beaker hoards in the northern Netherlands.[70] Rech has discussed this finds group extensively in its broader perspective.[71] His investigation was concentrated on northern Germany and Scandinavia and studied the Funnel Beaker culture and the Single Grave culture. Rech's study clearly shows that the intentional deposition of various artifact categories by the Funnel Beaker culture was widely practised. Especially thin-butted flint axes frequently appear in hoards.[72] The matrix varies since artifacts were deposited on the higher sandy grounds as well as in peat areas. Naturally, the range of artifact types found in the peat areas is more varied because the preservation conditions are better there than in the sandy soils. An important finds category in the peat areas, besides thin-butted axes, is pottery. Rech sees a clear decrease in hoards over the course of the Funnel Beaker

period. In the Single Grave culture this practice apparently dropped to a minimum.[73] The finds distribution on the western part of the Frisian-Drentian plateau does not contradict this picture when only the positively-identified hoards are considered: seven finds are attributed to the Funnel Beaker culture, two to the Single Grave culture. The question about the function of the hoards, both single as well as multiple, is difficult to answer, especially for the findspots on the higher grounds. Undoubtedly the finds in peat areas and rivers served a ceremonial function, but the higher grounds open up a wider range of possibilities. Various authors are of the opinion that the size of the axes (often longer than 20 cm) and the fact that many of them were never fixed to a shaft or put to use points to ceremonial use.[74] In this study the matrix in particular is employed as the criterium for the distinction between grave, hoard, or settlement finds (see section 2.4.2).

8.4.3 *Findspots in the study area* (maps II and II')
In the study area, 152 findspots have been attributed to the Middle Neolithic phase of the Funnel Beaker culture (table 11).[75] The largest part of them (60%) consists of isolated axes (29%) and other artifacts of stone, including flint. The distribution pattern seems to indicate that the whole area was inhabited during this period (map II). Concentrations round Oosterwolde, along the Oude Diep, and to the north of Havelte can be ascribed to the activities of Popping, Siebinga, and Voerman, respectively. In my opinion these concentrations reflect the actual density of findspots in the largest part of the area, with an exception perhaps being the region to the north of the Bergumermeer. The map formation factors, however, make it impossible to issue reliable statements about the area. The same holds for the areas between the Tjonger and the Linde and between the Tjonger and the Boorne. Finds are almost completely absent here, but then the archaeological visibility is practically nil (map II'). The investigation near Oldeboorn is illus-

68 For clan structures and totem classifications see Lévi-Strauss 1962.
69 The use of *hunebedden* as ossuaries is often emphasized. Kaelas even says that she knows of no examples to contradict this in her study area (Germany and Scandinavia) and says that use as a primary burial place is an exception (1983, 84).
70 Achterop 1960; 1961; 1972–73; Bakhuizen 1967; Bakker 1959; Van den Broeke 1979; Harsema 1979a; among others.
71 Rech 1979.
72 Rech 1979, 69.

73 Rech even goes so far as not to exclude the possibility that the disc wheels found in the peat in Drenthe (Van der Waals 1964) were deposited by the Funnel Beaker culture because he assumes that most intentional deposits are from the Funnel Beaker culture (Rech 1979, 56).
74 Jager 1981; Nielsen 1977; Rech 1979, 77.
75 As far as they are datable, the Late Havelte finds have been attributed to the Late Neolithic A in connection with the overlap between this phase and the beginning Single Grave culture.

Table 11 The western part of the Frisian-Drentian plateau: determination of site-type on the basis of individual specimens of different finds categories for the Middle Neolithic B. The columns and rows represent finds categories and site-types respectively.

site-type	finds category							total
	axe	hammer axe	grinding stone / quern	flint	pottery	bone	grave	
settlement	21	1	30	28	7	0	0	87
grave	18	1	0	0	5	0	9	33
hoard	6	3	1	0	0	0	0	10
unknown	15	2	2	1	1	1	0	22
total	60	7	33	29	13	1	9	152

trative in this regard.[76] Under a peat cover of varying thicknesses, findspots dating to the Middle Neolithic, Late Neolithic, and Middle Bronze Age were found during land reallotment activities. Surveys revealed that the banks of the Boorne were very regularly used as hunting grounds. Up to now comparable sites have not yet been found because they only come to light by way of unusual chance events. The finds near Oldeboorn affirm the probability that seasonal encampments were set up in the coastal areas and stream valleys which, just as at Hesselø, Sølager, and Bistoft, were intended for special hunting activities.[77]

The settlement distribution pattern seems to point to a locational preference for the transitional areas between higher sandy grounds and river valleys. This may also be related to the thick forestation on the higher grounds which took on a more open character only at a later stage after human intervention took place. Whether the relatively narrow ridge between the Tjonger and the Linde (2–4 km wide) was uninhabited is another question. This might be deduced from the fact that finds from later periods are also absent from this area. The only find is an Early Iron Age pot, possibly from a grave. The entire area, however, was until recently used as grassland and has a thin peat cover, so that post-depositional processes can also be proposed as the reason for the absence of finds here. Considering the Early Iron Age find this seems to be the most plausible explanation.

In fact there have been no excavations of Funnel Beaker findspots in the study area. Siebinga did investigate a few findspots, but of these only the finds remain. Nothing was recorded during the investigation. At the Zwartveen findspots, and also in the finds assemblages from around Fochteloo and Appelscha (Popping's '80

and 100 bunder', a bunder is a hectare'), there seems to be evidence of large sites, permanent or semi-permanent settlements. This is indicated by the discovery of grinding and polishing stones as well as the large number of flint artifacts, including axes and axe fragments. But smaller encampments are also known. The findspot near Oldeboorn, for example, could have been nothing more than a hunting or fishing camp. However, the locational preferences of the various site-types cannot be investigated because of the absence of differentiating criteria within the finds material.

Without map formation analysis, one would be inclined to differentiate a number of clusters within the occupation area: in Gaasterland, round Oosterwolde along the Tjonger and the Grootdiep, to the south of Marum, and round Havelte. It is clear, however, that these clusters were brought about by Siebinga, Popping, and Voerman's keen sense of detection, while the cluster in Gaasterland stands out because the surrounding area is thickly covered (map 11'). Most likely the finds distribution pattern in those areas with relatively high permeability is also representative of the areas with lower find permeability, with the exception of the north and north-west (see above).

8.5 LATE NEOLITHIC A (2900–2500 CAL BC; 4300–3950 BP)

8.5.1 General framework

The Late Neolithic in the Netherlands begins with the rise of the Single Grave culture. Its pottery was originally defined by Glasbergen as Protruding Foot Beaker pottery, now an obsolete term. Lanting and Van der

---

76 Fokkens & Van Gijn in preparation.

77 Johansson 1979; Skaarup 1973.

Waals, in various articles, specifically placed it in the broader context of beaker pottery.[78] The Single Grave culture is a part of the Corded Ware cultures which were widely spread out across northern Europe. Similarities in burial rituals are notable among these cultures, but there is no evidence of a common archaeological culture in the strict sense. Rather, what is involved is one common element: persons with the same sort of social status who everywhere are buried in a similar manner and with the same kinds of grave goods, while essential differences can be seen regionally in the nature and character of the settlements.[79]

Traditionally, the change from the Funnel Beaker culture to the Single Grave culture has been interpreted as an immigration of new inhabitants: Single Grave culture cattle herdsmen. In an earlier article I treated this subject in detail and proposed the thesis that the issue here is rather one of cultural continuity, a thesis which had previously been cautiously put forward by Bakker and Van der Waals[80] and is not exactly new outside the Netherlands either.[81] In this view, the apparent homogeneity of the beaker assemblage should be understood within the framework of exchange networks between certain individuals or groups.

In my opinion, the cultural change ushered in by the Late Neolithic is associated with the acceptance of a complex system of innovations which quickly diffused within an already existing network of relations. In this context it is striking that the distribution of the corded ware is approximately identical to that of the funnel beaker pottery. The seemingly drastic cultural changes are understandable in the framework of economic and social changes in the study area in which the transition from predominantly hoe agriculture to predominantly plough agriculture plays an important role.[82]

Sceptics of this model have objected that the ard was already known, and that ard marks have been found in Denmark and England that are much older.[83] Obviously this statement is correct, but that does not imply that at this early date the ard was an integrated part of the agrarian system and was accepted by everyone. The use of the ard in the Funnel Beaker context can be seen as a pioneer phase. It was only used in areas for which it was suited (thus eliminating the thickly-forested Frisian-Drentian plateau) and it was not yet used by everyone.[84] The introduction of innovations usually takes place according to a logarithmic curve: first comes a phase in which a relatively small number of individuals 'experiments' with the innovation. This is followed by a rapid increase in the number of users: the new technique becomes fashionable and eventually becomes traditional.[85] Finally, almost everyone has accepted the innovation, but every now and then a straggler still has to take up the practice. The speed at which an innovation will be adopted depends on a large number of factors which vary from innovation to innovation. Certainly one of the factors involved is the nature and extent of information networks. But it is always true that for general acceptance a threshold must be crossed. In other words, the time and circumstances must be ripe for change.

The reason that the ard was used on such a large scale is probably connected with the repeated use of the same fields. When the fallow periods become shorter, forest vegetation has no chance to return and clearings are created having low vegetation and a shallow, dense root system. In such a situation, especially when the vegetation consists of grasses, it is not particularly effective to set fire to a plot that is to be reused. The perfect instrument for breaking up the root system in this situation is the ard.[86] Hardly any occupation has been recognized on the

78 Lanting & Van der Waals 1976; Van der Waals & Glasbergen 1955.
79 Whittle 1985, 259.
80 Bakker & Van der Waals 1973.
81 Bakker & Van der Waals 1973; Fokkens 1986; Malmer 1962; Whittle 1985.
82 Champion et al. 1984; Fokkens 1982, 1986; Van der Waals 1984.
83 See Champion et al. 1984, 126; Fowler 1983, 7–8. The plough marks beneath South Street long barrow date from c. cal 3200 BC.
84 It is possible that during a pioneer phase the only available traction power was that provided by humans, who were later replaced by draught animals. In that respect it is striking that

the wheel made its appearance in our regions in the context of the Single Grave culture. A number of ox graves from this period suggest that oxen were not used as plough animals until the beginning of the third millennium (Champion et al. 1984, 159).
85 Abler, Adams & Gould 1972, 144.
86 See Boserup 1965, especially p. 24 ff, for an explanation of the various factors that play a role in the transition from long fallow to short fallow. It should be mentioned here that despite the criticism levelled at Boserup's theory on the relationship between population growth and the intensification of production, her work is very useful in providing a deeper perspective into the relationship between land use, agrarian techniques, and labour productivity.

higher sandy grounds of the Frisian-Drentian plateau before the Funnel Beaker culture (see section 8.2). Thus the Funnel Beaker farmers practised agriculture in a thickly-forested area in which clearings and fields without stumps did not emerge until after quite some time. If we set the time difference between the first appearance of the Funnel Beaker culture and the beginning of the Single Grave culture at five hundred years, we see a period in which the landscape probably slowly developed into an area in which plough agriculture was both possible and perhaps even desirable in connection with the growth of a denser root system.

The relatively rapid cultural changes which took place in the Late Neolithic, at least in the region north of the river Maas, can partly be explained by it being a period of almost complete acceptance of innovations, with plough agriculture using draught animals and the introduction of wagons being perhaps the most important.[87] Alterations in social relationships probably took place in connection with these changes, among them changes at the household level.

Many archaeologists work from the assumption that in communities which practised hoe agriculture women carried out most of the work, while in communities which practised plough agriculture the work was done by men. Carlstein is one of the few authors who has researched this and similar issues; he comes to the conclusion that there is indeed a certain correlation, but not enough to establish a working rule.[88] In temperate regions, however, it was probably men who played the most important role in plough agriculture. The transition from hoe to plough agriculture also brought with it a shift in the heaviest work period as well as a change in the total invested time necessary for ploughing, weeding and harvesting.[89] That means that when the plough was integrated into the economic system a role pattern shift could have taken place within occupation units.

When we attempt to connect these developments with the changes in the material culture which appear in the Late Neolithic, particularly those connected with burial customs, the following considerations are important, in my opinion. One of the most striking elements in the transition from the Funnel Beaker culture to the Single Grave culture is the replacement of collective graves with a more individual way of burial. The *hunebed* clans splintered into more individually-oriented units, which elsewhere I have linked with a greater emphasis on the domestic mode of production, together with a greater investment of labour in the land.[90] The size of the occupation units need not have changed, and it is possible that even the burial practices were not drastically altered. That is to say that the largest part of the population was probably always buried in individual flat graves within their own settlement area. Only a particular group of people in a society, possibly kin group elders or important persons in the clan descent line, were first interred in the *hunebedden* and later under barrows.

The use of barrows gave rise to a direct spatial relationship between graves and settlement area. The barrows form stable elements within each area. They remained recognizable because they were built in open, fallow fields; in later periods they were often reused as burial sites.[91] When the settlement was moved barrows were also constructed in the new settlement area. Clusters of barrows arose because an existing burial site continued to be used or because occupation and burial were resumed at a previously-used site.

The new burial practice, individual interment under a burial mound, was maintained until the Late Bronze Age, when the rise of urnfields once again announced a fundamental change in burial ritual. In principle, however, the urnfield represents the same occupation unit as a group of barrows spread out across a settlement area (see section 8.8.2).

The beaker problem

One of the problems which for many casts doubt over the continuity between the Funnel Beaker culture and the Single Grave culture is the appearance of beakers: the thin-walled, decorated, and heavily standardized pottery that figured so prominently in interments from the Late Neolithic and the Early Bronze Age, and, in the Netherlands, in settlements as well. Especially the fact that there is no transitional form between protruding foot beakers and Funnel Beaker pottery leads to scepticism over cultural continuity. In order to explain this

---

87 Van der Waals (1964) has shown that the wheel was indeed introduced in our part of the country by the Single Grave culture, which fits in with the common view of the wheel being introduced in Europe at the end of the fifth millennium BP (Piggott 1965).

88 Carlstein 1982.
89 Boserup 1965, 28 ff; Carlstein 1982.
90 Fokkens 1986, 16.
91 Casparie & Groenman-Van Waateringe 1980.

apparent paradox, I believe an analysis of the meaning of beaker pottery in Neolithic society is important.

First the functional aspect has to be considered: beakers are distinguished from beaker pots,[92] large to very large beaker types that are especially known in settlement contexts. Formerly beakers were therefore labelled as burial ceramics and beaker pots as settlement pottery, but after investigations in places such as Aartswoud, Kolhorn, Molenaarsgraaf, Oldeboorn, and Steenendam, that point of view can no longer be defended. It is a fact that in our area beaker pots are never or only sporadically to be found in burials, while beakers have been found at all settlement sites and not always in small quantities. It is my opinion that the distinction which should be made is not between settlement or burial ceramics, but between ware chiefly used in *food preparation* or storage (beaker pots) and ware chiefly used for *food consumption* (beakers).[93] It seems plausible that only one of these two categories, service ware, would be included in burials to hold food which the dead could eat during the journey to the hereafter.

A second important consideration in understanding the meaning of beakers is the heavily standardized form and decoration. There is regional diversity, which should not be surprising considering the extent of the distribution area, but the uniformity over sometimes vast distances during most phases between 2900 and 2200 cal BC is striking. This kind of uniformity, and the consistency of it in time and space, can only be explained by 'contacts' or fashion. Moreover, there must be a reason for such conformity. There may be an explanation in the symbolic meaning of the pottery used in the beaker communities. It is clear that this stylistic symbolism during the beaker period does not indicate an ethnic group; the distribution area is too large for that. In order to understand the significance of the beaker, attention should be given to two aspects: first, the fact that there is any decoration at all, and second, the standardization of the pottery.

The decoration of protruding foot beakers, and of funnel beakers as well, can be called fairly lavish. Much attention was given to decoration, and it was clearly intended to be seen. The same applies in fact to the beaker pots. In this respect they form a contrast with late Funnel Beaker pottery and Middle Bronze Age pottery, which is almost completely lacking in decoration and is crudely tempered.[94] The latter might be classified as functional pottery, but no one would imagine it to have been used as service ware despite the fact that it may well have served this function. If one begins with the idea, as Wobst does, that pottery decoration only has significance if people can see it and recognize its symbolism, then one may assume that in the Late Neolithic pottery played an important role in the transmission and legitimation of ideas.[95] The fact that pottery was used for this purpose indicates that eating and drinking, occasions during which pottery was displayed, were an important aspect of social life, even on a supralocal or regional level. The standardization of form and decorative patterns is related to this: by interpreting or copying the style, the potter identified with the prevailing ideology or tradition of which that style was a symbol.[96]

Beaker pottery can therefore be explained mainly in relation to its ceremonial role. Apparently it was important that the style did not depart too radically from a particular pattern that referred to a wide-spread tradition or ideology, which probably was first connected with an important innovation or a dominant group of people. Each use of the pottery was a symbolic reference and helped to reproduce the social system. As was mentioned earlier, the fact that it was pottery that was decorated implies that eating and drinking played an important role in society in creating, maintaining, and strengthening contacts. To some extent this is also reflected in the preoccupation with food which is apparent from excavations of causewayed enclosures from various periods and regions.

Women probably played an important role in these networks, not least as producers of the pottery itself.[97] Ultimately they helped through their conformity (whether under pressure from the community or not) to legitimate

92 Lanting (1973, 252 ff) used this as a collective term for pot beakers (belonging to the Bell Beaker culture) and barbed wire pots (belonging to the Barbed Wire culture). In fact this group also comprises the *Wellenband* pots (pots with short-wave moulding) belonging to the Single Grave culture.

93 As far as form is concerned distinctions should be made between bowls and dishes. There are even forms, especially among the bell beakers, which would hardly attract attention in a *Bierstube*.

94 Fokkens 1982.

95 Wobst 1977.

96 Wobst 1977.

97 It is fashionable to counter such statements with the argument that not all potters are women. Strictly speaking that is true, but usually potters are indeed women and this is certainly the case in communities which practise plough agriculture (Carlstein 1982).

the existing social structure. In addition, if eating and drinking were indeed important, women would have been partly responsible for maintaining the networks of social relations through the preparation of food. The waning in pottery decoration in Funnel Beaker phases F and G, just when the Single Grave culture was making its appearance, can be explained in this connection as a transitional process. The Funnel Beaker society, with its corporate tomb groups acting as core elements, slowly fell apart. As this happened, it became less important to maintain traditions, including the decoration of pottery. In abandoning traditional decoration, the makers in fact stressed the process of change: the old social order was no longer being legitimated.[98]

A new tradition, symbolized by the protruding foot beakers, was accepted as normative and became common property in a rather short period. The Protruding Foot Beaker pottery took over the function of the Funnel Beaker pottery which had lost its pronounced style during the transition period. If Late Havelte pottery is associated with the last 'convulsion' of the old tradition, it is hardly surprising that there is no indication of a takeover of style elements by the last phase of the Funnel Beaker culture from the Single Grave culture, by which the paradox of ethnic continuity and material discontinuity ceases to be a paradox.

The problem of the beaker assemblage can be elucidated with the same wording as that sketched above. The concept of beaker assemblage refers to the combination of grave goods which are regularly found in burials and which seem to be subject to style changes during the same time and on the same spatial scale as the beakers. In my opinion, the standardization of grave goods represents the striving toward qualification within prevailing traditions. The form of the interment should be seen as a pronouncement from the kin concerning the social persona[99] of the deceased. In their daily lives, all those who died were probably farmers or farmers' wives, but that is not apparent from barrow burials. The deceased is presented as he or she may have been seen occasionally, fulfilling a certain function during his or her lifetime. The men, for example, would be shown as fighting members of the clan. The kin emphasized a particular capacity of the deceased in the way the burial is carried out, probably the capacity which made him or her an accepted member of the community. Additionally, personal elements are reflected in the burial, which are signified by the quality and quantity of the grave goods. The barrow, in contrast to the flat grave, is connected with a social persona as well: the deceased is an elder or important person in the clan descent line. It is not necessary, however, to regard those buried in barrows as members of an elite.

The transition from the Single Grave culture to the Bell Beaker culture

The emergence of the Bell Beaker culture can be explained in a similar way as the transition from the Funnel Beaker culture to the Single Grave culture. Until the 1970s, it was almost unanimously assumed that the basis of this transition was migration from a core area. The first wave of migrants would have come from Portugal, with a second wave from Eastern Europe. The chief basis for these ideas was typological pottery analysis. It has become clear, however, that in the Netherlands and surrounding regions Bell Beaker pottery developed from Protruding Foot Beaker pottery via All Over Ornamented (AOO) pottery.[100] Today the migration model has been almost universally replaced by a model of continuity.[101] In addition, settlement research has shown that there is no evidence for a uniform Bell Beaker culture. The characteristic assemblage (bell beaker, copper dagger, wrist guard, flint knife, etc.) is limited to burials, and these seldom reveal a complete set. In general, except in the Netherlands, few beakers have been found in the settlements, and domestic ware differs sharply from region to region.[102]

These observations have led to new models for the explanation of the uniformity of the beaker assemblage. Shennan has shown that in central Europe there may be an association with local elites: the bell beaker being used as a status symbol. Shennan sees the appearance of local elites in that region as the only people in the society who have access to gold, copper, and costly pottery (the beakers). Exchange networks between the elites fostered the more or less selective spread of prestigious artifacts which have been found almost exclusively in graves, mostly men's graves.[103] Shennan relates the changes in material culture to the acceptance of innovations with which the beaker assemblage is associated. In that con-

98 Also see Tilley 1984.
99 Binford 1965.
100 Lanting & Van der Waals 1974; 1976.

101 Harrison 1980; Shennan 1977.
102 Shennan 1977; 1982.
103 Shennan 1976; 1977; 1982.

Table 12 The western part of the Frisian-Drentian plateau: determination of site-type on the basis of individual specimens of different finds categories for the Late Neolithic A. The columns and rows represent finds categories and site-types respectively.

site-type	finds category								total
	axe	hammer axe	flint dagger	grinding stone / quern	flint	pottery	grave	settlement	
settlement	15	2	1	1	15	4	0	2	40
grave	63	15	5	0	2	4	36	0	125
hoard	8	0	0	0	0	0	0	0	8
unknown	26	0	1	0	4	2	0	0	33
total	112	17	7	1	21	10	36	2	206

nection he lists metal production, the horse, and possibly fashionable eating or drinking customs which may have involved the beakers.[104]

Although Shennan's model may be correct for central Europe and England, it cannot be used as the basis for generalization. For our region there is nothing to indicate the development of a more complex society during that period, while in other regions that complexity appears to have been temporary. Perhaps these things are connected with the power position of a limited number of people which was achieved through the manipulation of scarce resources, among them copper. One might call them 'big men', or clever entrepreneurs. As soon as copper production was stepped up and more people had access to metal, their power monopoly ended and with it their power base. Usually it is not until the end of the Middle Bronze Age that we see society again becoming more complex in these regions, and then there are indications of a structural development (in central Europe in any case, and in England as well).[105]

Clarke interprets these developments more in the context of an exchange network, *the beaker network*, a point of view that has found little acceptance, however.[106] In his model it is essential to regard the clay used to make the thin beakers as a scarce product that was generally available only in the core areas at the production centres. There, many beakers are found in settlement sites as, for instance, is the case in the Netherlands. Outside the core area, where clay or beakers have to be imported, the beakers are expensive and are rarely found at settlement sites. In these areas the beaker can play a role in supporting status positions and in that capacity is included

in burials, which appears to be the case in central Europe.

No matter which model is used, it is clear that in various parts of Europe the bell beaker is associated with the definitive incorporation of metal and metal production into local communities. Butler and Van der Waals have convincingly shown this for the Netherlands.[107] The fact that a few graves in the Netherlands show that the deceased was a metalworker underscores the importance of his craft in Bell Beaker society. The observation that such graves only appear in the initial phase supports this idea. Because they are buried following the regional tradition, it also shows that they were local smiths and were buried by members of their own community.

The uniformity which marks the beginning of the bell beaker development, the maritime phase, visible in the style and distribution of early Bell Beaker pottery over almost all of western Europe, was lost after the maritime phase. There remained a clear reference to the prevailing tradition in both decoration and form, but regional developments occur. In the Netherlands this development begins with the bell beakers of Veluwe type, which are so closely tied to the Barbed Wire tradition that they are included in the following period (Late Neolithic B and Early Bronze Age).

8.5.2 *Settlement system*

The picture of the Single Grave culture in northwestern Europe is severely distorted by the absence of clear settlement areas on the one hand and by all the attention which the graves from this period have been given on the other. Investigation of settlements from the

104 Shennan 1977, 57.
105 Compare Champion *et al.* 1984.

106 Clarke 1976.
107 Butler & Van der Waals 1966.

Single Grave culture have taken place only in recent years. Notable among them are the investigations in West-Friesland[108] (Aartswoud, Kolhorn) as well as those in the northern Netherlands (Bornwird, Steenendam). The picture is still very sketchy, however, and partly distorted by the emphasis on investigation in wet environments. Investigations were concentrated in those areas because so far no pits or postholes from this period are known from the higher sandy grounds. In wet environments, however, culture layers are present or finds are imbedded in clay layers in which they remain preserved. That post holes were dug is apparent from investigations at Aartswoud[109] and Kolhorn.[110] Building structures, however, have so far not been recognized. The agrarian character of the settlements of West-Friesland and the northern Netherlands is certain in any case. In Aartswoud as well as in Kolhorn and Bornwird the indications are abundant.[111] The catching of fish and the gathering of plants and shells were also part of the food economy. In environments that did not directly lend themselves to agricultural activities, briefly-inhabited encampments for special activities can also be expected.[112]

8.5.3 *Findspots in the study area* (maps III and III')

A number of the 206 findspots in the study area have been attributed to the Late Neolithic, approximately 33% of the total number of identified findspots. Half of them consist of axes of flint and other types of stone, most of these found without further context (table 12). In conformity with the decision rules explained in Chapter 2, the complete axes found on the higher sandy grounds were interpreted as disturbed graves. The hammer axes were also generally interpreted as grave goods, except for two incomplete specimens.

Chapter 6 has already provided a discussion of the representativeness of the grave finds for the Single Grave culture in the northern Netherlands. It was established that the identified grave goods were not a good reflection of the total number of finds. This is all the more obvious when it is realized that 195 of the 206 findspots were

Table 13 The western part of the Frisian-Drentian plateau: number of findspots of the Funnel Beaker culture and the Single Grave culture respectively for which the function is determined by field observation.

culture	site-type			total
	settlement	grave	deposit	
Funnel Beaker culture	23	10	7	40
Single Grave culture	15	45	1	61
total	38	55	8	101

found in areas where the archaeological visibility is higher than 50% (map III').

If we make a comparison between the number of finds from this period and the preceding period (Funnel Beaker culture; tables 11 and 12), we may be inclined to postulate an increase in the number of sites in the Late Neolithic A based on the larger number of findspots. At this point a number of marginal notes are called for. In the first place, the Funnel Beaker settlement sites are much easier to recognize than those from the Single Grave culture. This is because the Funnel Beaker culture settlements manifest themselves as flint concentrations with fragments of sharpened axes, among other objects. On the other hand, graves from the Funnel Beaker culture outside the *hunebedden* area are very poorly recognizable, in contrast with the Single Grave culture barrows. In my opinion, the differences that are apparent in the tables between the grave and settlement finds in particular are to be attributed to both site formation processes as well as site distorting processes. These things become even more clear when we only look at those finds whose interpretation is based on field observations (table 13). It is taken for granted that hoards are extremely underrepresented since they were mostly placed in rivers or in *dobben*.

It should be established that for this reason statements about population density in both periods (Middle Neo-

---

108 The district of West-Friesland is situated north of Amsterdam in the Province of Noord-Holland, not in the Province of Friesland.

109 Van Iterson Scholten & De Vries-Metz 1981.

110 Kielman 1986.

111 Aartswoud: Van Iterson Scholten & De Vries-Metz 1981; Bornwird: Fokkens 1982.

112 The investigation carried out by J.W.H. Hogestijn in West-Friesland should be mentioned in this regard. Up till now only preliminary reports have been published, but Hogestijn claims to have clear indications of small temporary encampments as well as of larger (but perhaps not permanently inhabited) base camps. (See, for example, Hogestijn 1992).

113 Fokkens 1982.

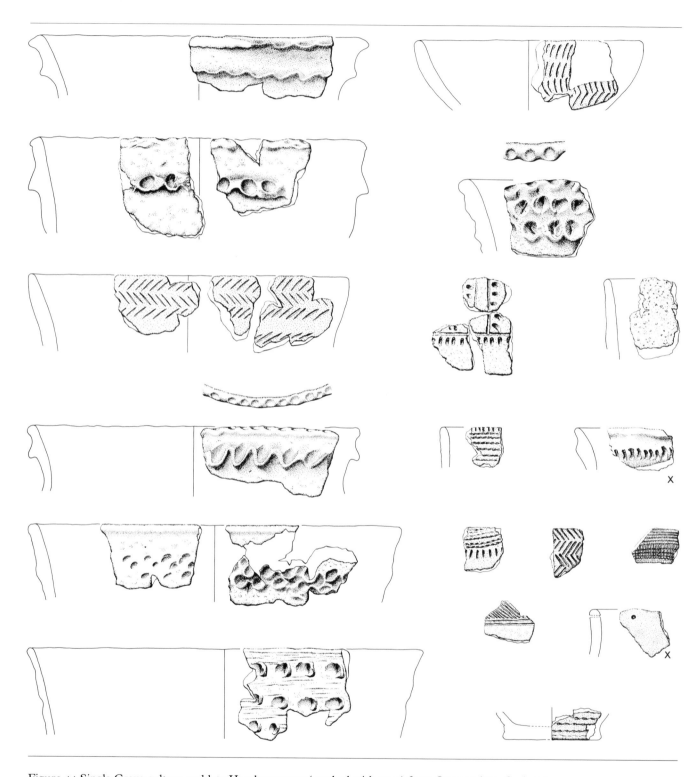

Figure 44 Single Grave culture and late Havelte pottery (marked with an x) from Steenendam. Scale 1:3.

lithic B and Late Neolithic A) are not permissible. The total absence of Funnel Beaker finds in the northern part of the area, in contrast to a large number of finds from the Single Grave culture or the early Bell Beaker culture, seems, however, to indicate that occupation extended further north during the Late Neolithic A than during the Middle Neolithic B. Indeed, the settlements near Bornwird and Steenendam (fig. 44) date exclusively from the last phase of the late Funnel Beaker period (and from the Single Grave period).[113] Pottery from the Drouwen phase is absent there. Moreover, axes identifiable with the Funnel Beaker period, usually a highly recognizable finds category, are also absent in this area.

Despite the scarcity of finds, it is clear that Gaasterland was still inhabited. Given the geological developments, however, this was probably the last period in which Gaasterland was inhabited, since at a slightly later date it could only be reached by crossing over peat areas.[114]

8.6 LATE NEOLITHIC B AND EARLY BRONZE AGE (2500–1800 CAL BC; 3950–3450 BP)

8.6.1 General framework

In this study, the second part of the Late Neolithic begins with the Bell Beaker culture, notably with the late phase, when local developments took place manifested in the appearance of epi-maritime beakers[115] and Veluwe bell beakers. This subdivision within the Late Neolithic has been made because the first clear traces of metal production appear in the context of the Bell Beaker culture, and because the other features of the material culture from this assemblage correspond perfectly with those of the Early Bronze Age.[116]

The centre of the Veluwe bell beaker distribution area is the Veluwe, where barrows constitute the main find context. However, this type of beaker is also found in Drenthe and north-western Germany, in the area between the rivers Maas and Waal in the river region, and in central Limburg.[117] It is a region within which uniform and continuous developments took place after the Single Grave culture. This is the case up to and including the last phase of the beaker cultures, that of the barbed wire beakers, whose distribution area also coincides with the area west of the river Weser described earlier.[118] There are few settlement data from this phase, however, and the burial rituals left few traces that are archaeologically visible.[119]

8.6.2 Metal production and consumption

The Bell Beaker period forms the beginning of metal production in the Netherlands.[120] The Wageningen hoard, initially ascribed to an Irish itinerant trader-bronzesmith,[121] was supposed to indicate the beginning of the Bronze Age. According to Glasbergen, the British immigrants who led to the rise of the Hilversum culture, which he considered to be Early Bronze Age, could be seen as the founders of a trading colony. This notion was nicely supported by the Voorhout hoard,[122] with its nineteen bronze objects of predominantly southern English types.[123]

This model of itinerant smiths has gradually become untenable, one of the reasons being ethnographic data.[124] However, its position in Dutch prehistory has not yet formally been replaced. The model assumes a sort of free market economy and system of proprietorship which does not belong in a tribal society. More probable is a network of local or regional bronze producers made up of members of local communities (section 8.5.1). That does not mean that all bronze was made locally. Regional production, as that demonstrated by Butler, chiefly concerned consumer goods.[125] Objects which required special craftsmanship, such as swords or complicated ornaments such as belt buckles, would

114 A now lost flint arrowhead found near Balk could easily have belonged to the Bell Beaker culture based on its description (broken off barbs). However, because the tang is described as wide and the person who made the description was not an expert in this field, it remains a possibility that the outward pointed sides were interpreted as broken off barbs. In that case the find would have belonged to the Single Grave culture. Given the assumption that Gaasterland was difficult to reach during the Bell Beaker period (Chapter 3), the arrowhead has been assigned to the Single Grave culture.

115 Lanting & Van der Waals 1976.
116 Lanting 1973.

117 Lanting & Van der Waals 1976; Van der Waals & Glasbergen 1955.
118 Lanting 1969. Barbed wire decoration also appears in northern France and Lorraine, however (information from the Clermont-Ferrand symposium, France, October 1992).
119 Lanting 1973.
120 Butler & Van der Waals 1966.
121 Butler 1963a, 104.
122 De Laet & Glasbergen 1959, 123–41.
123 Butler 1963a, 131 ff.
124 Rowlands 1971.
125 Butler 1961; 1963b.

probably have been made by only a few specialized smiths who were famous in their time. These smiths possibly worked by commission only, and their products would have circulated as prestigious gifts in exchange networks. It is not inconceivable that only the local elites had access to this form of distribution.

8.6.3 *Settlement system*

As in the case of the Single Grave Culture, it is difficult to come to an understanding about the settlement pattern of the Bell Beaker culture outside the delta, where numerous finds have been identified. Molenaarsgraaf is the model site, with houses, graves, and preserved bone remains.[126] The location indicates that in addition to agrarian settlements on the higher grounds, there were camps in the river valleys and delta areas being used for seasonal activities during this period. This practice undoubtedly continued on until the Middle Bronze Age. The investigation at Oldeboorn, among others, has been revealing in this regard (see below). The houses identified in Molenaarsgraaf may be of irregular structure, but they should certainly be regarded as house plans in my opinion. They are 18 to 20 m long, 6 m wide, and they have a central row of posts.

8.6.4 *Social organization*

The rise of metal production and the related new exchange networks must have meant an important change in the social organization in many areas. These changes are not universal for the Early Bronze Age, however. Increased complexity is evident in southern England and central Europe (Wessex and Únetie), but no such evidence can be found in our regions. Extremely rich graves have not been found, nor large-scale monuments which suggest organization at a supralocal level. Perhaps this is due to the peripheral location of the Netherlands in relation to the transit routes.

The first signs of the appearance of a separate category of graves are the Sögel and Wohlde graves. These comprise men's graves in particular, characterized by a short sword, a flanged axe, and sometimes other weapons such as spear heads or flint and bronze arrowheads.[127] These graves show that a certain group of men within the society possessed an important acknowledged position. There is no indication that this position was inherited or institutionalized in some other way. Probably they were local leaders who played an important role in maintaining the exchange networks of both prestige goods and commodities.[128]

The grave forms present the same picture as in the Late Neolithic A: individual interments under barrows, sometimes secondary interments covered by a mound enlargement, and occasionally some flat graves. Family barrows in the sense of a central interment under a barrow with a larger number of secondary interments in the body of the mound do not appear until the Middle Bronze Age. The kinship ties were not yet visibly expressed in burial rituals.

8.6.5 *Findspots in the study area* (maps IV and IV')

Flint arrowheads

A large number of the 102 findspots which can be ascribed to the Late Neolithic and the Early Bronze Age (almost 40%) appear to consist of one or more arrowheads in a mixed flint assemblage (table 14). Both the arrowheads with tang and barbs and the triangular arrowheads with convex or concave bases, all with surface retouche, are highly recognizable and frequently found. The reason that so many of these artifacts were classified as indications of settlements has to do with the fact that they are often part of a larger flint assemblage which, however, does not necessarily date from the same period. Once more than thirty of these artifacts were found in the same terrain: the driftsand area near Bakkeveen.[129]

The strikingly large number of flint arrowheads from this period is a phenomenon that requires an explanation. Naturally it is feasible that the distinct form makes them more visible from an archaeological point of view. But that also applies to arrowheads from earlier periods. On the other hand, it is also possible that the larger number reflects a more important role in society than

---

126 The houses (one of which had originally been dated to the Bell Beaker period) were reanalysed and dated to the Early Bronze Age by Louwe Kooijmans (Louwe Kooijmans 1974; pers. comm. 1991).

127 Drouwen and Hijken, for example; Beuker 1991; Butler 1969, 107 ff.

128 Lohof (1991, 267 ff) interprets the Sögel graves as a

reflection of personal acquisitions, possibly in combination with a symbolic function.

129 Popping described this find in *De Praehistorische vuursteenwerkplaatsen in Friesland* (1929). The finds illustrated in that article were accidentally rediscovered in a box without further finds identification in the former Bohmers collection at the Biologisch-Archaeologisch Instituut.

Table 14 The western part of the Frisian-Drentian plateau: determination of site-type on the basis of individual specimens of different finds categories for the Late Neolithic B and the Early Bronze Age. The columns and rows represent finds categories and site-types respectively.

site-type	finds category									total
	axe	hammer axe	flint dagger	cushion stone	flint arrowhead	bronze artifact	pottery	grave	settlement	
settlement	0	5	2	0	32	0	4	0	1	44
grave	3	10	3	1	2	0	0	15	0	34
hoard	1	0	4	0	1	2	0	0	0	8
unknown	0	4	6	0	5	0	1	0	0	16
total	4	19	15	1	40	2	5	15	1	102

in the previous period. An indication of this is the presence of arrowheads in graves (even though the actual number found is small), sometimes together with wrist guards: a complete set of archer's equipment. It is also striking that, in relation to Middle Neolithic arrowheads, a great deal of attention is paid to style in both form and surface retouche, which again shows that this was an important artifact.

I believe that this development can be explained in two ways. First, it is feasible that when the hunt became less important and the many-sided flint industry disappeared as a result, the rudiments received extra attention and this led to excessive forms.[130] A second explanation is that this kind of expressive design points to a specific social role for this type of artifact. The large number of arrowheads from this period and the archery equipment found in graves suggest that the latter was indeed the case. Although this, in connection with the special type of arrowhead, could be explained as an increase in hunting a particular kind of animal, it seems less likely in this context. Rather, the phenomenon should be understood as a sign that bows and arrows started to play a more important role as armaments in tribal warfare.[131]

Settlement traces

Although Lanting observes that the number of Veluwe bell beakers in the northern Netherlands is small,[132] this does not mean that the Veluwe bell beaker is not to be found in the north. The investigation at Oldeboorn was particularly important in this regard.[133] In 1980 in Oldeboorn on a sand outcrop 200 m to the south of the Boorne, a large amount of pottery, flint, and bone was found. The finds date from the Mesolithic, Late Neolithic (Bell Beaker culture), and Middle Bronze Age (Elp culture) (fig. 45). The palaeogeographic data show that the site lay on a sand dune, next to a blind arm of the Boorne, which probably already lay enclosed in peat during the Middle Neolithic. The bone spectrum, taken from an occupation layer dated to the Middle Bronze Age, indicates that the most important reason for residing at that site was probably to catch pike. A heavy overrepresentation of head parts was observed, which suggests that the animals were transported elsewhere after they were cleaned and their heads were removed.[134] This characterizes the Bronze Age site as a seasonal camp, probably used in the spring during the pike spawning season. The bones of large mammals were also

130 A remark already made by P.H. Deckers (J.D. van der Waals symposium 1985) in another context.
131 Tribal warfare is a notion that evokes images of battles and armies in the mind of the layman. Such warfare is more accurately characterized by controlled duels – raids – between groups, brief forays which can, however, result in substantial fatalities. Evidence of such an operation is the Wassenaar burial pit dated c. 3400 b.p. (1700 cal BC), which contains skeletons of five men, one woman, four children, and two of undetermined identity, one of whom had an arrowhead shot into the chest (Jungerius 1988, Louwe Kooijmans 1990).
132 Lanting 1973.
133 Fokkens & Van Gijn in prep; fig. 65.
134 Kastelijn 1982.

found, among them beaver, pig, and cow, which might indicate occupation of a longer duration at the site.[135]

The Bell Beaker finds consist of a few hundred sherds of Veluwe beakers and beaker pots (fig. 45). Strikingly, the beaker pots are tempered with stone grit, the bell beakers almost not at all. The spatial distribution of the pottery suggests that the Bronze Age occupation, which was probably intense but very limited in size, disturbed the late Bell Beaker occupation traces. Post holes or pits, other than those of natural origins, were not found. The natural location of the site leads one to suspect that this must also have been a temporary encampment during the Bell Beaker period, not an agrarian settlement. However, it is possible to draw parallels with Molenaarsgraaf, which has indeed been interpreted as a permanent occupation site.[136]

A site such as that discovered at Oldeboorn can be understood as representative of many such sites which still lie buried in the immediate surroundings as well as in other areas later covered by peat. The absence of pits, however, makes them extremely vulnerable and very difficult to detect. For example, only one settlement pit is demonstrated in the entire study area. This concerns a pit with barbed wire pottery found during the investigation of a barrow near Drachten.

Bronze finds

Only two bronze finds can be dated to the Early Bronze Age, i.e. two Emmen-type, low-flanged axes originating from peat areas and interpreted as hoards. These data do not lend themselves to inferences of a more general nature. They only serve to demonstrate that there was local bronze production in the northern Netherlands during this period as well.[137]

Stone hammer axes

Seventeen hammer axes of the Emmen type or a kindred form (*Arbeitsäxte*), unearthed as stray finds, have been identified in the study area. Dating of the *Arbeitsäxte* is difficult because few clear associations exist. Lanting reports a few associations with barbed wire pottery, but it

is clear that the type continued to be used into the Sögel or Wohlde period and can still be found in the Middle Bronze Age B.[138] The centre of the chronological distribution lies in the Early Bronze Age, however. Therefore the *Arbeitsäxte* are only shown on map IV.

Graves

Considering site formation factors, it can be established that Bell Beaker and Barbed Wire graves are less recognizable than Single Grave graves. The burial pits are shallower and the burial goods scarcer or less striking. Axes, which were extremely abundant in the Late Neolithic A, disappear entirely, even as grave goods.[139] Only four short flint axes with oval cross-sections are attributed to the Late Neolithic B and the Early Bronze Age.

Finds distribution

The distribution map (map IV) shows that in the areas where the visibility index is high, around the Bergumermeer, near both Marum and Oosterwolde, the finds density is also high. No finds have been identified in the extreme north. For the areas near Bornwird and Steenendam it is evident that this absence is a consequence of the advancing peat area.[140] Oligotrophic peat accumulation had probably already begun on the watershed to the east of the Bergumermeer during this period, but the absence of data makes this impossible to demonstrate.

Gaasterland became an island enclosed by peat during this period. This probably made it difficult to reach but not uninhabitable. In my opinion, it is this inaccessibility which kept Gaasterland from being inhabited after the Late Neolithic A (see Chapter 9). In order to reach the area, 15 to 20 km of moorland had to be crossed, a distance which could hardly be bridged by wooden trackways. It was not until the Roman period, when the salt marsh area reached almost to the Pleistocene soils and the peat area slowly dried up, that traces of human presence reappear on Gaasterland.[141]

In Chapter 9, the decreasing size of the habitable area will be dealt with in more detail, a development which

135 Clason 1981.
136 Louwe Kooijmans 1974.
137 Butler 1963b.
138 Lanting 1973, 229.
139 Lanting & Van der Waals 1976, 64.
140 Fokkens 1982.

141 Another problem in Gaasterland is water management. There are no brooks or water courses in this area. The boulder clay heights drain laterally into the surrounding peat and coastal area, and inhabitants would have had to turn to local seepage areas or wells for their water supply.

must have been noticeable for the first time during this period, although it is highly improbable that such developments took place within one generation only. It must have taken at least a hundred years for Gaasterland to become enclosed. But still, a response was necessary by the transfer of settlements.

8.7 MIDDLE BRONZE AGE (1800–1100 CAL BC; 3450–2900 BP)

8.7.1 General framework

Following Lanting and Mook's scheme, the Middle Bronze Age begins in the southern Netherlands with the Hilversum culture and in the northern Netherlands with the Elp culture.[142] Glasbergen traced the origins of the Hilversum culture to England and interpreted this as an evident example of immigration. The origins of the Elp culture, however, are understood as a continuous development from and successor to the Barbed Wire culture, influenced by the middle European *Hügelgräberkultur*. It is characterized by the burial of the dead under barrows in a fully extended posture instead of a crouched posture. It is clear that the *Hügelgräberkultur* is not an archaeological culture but a collection of archaeological culture groups which had only a few elements in common, particularly burial ritual. The northern Netherlands is part of the northern group (north-western Germany, Denmark), especially of the *Sögeler Kreis*, characterized by a number of distinctive men's graves.[143] The Drouwen grave is the best known Dutch example.[144]

It is remarkable that the Elp culture has never been presented as the immigration of a new group of people, because clearly this period was a time when a number of new elements made their entry while others disappeared. The disappearance of beakers, the appearance of the Sögel men's graves with the first 'swords', among other things, the fully-extended burial posture under barrows, the first appearance of obvious house plans: all these factors would have been reason enough in the past to conclude that the Elp culture represented an immigration of Sögel warriors. One of the reasons that this conclusion was not reached is, I believe, the Elp pottery,

the so-called *Kümmerkeramik*. This pottery is striking in its nondescript, 'ugly' appearance, at least in comparison with the beaker pottery which preceded it and the Late Bronze Age pottery which followed it. It is coarsely tempered, full of shrinkage cracks, and is mostly thick-walled; in this it resembles all Bronze Age pottery in north-western Europe. Besides this, it is undecorated, apart from the odd fingernail imprint. As a consequence, speculation about a possible origin is virtually impossible. In contrast, the Hilversum-Drakenstein pottery, which is comparable in workmanship and form, does make speculations about its origin possible, because a few pots are decorated in a characteristic way.

Despite the fact that Elp pottery is regarded as uninteresting, this appearance of a ubiquitous and, from a technological viewpoint, new type of pottery is a striking phenomenon. The beakers, i.e. the service ware (section 8.5.1), disappeared, and the pottery used in food preparation seems to have remained. From a technological viewpoint, Elp pottery is closer to the beaker pots than to the beakers: the former are also tempered with stone grit.[145] The disappearance of decoration from pottery is also striking. Against the theoretical background presented in section 8.4, this implies that pottery lost its important role at feasts or (far more probable) that feasts themselves lost their significance as unifying elements within the group, whereby the prominent role of service ware also disappeared.

My opinion is that bronze took over the symbolic role of beaker pottery. Bronze became the medium through which social position, extent of social and political contacts, etc. were 'transmitted'. Successful entrepreneurial endeavour and manipulation of social and political contacts (exchange networks) must have been important means of obtaining bronze. This is apparent from developments in the source areas of various bronzes. Apparently, at these higher levels of contact, other forms of symbolic communication became important. Although feasts have most probably played a role as well, the important role of hospitality on the family level, manifested in beautifully decorated beaker pottery, was over as far as its function in exchange networks was concerned. The role of the woman and the division of roles between the sexes in general surely must have changed as well. Today

142 Lanting & Mook 1977, 6–8.
143 Butler 1969.
144 Butler 1969; 1986.
145 This observation is based on examinations of the

Oldeboorn pottery, where all beaker pots are tempered with granite grit, while the beakers are mostly untempered. Van der Waals also points to the relations between Elp pottery and the late, undecorated beaker pots (Van der Waals 1965).

we would say it was a substantial step backwards for the woman.[146]

8.7.2 Metal consumption

According to Kristiansen, during the Middle Bronze Age the study area formed part of an exchange network that included West Jutland, Schleswig-Holstein, and the Elbe and Weser region.[147] He observes that until the end of the Middle Bronze Age, depositions (including swords) still regularly were made in graves, but that during the Late Bronze Age depositions took place almost exclusively in hoards. This observation seems to have been true for the Netherlands as well, although here the Middle Bronze Age was also a time of few grave depositions (and almost no swords), probably because of the peripheral location of our region within the exchange networks.

Hoards, especially those which come from the swamps and small bogs, therefore form the most important source of information about bronze circulation. The social context in which hoarding took place is a matter which can be interpreted in many ways. Depending on the theoretical model employed by the author, it can be demonstrated, for instance, that hoarding especially occurred during times of social stress,[148] or precisely in times of economic stability.[149] Whichever model is employed, is closely connected with the composition of the hoard. Conventions do exist in this respect, but they have very little foundation.[150] A number of types is generally accepted, such as scrap hoards, trade hoards, and ceremonial hoards, but these names often suggest more about the function than is warranted. From the northern Netherlands there are only a few indications of Middle Bronze Age hoards that have profane significance. Most finds unearthed in peat areas and brooks bear the mark of ceremonial hoards. This picture does not change until the Late Bronze Age, although the data from the northern Netherlands provide only a poor and vague indication for this. Elsewhere, however, it is clear that hoarding increased and that the form of the hoards changed essentially and became more excessive.[151]

8.7.3 Settlement structure and settlement pattern

The Middle Bronze Age is the earliest period in the northern Netherlands for which a number of settlements with house plans have been investigated. There are still too few of these to make any clear judgements about the settlement structure, but a number of elements continue to emerge with greater frequency. The investigation near Elp seemed to characterize the typical Middle Bronze Age house plan as an aisled byre-house of substantial length (30 m or more).[152] Since then it has been discovered that there was more variation in house length and type.[153] Originally Waterbolk thought that a farmyard always held both a large and a small dwelling at the same time. After reanalysis of the ^{14}C data, however, Waterbolk has come to the conclusion that the small buildings probably represent a separate Middle Bronze Age building phase. Now Waterbolk dates the long houses to the Late Bronze Age, but the dates show that this means only the very beginning of the Late Bronze Age (around 1100 cal. BC). In addition to the Elp type, an older Emmerhout type is distinguished in which the byre part is located in the middle of the farm.[154] In any case, indications of social differentiation within the settlement structure, such as those originally supposed, are no longer present in that sense.[155] The very long buildings of more than 60 m, which have been found in Elp as well as in Angelsloo, probably may not be interpreted as buildings with a central function, as Waterbolk suggested.[156] Harsema showed that for Elp, a reinterpretation of two

---

146 In connection with this kind of problems, outside the Netherlands a great deal of attention is being paid to the role of gender in society. The role division between men and women is of great importance, especially in societies in which domestic production methods are employed. This problem is always side-stepped in Dutch archaeological literature because it is assumed that such factors can hardly ever be deduced from the archaeological record. This is obviously as incorrect an approach as that which interprets everything in terms of social factors or structures. In the future it will undoubtedly be necessary to pay more attention to the problem of role patterns in order to come to more solidly grounded explanations for changes in the material culture.
147 Kristiansen 1978.
148 Bradley 1982; Hodder 1979.
149 Bradley 1984; O'Shea 1981.
150 See Levy (1982), however, for an attempt at a well-founded classification.
151 The number of bronze finds from the Late Bronze Age, including swords, increased considerably with the investigation by Roymans in the southern Netherlands. These finds indicate a clear increase in the number of intentional deposits in the rivers during the Late Bronze Age (Roymans 1991).
152 Waterbolk 1964b.
153 Waterbolk 1987a; 1989a.
154 Huyts 1992.
155 Waterbolk 1964b.
156 Waterbolk 1985a, 54.

houses built in precise alignment (possibly rebuilt) is also possible.[157]

The settlements seem to consist of individual farmsteads which were constantly being moved within a particular area, but every now and then returned to an abandoned settlement terrain. The data show that in most cases not more than one farm stood at any one time and that the clusters of houses that we find were the result of centuries of occupation of the same area and not an indication for the existence of villages.[158] This picture corresponds with that which was found on the Brabant sandy grounds and the bordering river region.[159] In Denmark, one has concluded to similar settlement patterns.[160] Only West-Friesland occupies a separate place, which is probably related to its isolated position and the occupation conditions specific to the area. In Bovenkarspel there is clear indication of colonization of the former salt marshes by a number of households which had settled close together. This village-like picture continued for a long period.[161]

8.7.4 Social organization

There is little reason to assume that society in the northern Netherlands became much more complex over the course of the Middle Bronze Age than in the period preceding it. Only a small number of rich graves has been identified. These do not, however, suggest a transition from the segmentary tribal structure to a centralized organization.[162] The family barrows reflect the importance of kinship ties, but the differences in grave goods or grave forms give no indication of dynastic aspirations of certain core groups or elites. Neither should one interpret the graves in barrows (which clearly underrepresent the total number of graves) as the last resting place of members of a top political echelon. The number of discovered barrows is much too large for that. The model that is applicable for the Late Neolithic barrows, that of the last resting place

for kin group elders, also applies to this period, although an increase in the number of barrows during the Middle Bronze Age B can indicate a further individualization of society.[163] A marked difference, however, is the presence of secondary burials in the barrows, supposedly of kin. This serves to emphasize the family ties (see section 8.8.2). Nevertheless, flat graves, sometimes in groups such as at Elp, continued to be used for interments.

Nothing is certain about the size of the households. The measurements of a number of large farms suggest that these were inhabited by extended families (ten to fifteen persons). In Elp, the dwelling parts of the houses are as long or even longer than the byre parts, that is to say 15 m or longer, while some of the houses had two hearths.[164] Smaller houses, probably with smaller residence groups, were found as well, however.

8.7.5 Findspots in the study area (maps V and V')

Up until now, the Frisian part of the Frisian-Drentian plateau has produced far fewer finds from the Middle Bronze Age than have been found in the Drentian part. Waterbolk saw this fact as a reason to conclude that depopulation took place during this period because of advancing peat accumulation.[165] The present investigation, however, shows that this definitely was not the case.

The number of identified findspots (table 15) may be considerably smaller than that from the preceding period, but there are various reasons for this which have to do with site deformation processes. In Chapter 6 it was explained that Bronze Age pottery is unremarkable and has been poorly preserved because of its brittleness. Even during large-scale reclamation projects, when so many finds from other periods were unearthed, pottery from the Middle Bronze Age was not readily noticed or collected. Another problem is that Bronze Age barrows often contain no grave goods, and therefore they are not recognized by laymen.

---

157 Harsema 1987, 109. This notion is correct in my estimation, certainly when considering the results of the recent investigation in Dalen (Kooi 1991) where houses up to 80 m in length were found. The excavator agreed that these are house plans created by several phases of rebuilding at exactly the same spot. The regular appearance of rebuilt houses in West-Friesland has already been demonstrated by IJzereef (IJzereef & Van Regteren Altena 1991).

158 Harsema believes that at Hijken and Noord-Barge there were a number of houses standing simultaneously (Harsema 1991). The argument for this, however, is not convincing, and his model cannot be accepted as normative.

159 Fokkens 1991a; 1991b; Vasbinder & Fokkens 1987.

160 Jensen 1987, 161.

161 IJzereef & Van Regteren Altena 1991.

162 Lohof 1991.

163 Drenth & Lohof in press.

164 It is usually assumed that the part of the house where stalls were not visible was the residential part. But this part could also have been used for storage functions, for example, which are no more archaeologically recognizable than is usually the case with residential areas. Hearths are often the only, albeit vague, indications of this.

165 Waterbolk 1965–66.

Table 15 The western part of the Frisian-Drentian plateau: determination of site-type on the basis of individual specimens of different finds categories for the Middle Bronze Age. The columns and rows represent finds categories and site-types respectively.

site-type	finds category						total
	grinding stone / quern	bronze artifact	pottery	grave	settlement	organic material	
settlement	3	0	2	0	1	0	6
grave	0	2	1	18	0	1	22
hoard	0	7	0	0	0	1	8
unknown	0	2	0	0	0	0	2
total	3	11	3	18	1	2	38

Settlement spots should be recognizable, but the nature of the features makes them poorly visible. The density of traces, apart from a few exceptions, is not great, and pits generally contain few finds.[166] Finally, the number of characteristic artifact groups is limited, certainly if *Arbeitsäxte* are included in the previous period. Querns and bronze artifacts remain the only highly recognizable groups, and even these are scarce. The finds distribution pattern such as that in map v was determined almost exclusively through the work of local archaeologists; accidental finds unearthed by laymen are few in number.[167]

Settlement traces

Only one settlement area has been investigated, that near Oldeboorn (fig. 45; section 8.6.5: settlement traces). This was probably not a permanently inhabited settlement but a temporary fishing camp. This observation adds an interesting element to the settlement pattern as it was sketched above. As far as I know, this is the first example of an extraction camp from the Middle Bronze Age. The circumstances under which the findspot was discovered suggests that it is certainly not a unique site and that such encampments may have been much more widely distributed. They ought to be searched for in ecological zones which were suitable for distinct types of exploitation during certain seasons.

Graves

Most of the findspots on the distribution map (map v) are classified as graves and hoards. The eighteen graves have all come to light through archaeological investigation. Many of them are in the vicinity of Havelte and were systematically excavated by Van Giffen during the Second World War.[168] They all lie along slopes of the Havelterberg, which in this area seems to have been a conscious choice of location. One of the barrows, the so-called Eupen Barchien, is noteworthy for the two dead bodies interred in central graves, one of which, according to Van Giffen, had a shafthole chisel as a grave good.[169] Tangential interments were found in the body of the mound, which in its entirety is characterized as a family barrow. Two barrows, or at least the remains of them, were discovered during the excavation of the urnfield at the Koningskamp.[170]

Metal

The bronze finds which can be dated to the Middle Bronze Age comprise eight palstaves, a bronze knife, and three bronze bracelets. Almost all were found during peat excavations, dredging in *dobben*, or widening of the river Tjonger.[171] The *Griffzungenschwert* (griptongue sword) found in the peat near Steenwijk was ascribed to the Late Bronze Age, although typologically it

166 The discovery history of the Elp settlement is illustrative of this. It began as the excavation of a barrow, as is so often the case in Drenthe (Waterbolk 1964b).
167 There was little interest in the Frisian sandy grounds at the Groningen Biologisch-Archaeologisch Instituut. The correspondence between Popping and Van Giffen reveals that the latter may have travelled regularly to Oosterwolde but only after Popping's 'fire alarms'. So the barrow excavations in the area surrounding Oosterwolde (Van Giffen 1925a; 1929) as well

as the well-known excavation of the settlements near Fochteloo (Van Giffen 1954) were only carried out at Popping's insistence. The same is true for Bursch's investigations near Marum (Bursch 1936).
168 The Germans built an air strip on the terrain in question (Van Giffen 1951).
169 Van Giffen 1951, 114 ff.
170 Kooi 1979, 83.

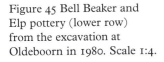

Figure 45 Bell Beaker and
Elp pottery (lower row)
from the excavation at
Oldeboorn in 1980. Scale 1:4.

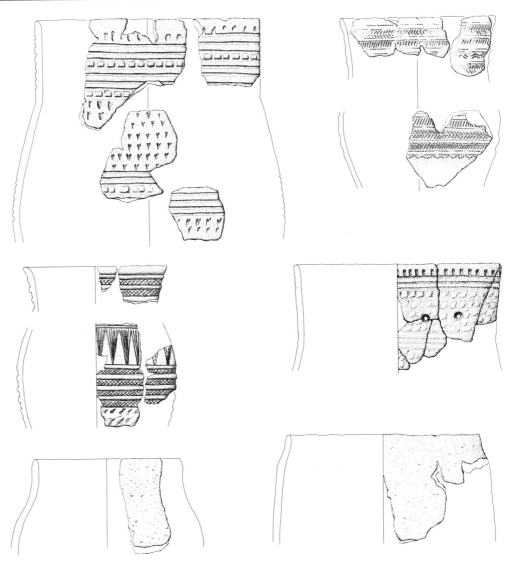

can also be dated to the end of the Middle Bronze Age.
The context makes clear that in almost every case, the
finds are ritual deposits of the same character as those
found elsewhere in northern Europe. The number of
hoards is no reason to suspect increased ceremonial activity which could be connected with heightened stress
resulting from a shrinking occupation area.

Finds distribution
In comparison with the previous period, the finds distribution is somewhat reduced in scope. The area around
the Bergumermeer in particular seems to be no longer
inhabited. There are no finds from later periods in this
area either. Also striking is the emptiness of the area to
the west of the Steenwijker Aa. Even so, there are Celtic
field systems in the vicinity of Noordwolde, which show
that the area had not become uninhabitable. The absence of finds from the Middle and Late Bronze Age in
this area must therefore first be understood through
map formation factors (map v').

8.8 LATE BRONZE AGE AND EARLY IRON AGE (1100–500 CAL BC; 2900–2450 BP)

8.8.1 *General framework*

The Late Bronze Age in the Netherlands begins when the first urnfields appear. Formerly these were interpreted as evidence of an invasion by urnfield people, but today the appearance of urnfields is understood to be the result of a change in burial ritual.[172] The idea of an urnfield *culture* as an encompassing concept was dismissed long ago; instead the notion is one of regionally differing groups which had roughly the same burial ritual in common.[173]

In the southern Netherlands the entire urnfield period is contained within the *Niederrheinische Grabhügelkultur*, whose most important distribution area is in eastern Noord-Brabant and the Kempen region, and the area along the rivers Maas, Rhine, and Lippe.[174] The elements characteristic of this culture are derived from the cemeteries (*Kerbschnitturnen, Deckeldosen, Eierbecher*, circular ditches which open to the south-east, etc.).[175] Little has been written about settlements, although to date many settlements have been investigated. One of the problems attached to the notion of a *Niederrheinische Grabhügelkultur* is the fact that the long Middle Bronze Age houses of the Oss 1 type continue far into the Late Bronze Age.[176] The transition to another type of house, the Oss 2 type, probably did not take place before 900 or 800 cal BC. Almost the only pottery to be found in the settlements is Drakenstein and Laren pottery, the types found in the urnfields are completely absent. A distinct change, evident in the settlement pottery as well, first appeared during the last part of the Late Bronze Age, approximately three hundred years later than the changes in burial ritual that mark the beginning of the *Niederrheinische Grabhügelkultur*. Therefore, in the settlement context it is preferable to speak only of a Middle or Late Bronze Age phase and to avoid the designation *Niederrheinische Grabhügelkultur*. In the cemetery context the term Lower Rhine urnfield group can also be used, as De Laet and Glasbergen have already done.[177]

In the northern Netherlands the problems are analogous. For the sake of clarity, Kooi proposed dividing the urnfield period into an Elp culture, a Sleen culture, and a Zijen culture. Verlinde criticized this division (rightly so, I believe), because these 'cultures' are defined only on the basis of burial ritual and associated pottery. Verlinde's alternative, to refer to the entire urnfield period in the northern Netherlands and bordering north-western Germany as an Eems culture divided into phases 1, 2, and 3,[178] is an even less satisfactory solution, however. It is burdened by the same problem as that in the southern Netherlands: that the settlements show little or no change before 800 cal BC. Therefore in this case it is also not recommended to speak of an archaeological culture, but of an Eems urnfield group, if necessary divided into an Elp, Sleen, and Zijen phase following Kooi's definitions.[179]

8.8.2 *The urnfield phenomenon*

Urnfields are cemeteries with cremated human remains which may or may not be stored in urns under low mounds of various shapes. They were not introduced suddenly,[180] but it is nevertheless apparent that a rapid and very general change in burial ritual took place. From the custom of burying the dead under large barrows and in secondary graves or flat graves it became common to bury the dead under small mounds. In the northern Netherlands, this was also the period when cremation became a general practice. Another new aspect is that many more dead were buried in archaeologically visible grave monuments than previously. In the Bronze Age the number of deceased people was underrepresented in the number of graves in barrows, but the impression exists that in the urnfields for the first time almost all the deceased were buried in an archaeologically recognizable fashion. The greater variety of monuments (at least in the Late Bronze Age) is striking, but even more so is the variety found in burial pottery. The difference between burial pottery and settlement pottery becomes more distinguishable in the sense that some types of urns (*Kerbschnitturnen, Deckeldosen, zweihenklige Terri-*

---

171 The fact that a concentration of finds has been uncovered around Oosterwolde again has to do with Popping's activities during peat cutting.

172 De Laet & Glasbergen 1959.

173 Verwers 1969.

174 Kersten 1948; Verlinde 1987.

175 Kersten 1948.

176 Comparable with the Elp type; Fokkens 1991; Vasbinder & Fokkens 1987.

177 De Laet & Glasbergen 1959.

178 This division then coincides with Kooi's Elp, Sleen, and Zeijen cultures (Verlinde 1987, 298 ff.).

179 Kooi 1979.

180 Kooi 1979; Waterbolk 1962.

nen, etc.) are rarely or never found in the settlement context.

Urnfields are often associated with one or more older barrows, which may indicate that the same group of people (a kin group) continued to bury their dead there. The graves became concentrated at a single location for a longer period of time, however, and in this way the first real cemeteries came into existence.

In my opinion, the explanation for these changes in burial ritual must be sought in changes in the social structure and, related to this, changes in the dominant ideology. The key to the explanation is locked in the change from interment in family barrows to interment under a 'private' barrow for everyone. If we assume that it was the family elders who were buried under barrows, then the secondary burials in the body of the mound can be understood as graves of the most important kin, important in the sense of proximity to the kinship line. From this point of view, the burial mound was a reflection of the kinship structure which was reinforced and legitimized each time someone was buried in or outside the mound. This is precisely the element that changed with the advent of urnfields. In the urnfields the family elder is no longer archaeologically recognizable as a distinct social *persona*, while all the other individuals buried are that much more recognizable. From the way the cemeteries were formed, however, it can be concluded that kinship ties still played a role. Both the shape and contents of the graves became more varied, which seems to indicate that personally achieved social positions became more important. Thus the graves reflect more differentiated status positions which were developing in the world of the living.

8.8.3 *Celtic field systems*

Another new development in the Late Bronze Age is the appearance of Celtic field systems. A Celtic field can be described as a system of small walled-in fields (*c.* 40 × 40 m) which can extend over a large area. The new element in this system is that for the first time coherent field systems are archaeologically recognizable, a consequence of the fact that individual fields are walled in. In the Netherlands, it is Brongers in particular who has carried out studies of Celtic field systems.[181] With the help of aerial photographs, Brongers mapped out the Celtic field systems visible on the Frisian-Drentian plateau. He also excavated a field system near Vaassen. Brongers dates the emergence of the Celtic field systems to the Early Iron Age on the basis of data derived from the Vaassen investigation. Other investigators have indications of an origin in the Late Bronze Age or even earlier.[182]

It is not known what agricultural system was used in the Celtic field systems. Brongers supposes that crop rotation was involved, but there are no palaeobotanical indications for this.[183] Kroll even finds indications to the contrary; during the Iron Age and the Roman period, the cultivation of hulled barley was dominant (more than 80% in the samples taken from arable land) and plants which to some measure would have been used in crop rotation are not present.[184]

Interesting discussions have taken place regarding the emergence of the Celtic field walls. It is Brongers's belief that the walls arose as stumps and stones were removed from the fields; the size of the lots would then be determined by the available manpower: 40 × 40 m is the surface area that one man can cultivate in one morning or afternoon.[185] Van Giffen was of the opinion that the walls were formed through the removal of exhausted soil from the fields.[186] Zimmermann contended, however, that this would have made cultivation impossible inside the walls unless the removed earth were replaced by new humus.[187] Zimmermann does not dispute the fact that cultivation took place inside the walls; there are plough marks to prove that. But the walls which he investigated belonging to a Celtic field system at Flögeln are so wide (up to 16 m)[188] and so rich in phosphate that he suspects that in the final phase of use only the walls were cultivated.[189]

181 Brongers 1976.
182 Waterbolk 1985b, 63; Zimmermann 1976, 79.
183 Brongers 1976, 60 ff.
184 Kroll 1975, 134.
185 Brongers 1976, 60.
186 The literal quotation given by Zimmermann (1976, 88) is 'Van Giffen 1951', with no further reference, however.
187 Zimmermann 1976, 88.
188 The width of the walls is a general distinguishing feature. Usually the base of the wall is more than 10 m wide. Other authors sometimes explain this width as being the result of the accumulation of weeds, stumps, and stones over the years (for example Harsema 1980, 95). Although this could easily have been the case when the field was first being exploited, it reveals a low opinion of the prehistoric farmer as a skilled worker to suppose that he would allow a large part of his cultivation area to disappear under walls.
189 Zimmermann 1976, 89.

The question is why the Celtic field system arose in the first place. Brongers believes that one of the basic elements was humus transport because there is a larger volume of earth in the walls than could have been taken from the space between them.[190] Brongers says in passing that a possible explanation lies in the fact that sod manuring took place on the Celtic fields, but he does not elaborate on this suggestion. Nevertheless it is not implausible to conjecture that sod manuring lies at the foundation of the new system. In my opinion, this would answer a great many questions.

Usually sod manuring is seen as a development which did not begin until the Early Middle Ages and goes hand in hand with the 'eternal rye cultivation'. It has become apparent, however, that in a few places sod manuring can be dated much earlier. The investigation at Archsum on the island of Sylt has made a particularly significant contribution in this area.[191] Sod manuring had been practised on Sylt since the Middle Bronze Age, and there are also fields raised through sod manuring on the more northerly islands of Föhr and Amrum,[192] these dating from the Iron Age.[193] In the southern Netherlands there are indications that sod manuring goes back at least to the Roman period. At Oosterhout and Goirle, sunken byres in houses from the second century AD are interpreted as remains of deep-litter byres.[194] This suggests that by this time the system was already completely developed.

In his work, Kroll describes different forms of medieval sod manuring which show that a broad variety of methods were applied. To begin with, virtually any kind of sod was used, varying from heath sods to clay and peat sods. The latter, however, were not among the favourites.[195] The methods used to mix the manure with the sods also differed widely. In some areas the sods (which in Brabant usually came from the fields) were brought to the farmyard and laid on piles of earth, *eerd-hopen*. After a period of time, the soil was brought into byre parts whose floors had been deepened, the so-called deep-litter houses. This process was repeated regularly. The sod-manure mixture was transported from the byres in the spring and spread over the land. This system was also utilized on farms where cattle were gathered into fenced-in areas instead of byres. In other regions the manure and sods were brought in separately and piled up into compost heaps. By lightly mixing the layers of manure and sods, a composting process took action which after a lapse of time produced a crumbly fertilizer.[196] The compost heaps were sometimes located in the farmyard, sometimes out on the fields.[197] A particular but frequently used method was to remove the humus layer from the field, mix it with stable manure, and after composting spread it out over the same or different fields.[198] Naturally, with this method the arable land was less raised than when the sods were brought in from outside. This practice was applied in areas where ploughs equipped with mould boards were not in use: without a mould board the sods are not turned, soil and manure are not mixed, and composting does not take place. When the ard is in use the simple application of manure on the fields is therefore ineffective.

It is apparent that the sod manuring practised at Archsum and the other islands is connected with the limited surface area of the arable land in these areas, which necessitates intensification. Therefore, the data from Archsum cannot be used to generalize, but they do show that sod manuring was a method that one was acquainted with in the Bronze and Iron Ages. When we return to the series of discussion points, a connection between Celtic field systems and sod manuring seems to explain many problems. It should first be established that the appearance of walls, which have made the Celtic field systems visible, is also probably the most distinctive new element in the cultivation system.[199] Brongers cal-

190 Brongers 1976, 62.
191 Harck 1987; Kroll 1975; 1987.
192 Kroll 1987, 113.
193 During the well-known excavation at Anlo it was established that long Gasteren-type beds (the Elp phase of the northern urnfield group) were built on an older arable layer. This layer was approximately 20 cm thick and dates from the Middle Bronze Age. This might be interpreted as an indication of sod fertilization, although the excavators did not conclude this at the time (Waterbolk 1960, 1985a, 45).
194 Buurman 1990; Verwers & Kooistra 1990.

195 Kroll 1975, 87.
196 Kroll 1975, 88.
197 This was probably the method used in Archsum, since the excavations there have not produced any traces of deep-litter byres (Kroll 1975, 96).
198 Kroll 1975, 87; 1987, 107. Kroll cites a source from 1858 which aptly characterizes this practice as 'Sisyphus work'.
199 The fact that the field systems are connected is in itself nothing new; this might simply be due to the long duration of the practice.

culated that there is more material present in the walls than could have been taken from the middle part of the field alone. From this he deduced that material must have been transported from outside the field.[200] In addition, Zimmermann established that the walls are often wide and have a much higher phosphate content than the fields themselves; he is also convinced of the transport of soil to the fields.[201] In combination with the knowledge that sod manuring was already being applied elsewhere at the same time, it can be hypothesized that the walls were in fact compost heaps, created with soil from the fields themselves, manure, and possibly sods from outside the fields, and grew during many years of use.

The division of the Celtic field systems into small parcels can be seen as a function of the manuring system. If it is assumed that the humus layer from the fields themselves was involved in the composting process, it is logical (seen from a twentieth-century perspective of work efficiency) that the units were not very large and were joined to each other. Probably one ought to imagine here not an annual procedure of manuring, but rather a procedure which took place every second or third year, or after a fallow period, as is known to have happened in historic times.[202] The composting of the fields then took place during the summer months, while the crops in other fields were in their growth phase. Zimmermann's point of view, that during the final phase of use (in the Roman period) the walls, which by that time had become quite wide, were also cultivated, is not a strange theory in the context of this explanation. In my opinion, the end of the

system is heralded by the use of the plough with a mould board which mixes the sods with the manure more efficiently.

In conclusion, there is one more element that can be linked to sod manuring: the appearance of podzolic soils which have been covered by drift sand. This connection has already been suggested by Van Regteren Altena.[203] Waterbolk originally proposed the idea that the ploughing of the adjacent Celtic field systems would have led to large-scale sand drift, but this has been refuted by Van Gijn's investigation.[204] This investigation shows that most drift sand covered surfaces can be dated within the period from the Late Bronze Age until the Late Iron Age.[205] Alternatively, the (temporary) removal of the topsoil of exhausted fields may have been a cause of the large-scale development of drift sand areas.

8.8.4 Settlement system

The settlement structures at the beginning of the Late Bronze Age are identical to those of the Elp culture: aisled farmhouses, some of them long, often with clearly recognizable stalls. Just as in the southern Netherlands, at some point a transition took place to farmhouses which were consistently lower and wider, usually accompanied by a number of granaries. Only five house plans have been published,[206] but they form a picture which is very similar to developments in the south. The Een house probably dates from around 700 cal BC, while the Peelo houses may be even older.[207] Just as with the southern Netherlands types, they have door openings located opposite each other in the long wall and more

200 Brongers 1976, 62.

201 Zimmermann 1976, 88.

202 Kroll 1975, 89.

203 Brongers 1976, note 5a.

204 A significant weak element in Waterbolk's original theory has not yet been pointed out: that ploughing with an ard does not result in uncovered arable land which is exposed to the wind. This situation occurs only when a plough with a mould board is used (see Waterbolk 1962, 45).

205 Van Gijn & Waterbolk 1984, 104, fig. 2

206 In Een (Van der Waals 1963), Peelo (Kooi & De Langen 1987), and Sellingen (Waterbolk 1989b).

207 The authors date the houses to the Early Iron Age. It is clear, however, that the terrain was also inhabited during the last part of the Late Bronze Age (Kooi & De Langen 1987, 164, fig. 11). By analogy with the results of the investigation in the southern Netherlands (Roymans & Fokkens 1991), it is not unlikely that the houses referred to as Peelo I and Peelo III can

still be dated to the period 850–700 cal BC. The Peelo II house is a later variant from a typological point of view, as well as by the radiocarbon date. The claim that the Een house also had an aisled part and a part with a central row of posts (Kooi & De Langen 1987, 156) is unfounded, in my opinion. The greater distance between the three posts at the eastern end and the next central post is not adequate proof, as is shown by one of the clearest house plans of this type in Oss (Van der Sanden 1987, 56, fig. 2). This house plan also illustrates another point. Kooi & De Langen and Van der Waals referred to the outermost row of posts in establishing the dimensions of these houses. In comparing this with the house plans in the southern Netherlands, however, it seems likely that in Een and Peelo the actual walls were not preserved (in the southern Netherlands these are sometimes visible as a shallow wall trench and sometimes as a wall of planks or posts). The actual width inside the walls is then c. 6.50 m rather than 9 m.

or less rounded extreme ends without roof-posts in the short wall, pointing to a hipped roof construction.[208]

The development in house plans from long byre houses to much shorter houses with little room for cattle might be linked to the appearance of Celtic field systems by suggesting that the splitting up of a large farm into two or more smaller ones which were more spread out across the farming area made manure transport more efficient. This is a purely speculative comment, however, and the current state of the investigation in fact does not allow such judgements. Nevertheless, it does appear that the extended families which were still inhabiting a number of Middle Bronze Age farms definitely broke up into nuclear families.

The settlement pattern of the Early Iron Age is comparable with the picture which has formed in the south. Based on the investigation at Hijken, Harsema sketches a picture of individual households 'wandering' through and along the Celtic field systems,[209] a picture that is corroborated by Kooi's recent investigation at Peelo.[210] Waterbolk theorizes that the ratio of settlement to urnfield was 1:1,[211] while Kooi stated that for each settlement territory (using Thiessen polygons) there must have been two or three urnfields.[212] The settlement unit which accompanies the average cemetery contained ten to fifteen persons,[213] which corresponds with two or three families or houses of the Een, or Peelo house 1, or Oss 2 type. So, according to Kooi's model, each Celtic field system would have accounted for four to nine families, or from 20 to 45 persons, an estimate reached by Harsema as well,[214] although from a completely different basis.

The emergence of coherent field systems and fixed cemeteries shows that the layout of the landscape was becoming increasingly more permanent. It can also be assumed that a territorial structure developed which is comparable in layout, but not in organization, to the medieval *marke*.

8.8.5 *Social organization*

After a period of less pronounced differentiation (at least as far as archaeological visibility is concerned), rich cemeteries and fortified settlements appear in central Europe, visible indications of the existence of elites. The extremely rich cemetery at Hallstatt shows that the accumulation of riches gained through monopolizing and manipulating important commodities which were to be found in that region (in particular, salt) constituted an integral part of society.[215] Although the real flourishing period did not take place until the Early Iron Age (Hallstatt C), it is nevertheless clear that these developments had already begun in the Late Bronze Age.[216]

It would be incorrect simply to assume a similar development in the Netherlands. Still, it is evident that there were contacts between our region and central Europe which, especially as far as the Early Iron Age is concerned, are evident in particular elements in the cemeteries. A number of very rich burials and exceptionally large burial monuments, especially to the south of the rivers Rhine and Maas, show that local elites existed here as well. Unfortunately very few of these 'chieftains' graves' have been carefully investigated, but the present state of knowledge reveals a consistent picture. What distinguishes the 'chieftains' graves' in particular is the presence of iron swords and parts from horse harnesses, wagon fittings, and bronze *situlae*. In the Netherlands there are six graves of this type from the Early Iron Age,[217] all in the valley of the river Maas. The bronze *situlae* as well as the iron swords, some with gold fittings, were certainly prestigious objects which were not manufactured locally; they must have come from central Europe, though the route they travelled may have been through Gaul. In addition, the provision of such objects as grave goods as well as burying horses and wagons follows the central European tradition.[218] The fact that these burials were carried out following this tradition indicates that the individuals involved possessed a certain institutionalized position. The swords (identified by Cowen as cavalry swords because of their length),[219] the wagons, and the horses suggest a 'knightly' status. The contacts of these individuals in the political sphere were such that they could participate in exchange networks with the wealthy Hallstatt region, a fact which was

208 Kooi & De Langen 1987, 159, fig. 8.
209 Harsema 1974, 1980.
210 Kooi & De Langen 1987.
211 Waterbolk 1987a.
212 Kooi 1979, 175.
213 Kooi 1979.
214 Harsema 1980.

215 Champion *et al.* 1984, 290.
216 Coles & Harding 1979, 377.
217 Baarlo, Meerlo, Mook, Oss, Venlo, Weert (Willems & Groenman-van Waateringe 1988).
218 Champion *et al.* 1984, 270, 275.
219 Cowen 1967.

emphasized by their relatives when they were buried. What was the power base of these 'chieftains'? There are no obvious centres of power or defended staple towns (although this could be a function of the present state of the investigation); nor are there rich cemeteries from which to conclude that the dynasty of a ruling class must have lived in the area. On the contrary, the cemeteries containing rich graves are generally very small[220] and the rich graves themselves are unique, even as far as the size is concerned.[221] It is Bloemers's conclusion that the variations in distribution as well as the absence of continuity reflect an unstable power structure.[222]

Obvious social stratification with a dynastic power structure was, therefore, not present. The picture is rather that of local chiefs taking turns in assuming a position of importance. With Hallstatt as an example, it does not seem unlikely to suppose that conducting military operations came to constitute an increasingly greater part of their power position, partly based on the monopolization and manipulation of important commodities. Roymans supposes that the trade in sea salt, important for the tanning of hides and the preservation of foods, was one of the most significant factors in the southern Netherlands.[223] Van den Broeke has convincingly shown that salt trading was carried out from the coastal regions, along the Maas and then inland.[224]

To what extent can indications for these kinds of development be found in the northern Netherlands during the Late Bronze Age and the Early Iron Age? It is not difficult to point to a few rich graves from the Late Bronze Age. The area around Drouwen and Emmen in particular has produced several finds which show that a certain accumulation of wealth occurred here.[225] The hoard of 'lady's jewelry' is particularly significant in this regard. Even in the context of the sometimes exceptionally rich hoards in the Scandinavian countries, it belongs to the top 16%.[226] Bronze finds which fit in the Hallstatt

sphere of influence are almost unknown in the northern Netherlands. An exception is a Gündlingen-type Hallstatt C sword[227] which was found in the Tjonger. It is not the northernmost sword of this type, but few have been found north of the Rhine.[228] The distribution pattern of these swords seems to indicate that they arrived in the north via the southern Netherlands, where a number of such swords have been found. As such it represents contacts with the southern Netherlands rather than with the Hallstatt region.

The finds show that in the northern Netherlands a number of individuals participated in the prestige networks of northern Europe, as was also true in previous periods. The impression exists, however, that the power base in northern Europe was somewhat different from that in the south. In particular the large number of hoards of exotic objects such as *lurer*, figurines, large ceremonial axes, etc., point to ceremonies in which metal was destroyed with great ostentation.[229] This is usually seen as a system in which the local elites act simultaneously as the ritual leaders. Ceremonies, such as the depositing of objects, are conducted by these elites and indirectly serve to legitimate their power position (see section 7.5).

A structure like this is stable as long as the power base – in northern Europe probably resting on the monopolization of the bronze exchange – remains intact. However, there is an inherent danger of escalation: as more bronze is brought into circulation, the elite must secure its power base to a greater degree by trying to obtain more exotic products. The destruction of a part of the supply by means of a ritual which the community both accepts and values can be a means of strengthening the power base (see section 7.5). The rigid standardization of forms and decorations (on ornaments in particular) in southern Scandinavia during periods V and VI and the shifting from grave deposits to ceremonial deposits in peat areas during the Late Bronze Age would indicate such an es-

220 Willems & Groenman-van Waateringe 1988, 27.

221 The diameter of the barrow near Horst was 19 m, of the barrow at Oss 53 m. The diameter of the average ring ditch, however, is not more than 6–8 m.

222 Bloemers 1986, 87.

223 Roymans 1991. Because ceramic salt containers are hardly ever found across the borders of the Netherlands, Roymans assumes that the salt was transported in bulk in containers of organic material. This argument does not hold much weight. Even less clear is how the 'chieftains' managed to control the salt trade in the southern Netherlands. A feasible alternative explanation is that the product being traded was not salt as

such, but products manufactured with the aid of salt such as cheese or salted hams.

224 Van den Broeke 1986.

225 Butler 1986; Lohof 1991.

226 Butler 1986, 157.

227 Cowen, however, is convinced that this is a sword of local make: 'Surely local work, but fully competent' (Cowen 1967, 440, pl. LIV: 3). The findspot cannot be more precisely described than 'in the Tjonger in the south-east of Friesland'. Boeles provided an illustration of the sword (1927, pl. V).

228 Cowen 1967, 392; Gerdsen 1986.

229 Coles & Harding 1979, 518 ff; Sørensen 1987, 99.

Table 16 The western part of the Frisian-Drentian plateau: determination of site-type on the basis of individual specimens of different finds categories for the Late Bronze Age and the Early Iron Age. The columns and rows represent finds categories and site-types respectively.

site-type	finds category						total
	hammer axe	bronze artifact	pottery	grave	settlement	field system	
settlement	0	0	1	0	1	0	2
grave	1	0	4	11	0	0	15
hoard	2	10	0	0	0	0	12
field system	0	0	0	0	0	39	39
unknown	5	3	0	0	0	0	8
total	8	13	5	11	1	39	77

calation,[230] certainly when it is remembered that this pattern does not continue into the Early Iron Age.[231] Kristiansen explains the disappearance of this system as the collapse of the exchange network that provided the managers with the necessary prestige goods.[232]

To summarize, the impression exists that during the Nordic Bronze Age the power base found its justification in a ceremonial leadership position rather than in economic monopolies. Although these two aspects are difficult to separate and the net effect for the power structure can be the same, the ceremonial leadership position nevertheless led to other kinds of hoarding practices for which the swamps and bogs (*dobben* in Friesland) of northern Europe assumed a central position. This is in contrast with the south, where the rivers are central. There, however, predominantly objects with a utilitarian character (swords, axes) are encountered. A large moor area such as the Peel, for example, has produced no finds which are comparable to the hoards in the Drentian and Frisian peat areas.[233]

8.8.6 *Findspots in the study area* (maps VI and VI')
A total of 77 findspots are known in the study area (table 16), including one settlement[234] and ten burial sites, either single graves or cemeteries. A large number of

Celtic field systems have come to light through Brongers's investigation.[235] Celtic field systems which are not connected but probably belong together (described by Brongers as separate field systems) are taken as one findspot in this study.

Distribution pattern
The distribution of the findspots in most of the regions shows continuity in relation to the Middle Bronze Age. This seems to be the case for the cemeteries as well: in a number of instances the urnfield is joined to older barrows,[236] giving the impression of settlement continuity as well as occupation continuity.[237]

The northern sandy area north of the Oude Diep and the Drait is completely lacking in finds, which probably reflects the actual situation. The oligotrophic peat accumulation in that area developed rapidly, partly through the presence of many *dobben* which functioned as peat accumulation centres. Although this region was probably not uninhabitable, the agricultural suitability in most places will have dropped drastically. There are no recognizable Celtic field systems there either, though this absence may have been caused by more recent peat coverings. That being said, traces of urnfields are also absent here.

230 Sørensen 1987, 92; 1989, 68.
231 In the northern Netherlands the earliest rich grave which is comparable with graves in the south is the Darp grave, which dates to the beginning of the Middle Iron Age (Kooi 1983).
232 Kristiansen 1978; 1989a.
233 It is not known to what extent the Late Iron Age and Roman period cult centres, which are regularly found in the southern Netherlands (Roymans 1990, 62 ff), may have had forerunners which fulfilled the role of the Drentian

and Frisian bogs (compare Van der Sanden 1990, 217).
234 Een: Van der Waals 1963.
235 Brongers 1976.
236 A fine example is the Wapse urnfield which joins two older barrows (Waterbolk 1957).
237 By this is meant that quite probably the same group of people continued to make use of the same area and the same cemetery.

Cemeteries

A number of the urnfields in the study area are excavated. In particular the cemeteries at Havelte, Oosterwolde, Ruinen, Vledder, and Wapse have been thoroughly investigated and published.[238] Kooi has dealt extensively with position, road patterns, territorial aspects and the like, and the present study cannot make any further additions to his work. There is one comment that can be made, however, regarding the distribution of the urnfields on the Frisian part of the Frisian-Drentian plateau.

The number of urnfields in the study area is very small in comparison with the Drentian part of the Frisian-Drentian plateau. Of only two urnfields the locations are known and their finds preserved: Donkerbroek and Oosterwolde. The others (De Legauke and De Vianen, both near Drachten) exist only on paper, and a small number exist only in oral tradition.[239] The much discussed Bornwird urnfield appears to have been an early medieval cemetery.[240] In my opinion, this scarcity of finds and the richness of the oral tradition must be interpreted in the light of the reclamation history. The reclamation activities carried out on the Drentian sandy grounds were not of the same disruptive magnitude as on the Frisian sandy grounds because the oligotrophic peat cover was less extensive. In addition, peat reclamation on the Frisian sandy grounds had been going on since the Middle Ages while the archaeological supervision of such activities was not introduced until the beginning of this century. These circumstances, in my view, go far to explain the absence of urnfields (and Celtic field systems) in Friesland. In the habitable areas the picture was probably comparable with the situation in the Drentian part of the Frisian-Drentian plateau.

There is still another possible line of reasoning to explain why so few urnfields have come down to us. This is connected with the size of the urnfields. The reports and the actual traces available to us give the impression that the urnfields were always small. The Oosterwolde urnfield, with a maximum of 38 graves, could act as a model.[241] This urnfield covers a period of 150 years at the most (from 750–600 cal bc) and according to Ascadi's formula this means a population of eight to twelve persons, if we take 30 years as the average life expectancy. That number is normal for this period.[242] It is therefore not the group of users but the duration of the use that makes the urnfield small. Although even in Drenthe small urnfields are certainly no exception,[243] the complete absence of large urnfields in Friesland and the related shorter duration of use might be connected with the changing landscape. This is a speculative judgement, however, that could only be substantiated by looking more carefully at the connection between the size and the physical-geographical position of the urnfields, which is too far outside the confines of this study.

Bronzes

Most of the bronzes discovered in the study area are finds without context, but it is often evident from the position of the findspot that the bronzes had been part of a hoard. This applies especially to the bronze objects found in peat or stream valley sediments, as for instance the 'sacrificial knife' from Appelscha.[244] Two bronze swords were found in the study area. The bronze Hallstatt sword from the Tjonger has already been discussed (section 8.8.5). Depositing goods in rivers fits entirely with the standard picture; it was not until iron swords made their appearance that deposits began to be made in graves.[245] The second sword was discovered near Steenwijk in 1912 close to an area of peat reclamation in a drift sand layer in the peat. According to the correspondence which took place in 1932 between the municipal collector of Steenwijk, A. Klijnsma, and P.C.J.A. Boeles, the sword was found together with two stone hammers

238 Kooi 1979; Elzinga 1973; Waterbolk 1965; Van Giffen 1938; Waterbolk 1957; respectively.

239 Elzinga 1973, 19.

240 Van Giffen 1918–19. The pots, which had been lost since the 1930s, were found in the Fries Museum by E. Knol, who dated them to the Early Middle Ages.

241 Elzinga 1973.

242 By using Ascadi's formula, Kooi reckoned that for the Wapse and Vledder urnfields, which were in use for a much longer period (1100–500 b.c.), there must have been a population of twelve to sixteen persons, or two to three families. The Ruinen cemetery was larger, with a population of

seventeen to twenty-one in the period 700–200 b.c. (Kooi 1979, 174).

243 On the contrary, in Kooi's list of urnfields it appears that of the 115 cemeteries, 85 date to one of Kooi's phases (9 early, 37 middle, 39 late), while only 40 were in use for more than one period, and 18 were in use during the entire duration of the urnfield period (Kooi 1979, 153–6). The doubtful cemeteries and those without continuity are not included in this calculation.

244 Butler 1973b.

245 Cowen 1967; Gerdsen 1986.

which had been drilled through and a fish-shaped object. These finds have not been preserved, but a photo taken by Boeles shows Late Neolithic hammer axes, thus not to be associated with the *Griffzungenschwert*. The sword dates from the beginning of the Late Bronze Age or somewhat earlier.

It is striking that the number of bronze finds from the Late Bronze Age, although few, is double that of the bronze finds from the Middle Bronze Age. This fits in with the general picture from the northern Netherlands (even Drenthe shows such an increase) and of the Nordic region in general.[246]

Settlement traces

Only two find assemblages can be identified with any certainty as settlements. The first is the Early Iron Age settlement near Een.[247] This concerns an investigation of limited size which tells us nothing about the settlement structure or pattern. Nevertheless, the excavated ground plan clearly fits in the wider framework of Early Iron Age houses. Second is a number of finds which indicates a settlement at Popping's findspot in the '80 *bunder*' near Fochteloo. There are no features known from this findspot, but seeing that there is a Celtic field system in the same area as well as the Roman period settlement investigated by Van Giffen (see section 8.10.3), it seems probable that the stray finds from this period also mark a settlement terrain.[248] The scarcity of settlement data from this period is not exceptional in the Netherlands, and it should be assumed that the occupation was just as dense as elsewhere.[249]

Flint sickles

Extra attention is needed for the flint sickles. This type of artifact is frequently found in eastern West-Friesland,[250] almost always as a stray find. Sometimes flint sickles are datable by their association with Bronze Age features, in particular features from the Late Bronze Age. In this region, they cannot be dated any later than that because eastern West-Friesland was uninhabitable after approximately 800 cal BC. Recent investigation of the wear traces left by sickles clearly shows that at least a

number of them were not used as sickles at all, but rather as instruments to cut the sods in the sandy clay.[251]

Flint sickles have also been found in the clay region of Friesland and Groningen. The question, however, is what date should be given to their appearance in that region. Waterbolk is of the opinion that they could have been brought there by farmers from West-Friesland or Texel, and they might thus be seen as the oldest finds in the *terpen* area.[252] This possibility presents itself because according to Zagwijn's reconstructions[253] the north-western Frisian clay region extended to Texel at the end of the Late Bronze Age and it was possible to reach the Frisian clay region from West-Friesland via the lake Almere and a supposed natural waterway, the 'primal Marne', connecting the Almere and the Frisian clay area.[254] As far as West-Friesland is concerned this theory is unlikely, however, because of the extensive oligotrophic peat area in south-western Friesland, even though it may have been possible to reach Gaasterland. In any case, it would have been possible (certainly by water) for the Texel farmers to visit the Frisian clay region. But there are no indications of human settlement in the Frisian clay region before 600 cal BC. Boersma is also of the opinion that the flint sickles in the Frisian-Groningen coastal region are not earlier than the last part of the Early Iron Age, and are probably later.[255]

In my view, the explanation for the appearance of sickles from different chronological contexts in the clay region of West-Friesland and the northern Netherlands must be sought in the similar physical state of the area in which the implement seems to have served a specific function: cutting sods. Only in an advanced phase of the Iron Age would iron tools take over this task.

It should be mentioned that not all flint sickles were found in the clay region. Siebinga found two sickles close together in the valley of the Oude Diep, probably a hoard, while another specimen comes from Weper, near Oosterwolde. A part of what is possibly a fourth sickle comes from Bakkeveen, although it might also be a fragment of a flint dagger. Naturally these specimens from the sandy area may date from the Late Bronze Age. However, considering that this type of artifact is gener-

246 Butler 1986; Sørensen 1987; section 8.8.5.
247 Van der Waals 1963.
248 Van Giffen 1958.
249 As in the Early and Middle Bronze Age, the amount of pottery in settlement pits and postholes is small, giving the settlement terrains poor archaeological visibility.

250 See note 108.
251 Van Gijn 1988.
252 Waterbolk 1988, 15.
253 Zagwijn 1986.
254 Waterbolk 1988, 12 ff.
255 Boersma 1988, 34.

ally found in the *terpen* area,[256] it is assumed that the occasional find from the surrounding countryside should be dated to the Middle Iron Age. On the basis of these considerations, the flint sickles are indicated only on the Middle and Late Iron Age map (map VII).

Hammer axes
Hammer axes of the Muntendam and Baexem types are another category of material which is difficult to date. These artifacts were certainly being used during the Late Bronze Age and Early Iron Age, as evidenced by find assemblages from Hoogkarspel and Den Burg.[257] The question, however, is how long did they remain in use. Achterop and Brongers argue for 400 cal BC, because this fits in well with their interpretation of the function of this artifact group in connection with a supposed topographical relation with the wooden trackway of Valthe.[258] Only one specimen with a late date is known, however: from the Ezinge *terp*.[259] But this could very well be an older specimen which for one reason or another was long in use. Considering that the most important usage phase, as far as is datable, is the Late Bronze Age and Early Iron Age, the Baexem and Muntendam type hammer axes are shown only on the map from that period (map VI).

8.9 MIDDLE AND LATE IRON AGE (500 CAL BC – 12 BC; 2450–2000 BP)

8.9.1 *General framework*
The outline of the Middle and Late Iron Age in the northern Netherlands and north-western Germany is first determined by the emergence of *terp* settlements in the coastal region where a salt-marsh area had developed after 900 cal BC. The emergence of *terpen* probably begins during the 6th century cal BC and is specific to the northern Netherlands and northern German coastal region.[260] Waterbolk has described the material culture of the *terpen*

as Proto-Frisian, succeeded by the Frisian culture.[261] The definition of these archaeological cultures is justified, considering the fact that an independent development in pottery style, settlements, and burial ritual does appear to have taken place. In the sandy area there are far fewer obvious elements of a separate material culture to point to; in any case it is usually neutral chronological indications which are used (Hallstatt and La Tène periods).

The fact that central European influences reached the northern Netherlands during the La Tène period is apparent from various finds, but it is equally evident that during this period the northern Netherlands lay on the periphery of the developments in central Europe. There are no indications of hill-forts or other central places during the Middle Iron Age, unless the 'fortified' settlements are considered as such (see section 8.9.3). Nevertheless, even on the settlement level differentiation gradually becomes evident, indicating that society had become more complex.

The burial ritual scarcely leaves any opportunities for analysis. It is true that a number of cemeteries have been thoroughly investigated, but the rectangular and circular ditches are without finds for the most part.[262] The ritual seems to have consisted of cremating the dead and throwing up a low barrow over the remains of the funeral pyre. Urns are scarce, and when they are encountered they are often not surrounded by a circular ditch.[263] The absence of grave goods makes it difficult to come to any conclusions about the social organization on the basis of the cemeteries.

8.9.2 *Emergence of the terpen*
For an explanation of the development of settlements in the *terpen* area, Waterbolk first looked to the colonists' supposed homeland: Drenthe.[264] The podzolic soils covered with drift sand play an important role in his line of reasoning. These were explained by concluding that in the Celtic field system the field plots were continuous, so forests could not function as windbreaks. Spring storms

256 Waterbolk (1988, 15) knows of 21 specimens in Westergo alone.
257 Achterop & Brongers 1979.
258 In this regard it should be mentioned that similarities in geographical distribution are not a reason to assume a chronological association and neither can a formal analogy with modern implements be a reason to assume a functional association.
259 Dated to 2295 ± 50 b.p., Achterop & Brongers 1979, 265.

According to J.N. Lanting, however, this date does not correspond to the layer in which the axe was found (pers. comm. 1989).
260 Boersma 1988, 34.
261 Waterbolk 1962.
262 For example Ruinen, Waterbolk 1965.
263 Wapse, Waterbolk 1957.
264 Waterbolk 1959; 1962.

blowing across the newly-ploughed fields would have led to enormous sand drift.[265] In addition, it could also be argued that advancing peat accumulation made the habitable area damper and smaller. It is logical to make a direct connection between the emergence of settlements in the coastal region and this 'environmental crisis'. For twenty years this was the accepted explanation for the development of occupation in the salt-marsh area, until Van Gijn and Waterbolk re-evaluated the available data, this time from an anthropological angle.[266]

The renewed investigation showed that many of the drift sand covered podzolic soils do not date from the Iron Age and that they could just as easily be either older or younger. It was also advanced that new, uninhabitable areas, such as the salt-marsh area at the beginning of the Iron Age, are almost naturally the object of interest. The alternative model proposes that the salt-marsh area came into use during a period in which transhumance was being practised. The cattle, who had less and less room for grazing on the sandy grounds, were brought to the salt-marshes in the summer. The people who brought them there were able to learn about the possibilities and limitations of the area, which finally led to the decision to live there permanently with an economy based on cattle-raising. The threat which peat accumulation and sand storms posed to the agricultural areas is not repudiated by Van Gijn and Waterbolk, but a direct cause-and-effect relationship is for them no longer an issue.

A nuance to the transhumance model came from Van der Waals.[267] Van der Waals has a background in ethno-archaeology with fieldwork in the Dogon region in Mali. It is his opinion that a change in the economic basis of an egalitarian tribal society, which he believes characterizes the Iron Age community, still had need of a catalyst. The kinship ties and traditions in such a society are so strong that what seems to us to be a reasonable decision is not taken in a casual way. Van der Waals therefore tries to show that the first inhabitants of the salt-marsh area were farmers with a mixed economy who, under pressure from a transgressive interval, passed into a more cattle-based economy.[268]

Although the archaeological foundation of Van der Waals's argument is not strong because of the absence of data from the earliest settlements in the salt-marsh region, it seems obvious that a catalyst must indeed have been present. We know that a transhumance system could have continued to exist for centuries without leading to permanent occupation in the pasture land.[269] The fact that in the sixth century BC a rapid development towards independent and aggregated settlements in the salt-marsh region took place suggests a cause that is connected not only with the attractiveness of the salt-marshes as pasture land. These settlements must have had their origin in specific developments, in particular the reduction in habitable land on the Frisian sandy grounds. Moreover it is incorrect to assume that the colonists came from Drenthe: the inhabitants of the Frisian part of the Frisian-Drentian plateau had many more reasons to exploit the salt-marsh region. Chapter 9 will examine this more closely.

In the light of palaeogeographic developments as reconstructed in this study, the transhumance and colonization routes indicated by Van Gijn and Waterbolk[270] should be somewhat revised. First, the arrows that point to Westergo and Oostergo should begin on the Frisian sandy grounds and not in Drenthe. Second, the Boorne and the northern sandy area should be seen as the most likely routes. It was probably possible to travel along the river or, at least, to pass over it. The southern route is much less probable because extensive oligotrophic peat areas lay there.

8.9.3 Settlement system

Although the excavations in Ezinge and Middelstum have received a great deal of publicity, actually very little information about the occupation in the *terpen* region is known from the Dutch excavation data. We can be quite precise about the number of settlements, but in fact little is known about the structure and the pattern because of a lack of detailed excavation reports. It is the investigations at Boomburg-Hatzum and Feddersen Wierde of our Wilhelmshaven colleagues in particular which now determine the picture. Settlements on the sandy grounds in northern Germany and Denmark have also been repeatedly investigated, especially regarding the Late Iron Age and the Roman period.[271] In Drenthe the investigations near Hijken and near Peelo should be mentioned.[272]

265 See note 204.
266 Van Gijn & Waterbolk 1984.
267 Van der Waals 1987.
268 Van der Waals 1987, 45.

269 Ingold 1987.
270 Van Gijn & Waterbolk 1984, fig. 10.
271 Kossack *et al.* 1984.
272 Harsema 1974; Kooi 1986; Kooi & De Langen 1987.

The data show that in the Middle and Late Iron Age the open settlement structure consisting of separate farmhouses which were constantly being moved within the field system is still present. During the last part of the Late Iron Age, however, a tendency becomes visible for the rebuilding of farmhouses on the same plot, and sometimes groupings of houses in clusters of two and three on one plot have been observed (Fochteloo). The German colleagues then speak of a *Mehrbetriebsgehöft* (farmyard with two or more farm buildings around it). Sometimes these are found within an encircling trench, such as in Hodde.[273] This picture corresponds with that which has been established for the area below the rivers Rhine and Maas. There, too, Late Iron Age farmhouses are more often rebuilt on the same place and aggregates of two or three buildings emerge.[274]

A separate category is the so-called fortified settlements from the Late Iron Age.[275] Waterbolk has drawn comparisons between this type of settlement on the one hand and hill-forts and *Viereckschanzen* on the other. His conclusion is that they were predominantly staple places for cattle and grain, possibly with a supplementary cult function.[276] Although not all the arguments for the staple place function are convincing (in the case of Rhee, for instance), the fact can hardly be avoided that what is being discussed here is an unusual type of settlement. The walling in of the settlements, sometimes clearly intended as fortification (Zijen II), can perhaps be seen in the light of hill-forts, but the nature of the fortification and the position in low-lying terrain limit the comparison.[277] A comparison with Celtic *Viereckschanzen* can be disputed because there is no encircling trench around the postulated central 'temple structure' in Vries, while such trenches are present at most Celtic cult sites.[278]

If the hill-forts are seen as regional centres, the seats of *pagi* or of subtribes, then the fortified settlements in the northern Netherlands instead represent units on the local level. The fortification must then be seen in the light of raids (chapter 9). Certainly their objective was not to harbour a subtribe inside a defensible fort in time of need. The structure is too small for that and the defences are not robust enough. In addition, the number of similar settlements in the same area is too large (three units within an area of 25 km²). Roymans comes to similar conclusions for the enclosed settlements in northern Gaul, where such settlements arise in the La Tène period as well.[279]

Although we hardly know what a 'normal' Late Iron Age settlement looked like, it can be assumed that its character was that of scattered farmhouses, as was the case in the previous period. The fortified settlements represent a higher level, making the differentiation in settlement types visible. For the first time, the growing complexity which is apparent in interments from the Early and Middle Iron Age (but which afterward is no longer visible) can also be observed in the settlement pattern and the settlement structure.

8.9.4 *Social organization*

In the Middle and Late Iron Ages there are increasing indications of the emergence of local elites. Their power base was probably founded on the manipulation of scarce commodities. It is not likely, however, that the influence exercised by these elites went beyond that of subtribes.[280] In the northern Netherlands, direct evidence of these leaders is scarce, but it does exist. One piece of evidence is the 'chieftain's grave' at Darp.[281] This interment does not stand alone, although most of the others are somewhat later.[282]

Other indications of growing social complexity are found in the settlements. Since the Middle Iron Age a hierarchy seems to have developed, but in the northern Netherlands only the lowest levels (fenced-in and open settlements) have been found so far. Higher levels, such as the later hill-forts, have been found only in the northern German region. Here in around 50 BC the Heidenschanze was constructed, with a fenced-in area of 10 ha at an extremely favourable geographic position as far as commerce and traffic are concerned.[283] It is not unlikely that such a site was indeed a *Herrensitz* with a supraregional function. Therefore, if this level was indeed present in the northern Netherlands more than

273 Hvass 1988.
274 Pers. comm. C. Schinkel; Simons 1989.
275 Waterbolk 1977.
276 Waterbolk 1977, 168.
277 Waterbolk 1977, 166.
278 Slofstra & Van der Sanden 1987.
279 Roymans 1990, 185 ff.

280 Roymans 1990, 261 .
281 Kooi 1983; Waterbolk 1977. The Ruinen-Wommels I type urn suggests a possible date of 550 cal BC or later (see Boersma 1988, 34), which is somewhat later than Kooi (1983) supposed.
282 Kooi 1983; Van der Sanden 1990, 222.
283 Haarnagel 1965; Kossack et al. 1984.

Table 17 The western part of the Frisian-Drentian plateau: determination of site-type on the basis of individual specimens of different finds categories for the Middle and Late Iron Age. The columns and rows represent finds categories and site-types respectively.

site-type	finds category							total
	flint sickle	bronze artifact	pottery	grave	settlement	field system	bone	
settlement	0	0	5	0	3	0	0	8
terp	0	0	104	0	0	0	0	104
grave	0	0	1	10	0	0	0	11
hoard	1	1	1	0	0	0	1	4
field system	0	0	0	0	0	39	0	39
unknown	2	0	1	0	0	0	0	3
total	3	1	112	10	3	39	1	169

one or two sites similar to the Heidenschanze are not to be expected.

8.9.5 *Findspots in the study area* (maps VII and VII')

If we rely only on archaeological finds, then findspots on the sandy grounds dating from the Middle and Late Iron Age are scarce (table 17). There are only 26 known findspots, not counting the Celtic field systems. The recognizable artifact categories are chiefly limited to pottery, probably originating from settlement sites that become more and more identifiable during this period. Although map formation processes certainly have been of influence, this does not alter the fact that the habitable area was considerably reduced in size and limited to the areas around the upper courses of the streams and the relatively well-drained parts of the sandy grounds. The drainage pattern increasingly must have determined the habitability and negotiability of the sandy area.

A number of cemeteries are known, some in the area around Havelte. Because these are almost exclusively pyre barrows containing no finds, precise dating is difficult. Probably many finds have been lost when the heathlands were reclaimed. The barrows near Havelte were investigated because they were threatened by the events of the Second World War, and Van Giffen had the opportunity to excavate them. One of the few thoroughly investigated cemeteries from this period is the cemetery at Ruinen.[284]

In relation to the clay area the number of settlement traces found in the sandy area is small. These concern pits or house plans found at Doldersum, Dwingeloo, Fochteloo,[285] and Weper. In addition, various concentrations of pottery were found which can be interpreted as settlement indicators. During this period the *terp* settlements in the salt-marsh area were still concentrated in Westergo. Probably most of the 104 *terpen* were smaller units containing only one or two farmsteads. The formation of larger villages in the salt-marsh area seems not to have occurred until the Roman period, just as on the Frisian-Drentian plateau (section 8.9.3).

8.10 ROMAN PERIOD (12 BC – AD 406; 2000–1650 BP)

8.10.1 *General framework*

The Romans entered the present territory of the Netherlands for the first time during the first century BC and occupied the area south of the Rhine. This set in motion a series of developments which could be felt much further afield, including the north. Tributes and alliances had to be negotiated, sometimes battles had to be waged, taxes were exacted, and new goods such as wine, chickens, and luxurious pottery became available. Money made its appearance, and new practices became fashionable.

Although the northern Netherlands are generally seen as a peripheral region in terms of these developments, it is evident that the Roman influence was felt there. Van Es calls the Frisian territory 'an invasion gateway to the heart of Germany' and thus of strategic importance.[286]

284 Waterbolk 1957.
285 Van Giffen dated these traces to the first and second centuries AD, but Waterbolk, after re-examination of the site, dates them to the pre-Roman period (pers. comm. H.T. Waterbolk 1990).
286 Van Es 1972, 31.

The region was required to provide troops and pay taxes. Cows (for both hides and meat) were bought by private individuals or by order of the legionary commanders, as attested by a sales contract found in one of the *terpen*.[287] Roman coins have been found in *terpen* in large numbers and bear witness to direct contacts, for they were probably not used as currency by the local population.[288]

A distinction should probably be made between the clay area and the sandy area regarding the intensity of the Roman influence. Despite reports of journeys on foot to the Elbe region, it seems unlikely that the sandy area served as a route of passage because it was too heavily covered by peat. Brooks may have served as transport routes, certainly if flat-bottomed vessels were used, but it would not have been possible to travel very far in this way. The coastal region must therefore be seen as the more important transit route and the inhabitants of this region as the more important trading partners for the Romans.[289]

Finds from the *terpen* show that trade played a role during this period, which probably led to surplus production.[290] The local elites must have found ways to use this to strengthen their power base. Economic competition will have played an increasingly greater role. Some settlements grew into villages, and each village seems to have had one person to act as the community representative who probably in turn was subordinate to a higher level of organization. This position differs to such an extent from that in previous periods that it appears to be institutionalized and appears everywhere (Feddersen Wierde, Fochteloo, Hodde, Peelo, Wijster). It probably can be compared with the position of the inhabitants of the houses in the southern Netherlands which during the Roman period grew into villas or houses with tile roofs and a porticus, such as at Oss.[291]

8.10.2 *Settlement system*

During the Roman period, clearly identifiable villages appeared for the first time. Most were small, such as at Fochteloo and Peelo; others grew to substantial village centres. Some residential centres became larger during the second century AD in particular, when there appears

to have been a flourishing period. From this very period a number of settlements have been investigated which go through the transition from small villages with a limited number of houses (three to five) in the first century to a large village with around twenty houses in the second and third centuries.[292] The best example of this is Wijster (see below), immediately to the east of the study area. The same development took place in the southern Netherlands and in the coastal region.[293] It is unlikely, however, that all residential centres followed the same course. The cases named here are probably exceptions that make visible a higher level in the settlement hierarchy.

An explanation for this development is not easy to provide. The arrival of the Romans, bringing with them a great demand for agrarian and other products, undoubtedly played a role. This explains the larger differentiation among the settlements, but it does not explain their sudden increase in size. Dismissing the possibility of a sudden population explosion, it must mean that the farmers moved their individual farms to enclosed areas in order to hold their ground as a larger unit in the undoubtedly tumultuous times.

The best example of a large village from the Roman period in the northern sandy area is Wijster.[294] The village is enclosed and consists of a number of contemporaneous houses. In the beginning (second century AD) there were six houses, but when the village was flourishing (period IIIb, AD 360–395) the number grew to 22. Because the phases follow each other quite closely, this should indeed have been approximately the actual number. Van Es assumes that each house was occupied by one extended family, thereby reaching an estimate of at least 250 persons or double that amount (in conjunction with unexcavated sections). In my opinion, however, this calculation is on the liberal side because there are no indications of extended families having lived in these houses. A number between 125 and 150 seems a more likely estimate. The development in size then roughly coincides with that supposed for Feddersen Wierde.[295] The investigation at Feddersen Wierde in particular shows a number of differences in the means of subsistence between the sandy area and the salt-marsh area. Of

---

287 Tolsum, see Van Es 1972, 205 ff.
288 Van Es 1960.
289 Van Es 1967, 535.
290 For example Haarnagel 1979.
291 Slofstra 1991; Van der Sanden 1987, 65.

292 See Kossack *et al.* 1984 for an overview.
293 Van der Sanden 1987; Haarnagel 1979.
294 Van Es 1967.
295 Haarnagel 1979.

Table 18 The western part of the Frisian-Drentian plateau: determination of site-type on the basis of individual specimens of different finds categories for the Roman period. The columns and rows represent finds categories and site-types respectively.

site-type	finds category								total
	bronze artifact	pottery	quern	coin	grave	settlement	field system	organic material	
settlement	0	1	2	0	0	2	0	0	5
terp	0	80	0	66	0	0	0	0	146
grave	0	3	0	0	2	0	0	1	6
hoard	6	0	0	9	0	0	0	0	15
field system	0	0	0	0	0	0	2	0	2
unknown	0	2	0	9	0	0	0	0	11
total	6	86	2	84	2	2	2	1	195

course the results of the investigations on Feddersen Wierde and Wijster apply to the Roman period, but there is no reason to assume that these differ substantially from the economy of the Middle and Late Iron Age. Inhabitants of the clay area probably specialized in cattle-breeding, certainly during the Roman period, while those of the sandy area had a more mixed economy.[296] Striking differences are the almost complete absence of sunken huts at Feddersen Wierde, while these were a permanent element of the sandy area settlements during the Roman period;[297] the differences in the number of granaries: only one per main building at Feddersen Wierde as opposed to more than one on the sandy grounds; the appearance of ploughs equipped with mould boards in the salt-marsh area, while the ard continued to be used in the sandy area.[298] The data on the economic strategies followed by the inhabitants of the clay area and the sandy area respectively, however, do not indicate that these people were in complementary positions that made them dependent on each other.

8.10.3 *Findspots in the study area* (maps VIII and VIII')
The number of known Roman period findspots from the sandy grounds is small: fifteen. Best known is the settlement at Fochteloo, with its so-called chieftain's residence. This is a 23 m long byre house with room for a maximum of 28 cattle, situated on a yard along with a number of outbuildings and a much smaller farmstead.

The residence was rebuilt a number of times on almost the same spot. From this arrangement, Van Giffen concluded that this was the home of a chief. A similar farmyard was found in Peelo and also given the name 'chieftain's residence'.[299] The term 'chieftain' is a rather unfortunate choice in this connection because it suggests a tribal chief with power on a regional level. The developments of the settlements in this period, however, show that these kinds of large, sometimes separately enclosed yards and houses were present in many settlements. It seems likely that a headman, or someone with a similar function on a local level, did indeed live here (section 8.9.4). Settlement traces were also found near Dwingeloo and Ruinen. Ard traces were investigated near Uffelte and Grijpskerk. The traces near Grijpskerk are part of settlements in the salt-marsh area even though they lay on a sand outcrop in that area.

Various indications of cemeteries from the Roman period are known, but most of these are merely isolated urns. Cemeteries from this period are difficult to identify because of the absence of grave goods.

The coins constitute a particular category of finds. They have been catalogued and dated by Van Es.[300] Unfortunately most reports do not provide exact findspot specifications, but the finds distribution pattern is striking. The known finds from the sandy grounds are relatively few, eighteen, in relation to the clay area. The well-known coin hoard from Onna, 86 coins dating from the

296 Van Es 1967, 406; Haarnagel 1979.
297 Sunken huts also appear in the *terp* settlements, however (pers. comm. H.T. Waterbolk).
298 Haarnagel 1979, 265.
299 Kooi *et al.* 1987.

300 Van Es, 1960. In the present study, all coins, even those dated to the last half of the first century BC, are included in the Roman period because this category of finds will be interpreted chiefly in that context. The precise dating is of minor importance here.

period up to AD 47, in fact is an exception in this category. The majority of these finds consists of a single
coin, sometimes a few. A number of them have been
found along the river Tjonger, even as far as the lower
course; others have been found on the sand islands between the rivers Tjonger and Boorne. These finds illustrate routes that ran through the peat area and over the
Tjonger, via Gaasterland or the Flevomeer in the direction of the salt-marsh area,[301] which were used by the
Romans or their purchasing agents, since the coins were
probably not used as local currency. Most of the coins,
66 specimens, were found in the salt-marsh area, however, and originate from the *terp* settlements.

In comparison with the previous period, the distribution
of *terpen* is extended most notably to the east and north.
Whether the increased number of *terpen*, from 104 to
146, indicates an actual increase in the population is still
a question. More specifically directed research on this
subject might provide clarity.

301 Certainly during the last phase of the Roman period, when
the Dunkirk II transgressive interval occurred, the clay region
probably extended far to the south. In some places it even
reached as far as Gaasterland and far into central Friesland

8.11 EARLY MIDDLE AGES

Most large villages on the sandy grounds of the north-
west European plain ceased to exist during the fifth century AD. They probably split into smaller units which are
more difficult to recognize. The social organization
changed, influenced by the rise of the Frankish empire.
This is also the period of migrations. Exceptionally few
finds are known from this period, a problem that applies
to the whole of the Netherlands. It does not mean that
there was no occupation, but that occupation was structured in such a way that archaeological visibility is poor.
This change serves as the terminus of this study. The
end is dictated on the one hand by the practical absence
of data, on the other hand by the need to possess an
adequate understanding of the new developments and a
well-founded knowledge of historical sources. The developments following the Roman period therefore require another approach, with more varied sources, than
was feasible within the framework of this investigation.

(Geological Map of the Netherlands 1:50 000, map sheets 11
west and east). In this way the peat area was drained and
negotiability increasingly improved.

Chapter 9

Occupation in a slowly drowning landscape

9.1 INTRODUCTION

The descriptions presented in Chapters 3 and 8 show that the gradually dominating peat accumulation and the shrinking of the habitable area are the most striking developments on the western part of the Frisian-Drentian plateau. It is true that peat formation was a significant factor throughout the region, but it was most drastic in the central part near the great Fochtelooër and Smildiger Venen and on the western part of the plateau. Departing from conditions in *c.* 4000 cal BC, peat formation continued until, by the Roman period, only 40% of the original area remained free of a peat cover and an even smaller part of the original area was suitable for cultivation. At first glance one has the impression that even though the period of time involved was quite lengthy, this process must have been noticeable to the population and could have been a cause for tension. The purpose of this chapter is to investigate whether there was noticeable tension between man and environment on the western part of the Frisian-Drentian plateau, and if so, how the inhabitants may have reacted.

9.2 RATE OF DROWNING

One way to ascertain whether there was tension between man and environment is to determine how fast the peat expanded over the sandy area. An attempt was made to answer this question by dividing the area into units that are physically and geographically defined (fig. 46). Thus the borders between the units are formed by brooks or watersheds. Next, the magnitude of the decrease in uncovered surface area was estimated in relation to the previous period based on the palaeogeographic reconstructions.[1] The result of these calculations is shown in table 19. It should be realized that the estimates are based on the applied geological model (see Chapter 3), and that

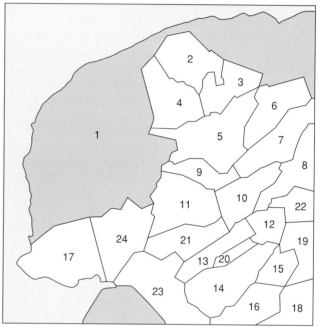

Figure 46 The western part of the Frisian-Drentian plateau: division of the study area into 24 physical-geographical units.

the drowning speed in the sandy area is chiefly determined by the premises of that model. For example, the rapid peat accumulation during the Early and Middle Neolithic is chiefly determined by the still rather rapid rise in the sea level. In the rather flat sandy area this led, within the framework of the model (seen spatially), to extensive peat formation in a short period of time, such as in area units 17, 24, 11, and 23. As the sea-level curve became less steep the fen peat ceased to expand in these areas, and the formation of oligotrophic peat, which

1 The estimate was produced by laying a grid with 1×1 km cells under the maps and adding up the number of grid units within each unit.

134

Table 19 The western part of the Frisian-Drentian plateau: estimated decrease of the surface of the habitable area per unit area per archaeological period. The figures are for km² unless otherwise indicated.

unit area	period							
	EN B	MN B	LN A	LN B / EBA	MBA	LBA / EIA	MIA / LIA	RP
2	80	68	54	43	27	25	24	22
3	85	75	75	74	65	61	60	55
4	137	101	76	72	60	38	35	30
5	191	173	162	162	154	131	114	62
6	99	88	88	78	74	61	48	24
7	105	103	103	99	96	78	70	25
8	85	85	85	85	83	75	66	10
9	60	27	20	20	20	13	13	1
10	103	103	103	103	103	91	67	15
11	142	74	35	28	27	2	0	0
12	58	58	58	58	58	57	41	39
13	64	64	64	64	64	64	58	35
14	153	153	141	141	141	129	123	95
15	50	50	50	50	50	50	47	43
16	77	77	77	77	77	74	68	45
17	184	92	84	74	65	64	64	61
18	56	56	56	56	56	56	56	45
19	56	56	56	56	56	45	43	11
20	19	19	19	19	19	19	19	19
21	81	63	60	46	45	21	17	5
22	62	62	62	62	62	47	37	18
23	99	7	0	0	0	0	0	0
24	152	81	57	45	40	34	30	21
total / period	2198	1735	1585	1512	1442	1235	1100	681
decrease / period		463	150	73	70	207	135	419
time span (in years)		1000	400	650	600	550	500	600
decrease / year		0.46	0.38	0.11	0.12	0.38	0.27	0.69
decrease / year / unit area*		0.04	0.03	0.01	0.01	0.02	0.01	0.03

★ only calculated in unit areas in which decreases occurred

slowly but surely had stretched out over the higher sandy grounds only after the Early Bronze Age, began accelerating. In the northern area units (2–6), the sandy grounds initially began drowning at a rather slow pace because the plateau there had relatively steep slopes. Only after the Middle Bronze Age did developments in the north speed up, when the oligotrophic peat on the watersheds expanded and the coastal peat reached the flat, bowl-shaped parts of the region. Oligotrophic peat formation in the eastern area units did not begin until after the Middle Bronze Age either. Peat formation before that time is barely perceptible, apart from the local bogs existing in depressions and *dobben*.

The calculations in table 19 show that during a period of five thousand years, the peat-covered area increased to at least 60% of the original uncovered area at an average speed of 0.3 km² annually. When this increase is calculated over a number of area units, however, we must then reckon an average of 0.1 to 0.4 ha per area unit annually. In other words: in each area unit (containing an average of 92 km²), a piece of ground the size of half a football field, sometimes a bit more, sometimes less, was disappearing every year. The above calculations seem to point to a development that was very gradual and that certainly was not traceable year after year. Even when calculated over a period of thirty years (one generation), no dramatic developments are indicated: 3 to 9 ha per area became overgrown with peat. Seen from this angle alone, there seems to be no reason to suppose that a field of tension existed. Considering that the farms were regularly moved, it is feasible that the inhabitants unwittingly anticipated these developments by gradually moving the parcels to the higher parts of the sandy areas.

9.3 CARRYING CAPACITY AND POPULATION PRESSURE

Generally it is assumed that the drowning of the western part of the Frisian-Drentian plateau led to population pressure. Waterbolk considered this the principal reason for migration to the *terpen* area.[2] Population pressure in the economic sense means that a field of tension exists between the available resources and the number of people that have to be fed. Archaeologists often use the carrying capacity model to describe the mechanisms which are at work within that field of tension. According to the model, each area possesses a certain carrying capacity which is usually calculated on the basis of the potential total biomass. The limits of the carrying capacity can be reached as the population increases or the amount of biomass decreases. According to the accepted theory, regulating forces then come into play: people migrate, famine develops, people switch to other production techniques (intensification), etc.

Numerous authors have shown that this description is too mechanical. It does little to allow for the fact that human beings are the main players in the model whose behaviour is far from consistently that of *homo economicus*. Social aspects also play an important role. In other words, carrying capacity models do not take into account the way in which prehistoric individuals perceived their environment, while it is just this perception which determines human activity. Nevertheless, carrying capacity models can be useful in directing the course of inquiry. They can define the framework within which calculations may take place.

The carrying capacity of a particular area can be figured in various ways. For agricultural communities, most cal-

culations are based on the amount of arable land necessary per capita, sometimes corrected for several overhead factors. If the surface area of the investigated region is divided by the resulting number, then the maximum carrying capacity (number of persons per area) is known. By calculating in this way, Kooi concluded that there was no reason to assume that during the Late Bronze Age and Early Iron Age in south-eastern Drenthe population pressure necessitated migration to the *terpen*.[3] He based his calculations on the assumption that each settlement required approximately 60 ha of arable land, while there were at least 300 to 400 ha available.

More advanced models have been developed under the heading of 'optimal farming' strategies. With such models, calculations are made (usually with the help of computer simulation) to determine how large an area must be to function as a dwelling and production area for an average farming unit for a certain period of time. The disadvantage of models like this is that they are based on an understanding of the individual as a creature who thinks and acts with optimal economic skill. Theories that are based on these kinds of models therefore lose much of their value when their overly twentieth-century approach is not sufficiently recognized. 'Optimal farming' models can be useful, however, to detect the limits of particular strategies in a particular environment, and that which is presented below must be read as such.

An example of an 'optimal farming' model is the work done by Gregg. Gregg calculated that for the Bandkeramik culture a village with six families or farms (totalling 34 persons) required an area of 6.07 km² to exist.[4] Another example is IJzereef's study of the Bronze Age in West-Friesland.[5] The first model was designed for the loess during a period in which hoe agriculture was used, the second is based on archaeological finds in the clay and sandy clay region of West-Friesland during a period in which the ard was used for ploughing.

For the sandy soils worked by plough agriculture (with the ard) there are other values that apply. Therefore the following section will present a number of calculations aimed at giving an impression of the extent to which agrarian activity on the sandy grounds (with varying ra-

2 Waterbolk 1965–66.
3 Kooi 1979, 170.
4 Gregg 1988, 167. Within this area distinctions were made for arable land, land for houses and gardens, pasture land, meadowland, and woodland used to meet various needs and to

supply building materials. The largest part of the area is taken up by woodland which was also used as forest grazing and which, as a result of degradation in the simulation, has to cover a large area of more than 5 km² in total (Gregg 1988, 165 ff).
5 IJzereef 1981.

tios of arable farming to stock breeding) could have laid claim to the landscape. This is no more than an estimate which is necessary in order to be able to make well-founded judgments about the relation of man to environment in the study area.

9.4 A QUANTITATIVE MODEL FOR AGRICULTURE IN THE NORTHERN SANDY AREA

The following model is an attempt to quantify a number of aspects of the agricultural system from the Bronze Age and the Iron Age. The first task is to analyse how large the households were during each distinct period. A household is understood as the group of people living together in one dwelling unit. Strictly speaking this does not necessarily mean a family, but under actual circumstances that is generally the case.

The next step is to calculate the minimum number of calories needed for a household to stay alive. Then an investigation is made to determine to what extent stock breeding and arable farming can meet this need. An important part of this calculation is the verified size of prehistoric byre houses, upon which are based estimates of the size of the households and the livestock. These give an indication of the share that livestock could have contributed to the food supply. The rest is assumed to have been supplied by arable farming. In this way the structure of the farming economy is assessed. The calculation tables which are thus generated can then be used to determine the surface area of the assumed agricultural system. Finally, on the basis of the presented quantitative model an attempt is made to come to a conclusion about the carrying capacity of the Frisian-Drentian plateau's sandy grounds and about population pressure.

9.4.1 *Size of households*

Estimating the size of the households per farm is usually a question of speculation. No systematic investigation has yet been carried out for the aisled byre houses in the Lower Rhine basin. Such an investigation is indeed almost impossible because direct indications are generally not to be found. Usually an attempt is made to calculate the size of the households on the basis of the

surface area of the houses themselves. However, for the Early Neolithic houses of the Bandkeramik culture Soudsky worked from the principle that the hearth was the focus of the family, and he multiplied the number of hearths in the dwelling part of the house by the number of families. For each hearth there seems to have been an average of 6 m of house available (with a width of 6–7 m). The house lengths vary somewhat, but there is a tendency toward long houses, which means that the households comprised extended families (couples from several generations with their children). The number of persons in such a household averages fifteen.

It is questionable, however, whether this model is applicable for later prehistoric periods, one reason being that beginning with the Bronze Age the types of houses built were farms with a byre included. Initially these structures were rather long (20–30 m), but at the end of the Late Bronze Age they became substantially shorter (10–20 m). Of the houses at Elp, the supposed dwelling parts are generally more than 10 m long, in any case those which Waterbolk now dates to the first part of the Late Bronze Age.[6] There even seems to be a tendency for the dwelling parts to be longer than the byres, while some houses have two hearths. It is quite possible that these large farms offered sufficient room for extended families and that the households comprised ten to fifteen persons.[7]

During the Late Bronze Age and the Early Iron Age the length of the houses decreased and remained 10-20 m throughout the entire Iron Age. In instances where the byre is archaeologically recognizable, however, it appears that the shortening has particular bearing on the dwelling part of the house. The ratio of dwelling to byre is regularly 1:2, although the number of stalls in several cases is also very small.[8] The length of the dwelling parts, 4 to 8 m, seems to indicate that they were generally inhabited by nuclear families.[9]

The caloric requirements for households of varying sizes is shown in table 20. This has been determined on the basis of age according to a table published by Gregg following the norms of the World Health Organization. For infants that requirement is 1000 Kcal per day, for adult males it is 3000–3500 Kcal per day.

6 Waterbolk 1987a.

7 It is important not to dismiss the possibility that farms were lengthened over the course of their existence. This, however, would confirm the hypothesis that they were inhabited by

extended families rather than the other way round.

8 Compare Harsema 1980, 24–5.

9 Two to four adults and three to four children under sixteen years of age.

Table 20 Estimated caloric requirement according to household size. Based on Gregg 1988, table 1.

age class	household size					
	6 persons		10 persons		15 persons	
	number	Kcal / day	number	Kcal / day	number	Kcal / day
0–4 years	2	2 000	1	1 000	3	3 000
5–9 years	1	1 500	2	3 000	3	4 500
10–15 years	1	2 500	2	5 000	2	5 000
adult	2	6 000	5	15 000	7	21 000
total Kcal / day		14 000		24 000		33 500
total Kcal / year		5 110 000		8 670 000		12 227 500

Table 21 Expected annual milk surplus per herd size. Based on IJzereef 1981 and Gregg 1988, table 12.

	herd size			
	10 animals	20 animals	30 animals	40 animals
number of cows / herd	5	7	11	16
number of milk cows	4	5	9	13
annual milk surplus in l (150 l / cow)	600	750	1350	1950
annual milk surplus in Kcal (660 Kcal / liter)	396 000	495 000	891 000	1 287 000

Table 22 Caloric value of meat, fat, and 'rest' products from cattle of different age classes. Based on IJzereef 1981.

	age class		
	0–1 year	1–3 years	adult
average living weight (kg)	35	80	200
meat (kg)	14 (40%)	28 (35%)	60 (30%)
fat (kg)	3.5 (10%)	12 (15%)	40 (20%)
'rest' products (kg)	3.5 (10%)	8 (10%)	20 (10%)
unusable (bones, etc.; kg)	14 (40%)	32 (40%)	80 (40%)
caloric value, meat (Kcal / kg)	1 430	1 700	1 970
caloric value, fat (Kcal / kg)	8 000	8 000	8 000
caloric value, 'rest' products (Kcal / kg)	2 000	2 000	2 000
total caloric value per animal	75 040	159 600	478 000

9.4.2 *Composition of farming activities*

By composition of farming activities is here understood the ratio between arable farming and stock breeding in the mixed farm economy. This ratio is difficult to estimate. Bones can be an indication of the share that livestock contributed to the economy, but usually these have not been found, and so one is dependent on estimates of stable space by which, however, only the contribution made by cattle can be calculated. But considering the fact that cattle were the dominant livestock (at least during the Middle Bronze Age), this need not be problematic. IJzereef is of the opinion that the best model for food production in the Middle Bronze Age in West-Friesland should be based on proportions of 50% meat,

Table 23 Caloric weight of butchered cattle of different age classes per herd size.

age class	herd size							
	10 animals		20 animals		30 animals		40 animals	
	number	Kcal	number	Kcal	number	Kcal	number	Kcal
0–1 year	–	–	1	75 040	2	150 080	3	225 120
1–3 year	1	159 600	3	478 800	7	1 117 200	8	1 276 800
adult	1	478 200	2	957 600	3	1 434 600	4	1 912 800
total	2	637 800	6	1 511 440	12	2 701 880	15	3 414 720

10% milk, and 40% agricultural products, perhaps with a somewhat larger portion of dairy products later on.[10] For the sandy grounds, Harsema sees a totally different ratio between arable farming and stock breeding: 90:10.[11] However, no bone spectrums have been recovered from the sandy soils, making this estimate difficult to substantiate. Although the house plans from the Early and Middle Iron Age generally indicate little stable space, this says little about the ratio of arable farming to stock breeding. The quantitative model below will show that the ratio presented by Harsema puts too much emphasis on arable farming.

The following is an ideal model that attempts to estimate the maximum yield from the agricultural system in caloric values. In this way, an attempt is made to assess the composition of farming activities. First the yield from the livestock component is calculated. If this figure is based on the caloric value of cattle, then two aspects must be taken into account: meat and milk. IJzereef posits a milk surplus of 100 l per cow per year.[12] That is considerably less than Gregg, who figures a lactation period of two hundred days and a surplus of 1.8 l per day, resulting in 340 l per year.[13] It must also be realized that Gregg is working from the assumption that only 50% of the cows produced a surplus of milk. IJzereef's low number can partly be explained by the fact that the

Bronze Age cows that are the subject of his investigation weighed considerably less than Gregg's assumed weight for cows. Accordingly to IJzereef, Bronze Age cows weighed an average of 120 kg,[14] while Gregg assumes a weight of 550 kg. If we figure that a cow weighing less will also give less milk, then IJzereef's and Gregg's numbers are in rather close agreement, although IJzereef's estimate – really an educated guess – is on the low side. A milk surplus of 150 l per cow seems more acceptable and more in agreement with the weight ratios between modern and Bronze Age or Iron Age cows. Table 21 shows what kinds of caloric values milk can produce with varying numbers of livestock and with a milk surplus of 150 l.

In addition, IJzereef gives very precise calculations for the caloric value of meat and fat. In this study only the calculations for cattle are followed, using the sizes and weights of the West-Frisian Bronze Age cow (table 22). It is assumed that these sizes applied to the northern Netherlands as well. The estimate of the number of animals slaughtered per year (table 23) is based on Gregg's tables 17 and 18[15] and not IJzereef's tables, because the latter are not ideal models but are reflections of the situation encountered in Bovenkarspel.

Finally, it is possible to calculate the maximum portion of the dietary requirement that could have been taken up by

10 IJzereef 1981, 191.
11 Harsema 1980.
12 IJzereef 1981, 183.
13 Gregg 1988, 107.
14 Gregg 1981, 104; IJzereef 1981, 60. Although this figure is much lower than all previous estimates, there seems to be little

in this calculation to dispute considering the quality and the quantity of the bone material that IJzereef had at his disposal. Moreover, most of the cited values are for adult steers, which according to IJzereef, in Bovenkarspel varied in weight from 150–360 kg.
15 Gregg 1988, 107.

Table 24 Maximum contribution of livestock in caloric requirements per year expressed in percentages per herd size in relation to household size.

herd size	household size and caloric requirements								
	6 persons 5 110 000 Kcal			10 persons 8 670 000 Kcal			15 persons 12 227 500 Kcal		
	meat	milk	total	meat	milk	total	meat	milk	total
10 animals	12.5 %	7.7 %	20.2 %	7.3 %	4.5 %	11.8 %	5.2 %	3.2 %	8.4 %
20 animals	29.6 %	9.7 %	39.3 %	17.4 %	5.7 %	23.1 %	12.4 %	4.0 %	16.4 %
30 animals	52.9 %	17.4 %	70.3 %	31.2 %	10.3 %	41.5 %	22.1 %	7.3 %	29.4 %
40 animals	66.8 %	25.2 %	92.0 %	39.4 %	14.8 %	54.2 %	27.9 %	10.5 %	38.4 %

animal products. The assumption here is that dairy products were also being used, which strontium analysis has shown to have indeed been the case in West-Friesland.[16] The following considerations play a role in the calculations. In Bovenkarspel, the total amount of livestock during the colonization phase consisted of 78% cattle, 6.7% pig, 12.7% sheep, 0.8% goat, 1.5% dog, and 0.1% horse. During the late occupation phase (the Late Bronze Age), the proportions were 62.8% cattle, 9.1% pig, 22.7% sheep, 1.6% goat, 3.8% dog, and 0.1% horse.[17] The portion of game and fish was small during all periods. The figures for the northern Netherlands cannot simply be extrapolated from these proportions, however, because Bovenkarspel lay in an entirely different landscape, much more comparable with the Frisian salt-marsh area than with the sandy area. The proportion of sheep and pig within the total amount of livestock might have been higher on the sandy grounds. However, this is no reason to suspect that large flocks of sheep existed. The landscape may have been open, but the extensive heathlands that could have supported such flocks probably had not yet developed. The bone spectrums from the western Netherlands indicate that an average of 20% of the total amount of livestock was sheep and pig, peaking at 45% at Assendelft Q.[18] In this last case, however, the percentage is calculated on the basis of a small sample. Taken as a whole, these figures are of limited value for the Drentian sandy grounds. Theoretically, the decrease in the amount of stable space during the Late Bronze Age and Early Iron Age might

point to a reduction in the proportion of cattle within the total amount of livestock. This reduction may have been compensated for by an increase in the portion of arable farming in the farming activities. To fully satisfy caloric requirements, however, high yield factors would then be necessary. For example, table 24 shows that a herd of ten cattle can provide for 20% of the caloric needs for a family of six persons. The remaining 80% could only have been provided by products of arable farming if the yield factor was much higher than the traditionally assumed harvest of three times the amount of sowing seed (section 9.4.3). In such a case 12.9 ha of corn would have to be cultivated, an amount that cannot be harvested by a family of six. A small flock of sheep would then have to be postulated to make up the deficiency. If the harvest factor is changed to 10, however, then it is possible to supply 80% of the dietary requirement with products of arable farming.

On the other hand, it is feasible that the decrease in the amount of byre space was a consequence of the splitting up of the large Middle Bronze Age farms into smaller units. The fact that the dwelling space also became smaller can be advanced to support this hypothesis.

With the information summarized in table 24 it is possible to estimate the composition of the farming activities on the Frisian sandy grounds. It is assumed that the milk was utilized and that at least 10% of the caloric requirements came from other animal products (sheep and pigs). A farm with at least thirty cows and a household of ten to fifteen persons (the average presumed size for

16 Van Wijngaarden-Bakker 1988, 163.
17 IJzereef 1981, 194.

18 Van Wijngaarden-Bakker 1988, 156.

the Middle Bronze Age) can derive 40–50% of its caloric requirement from cattle breeding using an optimum strategy. For the Iron Age, with households of five to eight persons and farms with ten to twenty cows, this dropped to a maximum of 30–40%. Very small farms, which certainly existed at that time, must have produced a higher proportion of products of arable farming unless deriving extra animal products for example by keeping larger flocks of sheep. The latter should not be discounted as an unlikely option, although unfortunately it is not demonstrable on the basis of bone spectra. Another factor which is equally difficult to quantify is the portion of supplementary crops such as tickbean and gold of pleasure.

9.4.3 Size of the area required for living and farming

Calculating the minimum amount of land necessary to run a farm opens up an even larger field for speculation than the size and composition of farming activities. The biggest problem is that only rough estimates can be made, all the more difficult because it is not known how intensively the prehistoric farmer used his land. Moreover, it is almost impossible to include all types of land use in the calculations. For the northern sandy grounds, minimally, the following types were important and are therefore included in the calculations: settlement area; arable land; land for sod cutting; meadowland (after the Late Iron Age); pasture land (grassland, woods, heath); forest for timber (buildings, fences, trackways, and boats) and firewood; forest used as grazing and for leaf fodder.

Settlement area

The size of the settlement area is really not very important in the quantitative models because the surface area is relatively small. The scattered farms which 'wandered' over the landscape until the Roman period would have had plots of land no larger than 0.5–1 ha.

Arable land

Calculating the dimensions of the arable land is a substantial problem. Most studies make use of medieval data on crop yield factors[19] and the necessary amount of sowing seed. Slicher van Bath's agrarian history of western Europe is the most frequently cited source.[20] On the basis of this work, the crop yield factor is usually believed to have been 1:3 or 1:4. A weight of 100 to 200 kg of sowing seed per ha and a yield of 800 to 1000 kg per ha (for barley and emmer wheat respectively, with a crop yield factor of 1:4) is further cited to provide 'hard' figures. There is, however, the tendency to lean towards the most unfavourable figures, probably based on the idea that the prehistoric period was less rose-coloured than the Middle Ages. The crop yield factor is then usually set at three, the lowest figure that Slicher van Bath came across for wheat.[21] This figure, however, does not take into account the fact that these proportions apply in general to broadcast sowing in fields prepared with ploughs equipped with mould boards. In addition, the statistics are influenced by a variety of administrative factors.[22]

Remarkably enough, in making their calculations most archaeologists pass over the results of experimental investigation. Here the work of Reynolds in particular has produced spectacular results.[23] Reynold's experiments, conducted over a period of eight years (1973–1980), show crop yield factors that vary from 1:7 to 1:59, with an average of 1:32 for spelt and 1:34 for wheat, without the use of fertilization. Reynolds describes the soil on which he had conducted his experiments as the poorest imaginable, while it had not been cultivated in at least a century.[24] Most archaeologists do not dare to work with these figures because they seem so extremely high.[25] Reynolds himself cannot explain the reason for these high values, although he suspects that they are due in part to sowing into rows of furrows made with an ard. Historical sources also tell us that these methods led to higher yields.[26] In my opinion, a crop yield factor of at least 1:10 can therefore be expected based on the use of 60 kg of sowing seed per ha, the amount which, according to Reynolds and IJzereef, is optimal for sowing in rows.[27] Table 25 calculates the minimum amount of cultivated arable surface area for various crop yield factors that is necessary to meet the caloric require-

---

19 By crop yield factor is meant the ratio of sowing seed to harvested yields. (Slicher van Bath 1978).

20 Slicher van Bath 1960; 1978.

21 Slicher van Bath 1978, 81 ff.

22 Slicher van Bath 1978, 82 ff. For example, to return lower yields could result in lower taxes.

23 Reynolds 1987.

24 Reynolds 1987.

25 Moreover, Reynolds's work is not well known due to the inadequate publication of the quantitative data.

26 Slicher van Bath 1978, 37.

27 IJzereef 1981; Reynolds 1987.

Table 25 Quantitative model for the necessary amount of arable land on the basis of caloric requirements for a household of five to ten persons (caloric requirement 7,000,000 Kcal / year) and ten to fifteen persons (caloric requirement 10,000,000 Kcal / year) in relation to various crop yield factors. The figures for the surface areas are in ha.

		crop yield factor						
		1:3		1:10		1:20		1:30	
available for consumption per ha (kg)		120		540		1140		1740	
percentage of arable farming:		100%	50%	100%	50%	100%	50%	100%	50%
household size									
5 – 10 persons		17.6	8.3	3.9	2.0	1.9	0.9	1.2	0.6
10 – 15 persons		25.3	12.6	5.6	2.8	2.7	1.3	1.7	0.9

ments.[28] The factor of 1:3 is added for comparison, but it is regarded in this study as unrealistically low.

A crucial question is whether the crops were fertilized or not. IJzereef is convinced that in West-Friesland fertilization was being applied as early as the Bronze Age.[29] In addition, Harck demonstrates that on Archsum fertilization through composting was being carried out during the Bronze Age.[30] Therefore it is likely that fertilization, in whichever form, was an integral part of the agrarian system beginning with the Bronze Age. That does not mean that every field was fertilized each year and was under permanent cultivation, but that a high crop yield factor may be assumed.

Most authors assume that the poverty of the sandy soils made a field system based on a two-field or three-field rotation necessary. The amount of arable land calculated in table 25 should therefore be doubled or tripled to satisfy these conditions. In order to fit sod manuring into the model, at least double the amount of land is necessary for sod cutting.[31] The Celtic field systems require a relatively small amount of land for sod cutting for compost because it is assumed that the fields themselves were the most important source of sods (section 7.8.3). Data concerning the amount of manure necessary per ha

are also available from historical sources. Farmer Hemmema from Hitsum, who kept financial records for his farm at the beginning of the sixteenth century, carefully accounted for the amount of manure he used because he had to buy part of his supply from his neighbours.[32] From these data it can be calculated that in the Middle Ages 60,000–70,000 kg of manure were spread over each ha (80–100 hauls or wagon loads).[33] A cow produces approximately 5000 kg of manure (if all of it is collected); therefore the manure of approximately fourteen cows is needed for 1 ha. If the manure was mixed with straw, less was required, but this kind of manure was considered to be of an inferior quality. These, however, are data that relate to direct fertilization without composting. For sod manuring, Kroll also quotes figures of 30–100 hauls of manure and a ratio of manure to sods of 1:2 to 1:10.[34] IJzereef, on the basis of research into the literature, comes to the conclusion that 10,000 kg of manure per ha for one harvest is a much better figure than the above-mentioned 60,000–70,000.[35] For the Bronze Age he estimates manure production of 2475 kg per cow for animals confined to the byre for a period of 180 days. Even if only half of that could be collected, ten cows could produce enough manure to fertilize 1.25 ha. Using the numbers quoted by

28 The caloric value of grain is fixed at 3300 Kcal (IJzereef 1981). For the Middle Ages, 250 kg of bread grain per year was considered sufficient for an adult in a household that was 100% dependent on grain products (Slicher van Bath 1978, 76). This works out to 2260 Kcal per person per day, somewhat lower than the norm applied here (3000 Kcal per person per day).
29 IJzereef 1981.
30 Harck 1987.
31 According to Kroll (1975, 90), five to twenty times the surface of the arable land was necessary in the Middle Ages,

depending on the intensity of the fertilization. Slicher van Bath (1978, 237), however, prefers proportions of 1:2 to 1:7 for the proportion of arable field : sodded ground.
32 Slicher van Bath 1978, 52 ff.
33 The calculation of kgs per haul involves a number of problems, as Kroll (1975) and Slicher van Bath (1978) demonstrate.
34 Kroll 1987.
35 IJzereef 1981, 190.

Table 26 Estimated amount of pasture land per herd size. The figures for the surface areas are in ha.

type of pasture	herd size			
	10	20	30	40
forest (65%, 2 ha / individual)	6.0	12.0	18.0	24.0
marshland (30%, 1 ha / individual)	3.0	6.0	9.0	12.0
stubble field (5%, 1 ha / individual)	0.5	1.0	1.5	2.0
total	9.5	19.0	28.5	38.0

Kroll and Slicher van Bath, however, 70 Bronze Age cows would be necessary for the same surface area. That is a very high number, and I assume that IJzereef's calculation comes closer to the truth.

Pasture land and meadowland

Because there are so many different kinds of pasture, it is difficult to calculate how much land the cattle must have needed to graze. Cattle today graze on 0.7 ha of grassland per animal, but the quality of the pasture is much higher than it was in prehistoric times.[36] In this regard Henning quotes a number of interesting figures which relate to eastern Prussia in the seventeenth century. Henning is of the opinion that a cow needs the same area of pasture as a horse, two calves or foals, or ten sheep. Such an area comprises 1.16 ha of stubble field per cow, 0.87 ha of marshlands, 0.28 ha of deciduous forest, 0.58 ha of pine, birch, or beech wood in marshlands, or 1.18 ha of pine, birch, or beech wood on dry ground.[37] Naturally, these were areas which had been grazed for centuries and must have been quite open. Slicher van Bath's figures run in the same order of magnitude, at least for grassland. Based on the same sources, Bakels concludes that in the Early Neolithic an adult cow needed at least 1.5 ha of grassland.[38] Gregg's figures, based on the work of Bogucki, are quite

different.[39] Bogucki derives his calculations from current statistics for cows that graze in the American pine forests. These animals need 2.0 ha or more of pasture per month.[40] Bogucki assumes that there was more nutrition available in the European deciduous forests, and therefore reaches the figure of 1 ha per month or 8 ha per year for Neolithic Europe. This results in a strikingly large area of required forest grazing in Gregg's model: 265 ha for a herd of thirty cows. It is true that the Early Neolithic forests were very dense and therefore had less nutritious undergrowth, but the truth probably lies closer to the middle than to the extremes of 1 and 8 ha per year. If the highest extreme is halved, it means that the small Bronze Age cow probably needed no more than 2 ha of forest grazing per year. For grassy pasture land the figure of 1 ha, which IJzereef uses, can be retained, although that figure may be on the high side.[41]

It is almost impossible to reliably estimate the proportions of various landscapes (forest, heath, marshlands, farmland, etc.). Van Zeist is of the opinion that until the Bronze Age only a small amount of grassland appeared in the sandy area.[42] Heath began growing during the Neolithic and would have reached a limited size, but there was probably no extensive heath because the area had not undergone enough intensive development. Moreover, heath is not a major grazing region for cattle because they require feed with higher nutritional value.[43] Forest, marshlands, and fallow fields must therefore have been the most important sources of nutrition for cattle in the summertime, probably in that order of importance. Forests existed in abundance, the marshlands were located beside the stream valleys, and stubble fields were probably only small in surface area. In this study, the ratio forest:marshland:stubble field is set to 60:35:5. Table 26 shows how large the necessary pasture area must be when this ratio is used.[44]

Winter forage for the cattle is an even more important factor in the farmland. Gregg postulates that during the

36 Bakels 1982, 10; IJzereef 1981, 177.
37 Henning 1969, 46.
38 Bakels 1982.
39 Bogucki 1982, 107; Gregg 1988, 106.
40 It is not clear how these extremely high values were reached. It would imply that the modern American cow needs approximately fifteen times as much forest pasture as the European cow in the seventeenth century.
41 IJzereef 1981, 177.
42 Van Zeist 1991.

43 Van Wijngaarden-Bakker 1988, 158.
44 Sheep are not included in the calculation because it is understood that a flock of ten to twenty animals can graze on the available heathland without difficulty. For a larger flock extra heathland should be calculated, but it is assumed that sheep breeding did not play a real role until the Roman period (compare Harsema 1980, 41). The pasturing of pigs is also of minor importance in relation to the demands that cattle make on pasture.

Table 27 Quantitative model for the amount of farmland per farm per herd size using a crop yield factor of 1:10. The figures for the surface areas are in ha.

	herd size							
	10 animals		20 animals		30 animals		40 animals	
household size (persons)	6–8	10–15	6–8	10–15	6–8	10–15	6–8	10–15
ratio stock breeding : arable farming	30:70	20:80	45:55	30:70	75:25	45:55	95:05	55:45
type of farmland								
arable land for grain cultivation (= straw supply)	2.9	4.5	2.3	3.9	1.4	3.1	0.8	2.5
fallow land (= stubble field)	5.8	9.0	4.6	7.8	2.8	6.2	1.6	5.0
marshland (cattle pasture)	3.0	3.0	6.0	6.0	9.0	9.0	12.0	12.0
forest (cattle and pig pasture) / forest (leaf fodder and wattle)	12.0	12.0	24.0	24.0	36.0	36.0	48.0	48.0
forest (timber)	2.0	3.0	2.0	3.0	2.0	3.0	2.0	3.0
heath land (sheep pasture)	2.0	2.0	2.0	2.0	2.0	2.0	2.0	2.0
settlement area	0.5	0.5	1.0	1.0	1.0	1.0	1.0	1.0
total	25.3	35.0	41.9	47.7	54.2	63.9	67.4	75.5
pasture land as percentage of total	67.2%	51.4%	76.4%	69.2%	86.7%	75.1%	91.2%	83.4%
pro memoria								
area used for sod cutting (ratio to arable land under cultivation 1:3)	8.7	13.5	6.9	11.7	4.2	9.3	2.4	7.5
arable land for grain buffer supply	2.9	4.5	2.3	3.9	1.4	3.1	0.8	2.5

four winter months in which the animals were kept in byres, 60% of their feed consisted of hay and 40% of straw.[45] Recent data show that in the Alps an adult cow gets through the winter with 400 kg of hay on an exclusively hay diet, and that the best meadows produce 4000 kg per ha. Marshlands, however, produces 1470 kg per ha, and this is the figure that Gregg uses.[46] The problem arises with the cutting tool that was necessary for gathering hay, preferably a scythe.[47] Scythes were not introduced until the end of the Iron Age, so it must be assumed that in the previous period leaves and twigs were the most important source of winter forage. According to Pott, this form of hay production, 'leaf fothering' or *Schneitelwirtschaft*, together with forest grazing in north-western Europe, constituted the most important use of deciduous forests during the prehistoric period, but it was still being widely practised during the historic period.[48] The branches with their leaves were cut and dried in the late summer; the stripping off of the leaves just before they began to turn colour was also

45 Gregg 1988, 107.
46 Gregg 1988, 107.
47 Apparently Gregg assumes that the sickles used by the people of the Linear Pottery culture for harvesting grain were also used for haymaking. The use of these sickles as grass-cutters has not yet been demonstrated. Perhaps future experimental archaeological research and investigation of use wear traces can focus attention on this aspect. It is not likely that flint sickles continued to be used for harvesting during the Bronze Age and Early Iron Age (Van Gijn 1988); whether bronze sickles can be used for this purpose has never been investigated, as far as I know.
48 Pott 1990, 1.

a known practice which – as historical sources tell us – was carried out during the Late Iron Age and probably much earlier.[49]

I have found no data on the amounts of foliage and the requisite surface area of woodland that were necessary for winter forage. It is plausible that much of the necessary foliage could be cut from the forest grazings and along the stream valleys without assuming a need for extra large areas of woodland. On the other hand, it is also true that the combined practices of grazing cattle and extracting foliage exhausted the forest and brought about a change in its character.[50] For purposes of regeneration it is therefore supposed that a wooded area that was used for a year of grazing was left unused at least for the following year. That means that the amounts of necessary woodland calculated in table 26 must be doubled in table 27.

Forests as a source of wood

Forests were important not only as pasture areas but also as sources of wood suitable for a wide range of uses. Timber for buildings, fences, trackways, and boats is naturally an important factor, but the demand for firewood – especially since the beginning of metal production – must have constituted an enormous assault on the forests. The area of woodland that was necessary for construction wood is difficult to determine because the density of suitable trees differs according to the type of forest. From Bakels's figures it appears that a minimum of 1 ha was required for one house, and that the area probably must have been much greater to meet the total wood requirement.[51] In table 27, 2 ha is regarded as the minimum area of forest that was needed.

9.4.4 *The quantitative aspects summarized*

When all the foregoing data are combined (table 27), an evaluation of the total land use for living and farming can be made. In doing so it must again be emphasized that this is a rough estimate involving an ideal model with minimum values. In my opinion, the most striking result of the above calculations is that with a basic crop

yield factor of 1:10 instead of 1:3 it is the pasture land and meadowland and not the arable land that constitute the crucial land use factor. With a herd of ten cows, approximately 50% of the land usage is taken up by the cattle, but with twenty cows, 80% is required based on the needs of a nuclear family (table 27). If the values from the model are applied to the Celtic field system, the following picture unfolds. When the three-field system is applied, then the cultivated area for a farm with six to eight persons and ten cows must have comprised 8.7 ha of arable land. If the provision of a buffer supply is included in the picture,[52] then the necessary area was approximately 12 ha. The average Celtic field system, which Kooi believes goes with two to three urnfields (representing two to three families each),[53] must have been at least 35–52 ha, or 48–72 ha if a buffer supply is taken into account. If it is assumed that only one Celtic field system existed for each urnfield, the model which Waterbolk uses, then no more than 17–26 (or 24–36) ha of arable land had to be available at one time.[54] Most Celtic field systems are greater in area, some as large as 100 ha, but it should be assumed that such surfaces were not utilized at the same time.

The quantitative model indicates that if one considers only the amount of available arable land (as most authors do), the limits of the environment's carrying capacity were not reached in prehistoric times. If per urnfield a territory of approximately 300 ha was available, then there was indeed sufficient space.[55] Kooi's conclusion that there was no question of population pressure during the Iron Age would be justified following this reasoning. The question, however, is whether the necessary area of farmland was indeed available within these territories. The answer to this question is easily confirmed for the arable land, but the presence of sufficient pasture land was probably a crucial point, just as it was the case in the *marken*.[56] The question, then, is not whether it was possible for arable farming to support the increasing population pressure, but whether the system was flexible enough to support the strain that resulted from the diminished amount of pasture land.

49 Pott 1990, 5.
50 Pott 1990.
51 Bakels 1978; 1982.
52 Gregg proceeds from the supposition that farmers keep, as a minimum, one year's buffer supply of their most important product. That means that they grow twice as much as they need for one year. The consequence of this is that double the

amount of land is needed for cultivation. In table 26 this option is mentioned as a reminder.
53 Kooi 1979, 175.
54 For example Waterbolk 1987.
55 Kooi 1979.
56 Slicher van Bath 1978, 237.

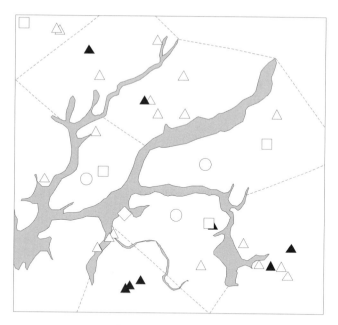

Figure 47 The area around the upper course of the Tjonger in the late Neolithic A. Only in the case of black symbols is the interpretation certain. Legend: triangles: graves; squares: settlements; diamond: hoard; circles: findspots of undetermined nature; broken lines: hypothetical territory boundaries; shaded area: stream valleys.

9.5 TERRITORIALITY AND POPULATION PRESSURE: A REASSESSMENT

When the Frisian-Drentian plateau is considered in its entirety, there is no reason to suppose that in any of the periods studied the limits of the carrying capacity were reached. The economic structure seems to have been stable and, in absolute terms, it offered adequate room to absorb a population forced to leave the peripheral areas. The question, however, is not only whether absorption was possible, but whether it was socially acceptable: how flexible was the territorial structure? For an answer to this question it is necessary to analyse whether the social structure made it possible to absorb gradual population shifts, or even migrations, or whether those

kinds of developments would necessarily lead to tension and conflicts. First, an assessment will be necessary of the scale on which occupation shifts took place.

In Chapter 7 it was stated that a territorial structure had been present on the Frisian-Drentian plateau since the Neolithic. Initially that must have been a very loosely-woven network in which many areas were undivided and, to a certain extent, unused. The same situation can certainly be assumed for the Late Neolithic and Middle Bronze Age. One of the few periods in which the finds distribution permits comment is the Single Grave phase of the Beaker cultures. In this period occupation was spread out over the entire plateau (map III), but not much can be said about the population density. The distribution map covers about five hundred years of occupation and is highly incomplete due to distortion. Only the region around the upper courses of the river Tjonger seem to offer a fairly representative picture.[57] If, by way of exercise, the territories are differentiated on the basis of natural landscape units (fig. 47), each seems to average 15 km². Findspots have been found in all the territories differentiated in this way (predominantly finds associated with graves), with the exception of the north-eastern part. That part forms the presumably uninhabited watershed between the rivers Tjonger and the Peizerdiep. If the finds in each territory are regarded as representative of a settlement unit of ten to fifteen persons, then the number of persons who lived in this area (measuring about 150 km²) was between 100 and 150.[58] It is important to remember, however, that in fact we do not know anything about the settlement system, and that figures such as these are no more than an educated guess which certainly may not be extrapolated: probably the region around the upper courses of the Tjonger were relatively densely populated.

The question was whether the social organization of the society could absorb shifts in the population pattern. The Late Neolithic society can be characterized as a tribal community consisting of self-supporting and autonomous kin groups which were predominantly exogamous. In section 8.5.1, it was shown that relations on the household level probably played a large role. We may

57 There are more clusters that can be pointed out, such as those around the Havelterberg, around the Bisschopsberg, and between the upper course of the Oude Diep and the upper course of the Lits, but the unavoidable question is whether or not research processes are responsible for the clustering. In any case, the cluster around the Havelterberg is the result of the

activities conducted by Voerman and published by Jager (1992).

58 Less than one person per km². For comparison, Kooi (1979, 174) calculated a density of three to four persons per km² for the urnfield period in Drenthe.

thus imagine an extensive network of social relations. It may be assumed that since the introduction of the ard traditional usage rights applied in certain areas, which means that marriage relationships played an important role as social binding agents.[59] The flexibility of the system, social as well as spatial, is contained within this framework. As long as people managed to live within a network of kinship ties, it was probably not difficult to come up with conflict-free solutions to spatial problems. As long as the population in the peripheral areas moved in gradually, there would have been little reason for conflicts. Another situation developed when a particular region such as Gaasterland and the area around St.-Nicholaasga became closed off from the other parts of the plateau by peat accumulation. In that case, the contacts with kin groups that were necessary for social reproduction became endangered. I believe that such a situation arose when these regions were abandoned in *c.* 2500 cal BC. In this case it is not very likely that a gradual movement in the direction of the eastern high sandy grounds took place because in principle there was enough room for a rather large community within these areas (table 19). The threatening isolation of Gaasterland and the already problematic drainage of that area (there are no streams, and the outcropping boulder clay made it ill-suited for arable farming) probably led to the eventual departure. It is likely that this process took place within a few generations. The distribution area of find-spots from the Late Neolithic B and the Early Bronze Age (map IV), however, permits no speculation about the exact moment of this small migration or how it progressed. Presumably it was not a large-scale operation because the region was never densely populated. If there were conflicts, they were probably of a local nature.

Another region that was probably abandoned without it having become completely uninhabitable is the sandy area north of Bergumermeer. It is difficult to pin down a time frame for this occurrence or even an approximation. If we assume that two arrowheads from Oostrum reflect the tip of the iceberg (and the map formation analysis gives every indication that this is so), then this zone was probably still inhabited in the Early Bronze Age. No more finds are known, however, from the Middle Bronze Age and later, and although the archaeological visibility here is low, it can be assumed that this area was then abandoned. The population would have found a new place to settle further south, but again there is no visible indication of the time or the place.

We find that the area north of the Oude Diep is completely without Late Bronze Age finds, and that the zone between the Boorne and the Oude Diep is without Middle Iron Age finds. It is quite possible that this was one of the most important routes to the *terpen* area and that the former inhabitants had moved to that area themselves.

Although the limits of the area's carrying capacity had not been reached, there are enough elements embedded in the developments just described that could have led to increasing tension between groups of people. The grazing of cattle in an area becoming increasingly smaller could have been particularly problematic. Reducing herd sizes and expanding field systems may not have been possible because the system had become dependent on manure production. Certainly in later periods, when the peat was pressing in on all sides, it would have been more and more difficult to come up with conflict-free solutions to problems. In addition, the social structure had become more complex since the Early Iron Age and the territorial structure assumed a more permanent form: the landscape increasingly was becoming a man-made landscape.

The obvious conclusion would be that the tension between inhabitants and environment was solved by the environment itself: after all, the coastal region had become suitable for use just in time. Evidently, the people who were driven out by peat accumulation would have settled in that new area, thus avoiding conflicts with groups of people living on the sandy grounds! However, this kind of reasoning ignores the fact that exploitation of the sand environment demands a completely different economic strategy from exploitation of the clay environment. For this reason, the transfer from one landscape to the other is not something to be taken for granted. In addition, farming communities generally are quite attached to the land that they have always cultivated. Moving to a totally different area, no matter how good the economic perspectives may have been, would not have been a simple matter.

So we are back to one of the problems that has long been a topic of discussion: why was the salt-marsh area colonized, and how should we envisage that colonization process?

59 Goody 1976.

9.6 THE SALT MARSHES: NEW LAND, NEW PERSPECTIVES

We might call Waterbolk's original model, designed to explain the colonization of the salt-marsh area, the environmental crisis model. Its basic premise is that the inhabitants of the western part of the Frisian-Drentian plateau, compelled by advancing peat accumulation, settled in the bordering Drenthe area as early as the Middle Bronze Age. This led to population pressure in that region, resulting in overexploitation of the environment. The danger of reaching the carrying capacity was threatening, and it is taken for granted that the population moved to the clay area – when the salt meadows became inhabitable. In Chapter 8, it was demonstrated that Waterbolk's basic assumption was incorrect: in fact the western part of the Frisian-Drentian plateau was never completely uninhabitable. He appears to have been misled in his interpretation, due to his not including all the finds categories in the picture and to his not taking map formation processes into account.

In Waterbolk's environmental crisis model, the population pressure is the driving force of social change. It is in fact an ingenious model, because Waterbolk did not only assume the overpopulation of the area but he offered proof: the layers of arable covered with drift sand. Van Gijn's investigation, however, showed with certainty that the double podzol sections cannot be dated solely to the Early Iron Age crisis period posited by Waterbolk.[60] So an alternative explanation for migration to the salt-marsh area had to be found. Van Gijn and Waterbolk presented a model to this end in which the salt-marshes were first explored during a period of seasonal grazing before the decision was made to move there permanently.[61]

This transhumance model has its attractive aspects, especially for the initial period, even though it is still based on the assumption that the western part of the Frisian-Drentian plateau had already been abandoned by the Middle Bronze Age and that the original inhabitants had withdrawn to the higher sandy grounds of Drenthe.[62] Seasonal grazing would therefore have taken place mainly from Drenthe. The present study makes clear that the first people to utilize the north-west Frisian clay regions probably did not originate from the eastern but from the western part of the Frisian-Drentian plateau. Indeed, it is quite possible that the salt-marshes were used as seasonal grazing land. It was a new type of landscape whose grassy growth made excellent pasture. The farmers living in the area that bordered on the clay region would certainly have wasted no time putting the land into use. The transition to transhumance is not obvious in this connection, but it is conceivable.

In section 8.9.2, it was already noted that seasonal grazing is a stable system that can persist for centuries without requiring the population to settle in the pasture area. In the present case, the salt meadows were colonized around 550 BC, long after the salt-marsh area came into being. This is not an obvious development, and it demands an explanation.

A factor that undoubtedly presented a problem was the suitability of the clay region for arable farming. The Iron Age colonists who settled there had traditionally practised mixed farming and had always been self-supporting. If they wanted to live permanently in the clay region, then arable farming would have to have been possible there as well. The alternative would have meant regional specialization: the sand farmers could create a surplus of arable products and trade with the clay farmers for their surplus of cattle products, which included manure. This kind of situation would be quite conceivable, certainly in our modern way of thinking, but as a solution at the time of the colonization phase it is out of the question. Regional specialization is something that grows gradually and not something that people decide to. In addition, it creates a relationship of dependence that may have been undesirable. The colonists of the clay region therefore needed the assurance that in their new living area they would have more or less the same opportunities to keep a mixed agrarian farm going as they did on the sandy grounds. They may have tested this possibility during the seasonal grazing period.[63]

The fact that around 550 BC a number of farmers decided to move to the clay area was probably a radical historical decision. The question whether the motivation for the move was the advancing peat area or the good perspectives of the salt-marsh area cannot be answered. A local conflict seems out of the question as a motivation, because it must then be supposed that such a conflict played itself out along the entire Dutch and northern German coastal area.

60 Van Gijn & Waterbolk 1984.
61 Van Gijn & Waterbolk 1984.

62 Waterbolk 1965–66; section 1.4 of this publication.
63 Van Gijn & Waterbolk 1984.

The number of colonists involved in the pioneer phase cannot be known.[64] Local leadership presumably played an important role in this process. Those decisions that were made will have had the character of collective decisions and have required a substantial measure of organization. In my opinion the organization and the decision-making process were guided by a few persons who managed to obtain the loyalty of a group of people on a micro-regional scale. The chieftain's grave at Darp was possibly the last resting place of such a person, although this kind of prestigious burial may point to the existence of leadership at a still higher level.

As far as we now know, the first settlements were concentrated in the southern part of Westergo and a small area in Oostergo (around Hogebeintum). In my opinion, the first settlers originated from the bordering Frisian sandy grounds, and when settlement proved to be successful, colonization took place within a short period of time. That the colonization was a success is evident from the fact that rather quickly characteristic pottery and burial traditions developed which are clearly different from those of the sandy area. This suggests that quite rapidly endogamous communities grew up which probably possessed few kinship ties with the communities of the sandy grounds.

It is not inconceivable that the fortified settlements as well as the *terp* settlements with their many granaries, such as the one at Middelstum,[65] should be interpreted in the light of this regionalization. Gradually, colonization of the salt-marshes could have led to a new kind of conflict in spite of the fact that the population was self-supporting. These conflicts could only have been resisted by a stronger form of organization. Chieftains' houses in the *terpen* and on the sandy grounds, fortified staple places, etc. can be seen as reflections of this development. Although they also fit into the increasing complexity of communities all across western Europe, in my opinion the specific forms in Drenthe and north-western Germany ought to be seen in connection with the slowly developing regional specialization of the coastal region and the sandy grounds.

64 In order to obtain a picture of this period, however, systematic investigation must be carried out into the appearance of Ruinen-Wommels I type pottery with and without sand/grit tempering. It is hoped that Taayke's work will look into these kinds of problems (see Taayke 1988, 54).
65 Boersma 1988.

References

Abler, R., J.S. Adams & P. Gould 1972: *Spatial Organization: the Geographers View of the World*, Londen.

Achterop, S.H., 1960: Een depot van vuurstenen bijlen bij de Reest, *NDV* 78, 179–89.

Achterop, S.H., 1961: Een depot van bijlen uit Boerakker, gem. Marum, *GV* 1961, 158–64.

Achterop, S.H., 1972–73: Stenen bijlen uit de omgeving van het Oude Diep bij Marum, *GV* 1972–73, 143–61.

Achterop, S.H., & J.A. Brongers 1979: Stone Cold Chisels with Handle (Schlägel) in the Netherlands, *BROB* 29, 255–371.

Andersen, S.H., 1975: Ringkloster: en jysk indlandsboplads med Ertebøllekultur, *Kuml* 1973–74, 11–108.

Ascher, R., 1968: Time's Arrow and the Archaeology of a Contemporary Community, in: K.C. Chang (ed.), *Settlement Archaeology*, Palo Alto Ca., 43–52.

Bakel, M.A. van, R.R. Hagesteijn & P. van de Velde (eds) 1986: *Private Politics: a Multi-disciplinary Approach to 'Big-man' Systems*, Leiden (Studies in Human Society, 1).

Bakels, C.C., 1978: *Four Linearbandkeramik Settlements in their Environment: a Paleoecological Study of Sittard, Stein, Elsloo and Hienheim*, Leiden (APL, 11).

Bakels, C.C., 1982: Zum wirtschaftlichen Nutzungsraum einer bandkeramischen Siedlung, in: J. Pavúk (ed.), *Siedlungen der Kultur mit Linearkeramik in Europa: internationales Kolloquium Nové Vozokany 17.–20. November 1981*, Nitra, 9–16.

Bakels, C.C., 1986: Akkerbouw in het moeras?, in: M.C. van Trierum & H.E. Henkes (eds), *Rotterdam Papers*, v: *a Contribution to Prehistoric, Roman and Medieval Archaeology: teksten van lezingen, gehouden tijdens het Symposium Landschap en bewoning rond de mondingen van Rijn, Maas en Schelde te Rotterdam van 5 t/m 6 oktober 1984*, Rotterdam (Rotterdam Papers, 5), 1–6.

Bakhuizen, S.C., 1967: Drie grote vuurstenen bijlen uit de provincie Groningen, *GV* 1967, 125–38.

Bakker, H. de, & J. Schelling 1966: *Systeem van bodemclassificatie voor Nederland: de hogere niveaus*, Wageningen.

Bakker, J.A., 1959: Veenvondsten van de Trechterbekercultuur, in: J.E. Bogaers, W. Glasbergen, P. Glazema & H.T. Waterbolk (eds), *Honderd eeuwen Nederland*, The Hague (Antiquity and Survival, 2: 5–6), 93–9.

Bakker, J.A., 1979: *The TRB West Group: Studies in the Chronology and Geography of the Makers of the Hunebeds and Tiefstich Pottery*, Amsterdam (Cingula, 5).

Bakker, J.A., 1982: TRB-settlement Patterns on the Dutch Sandy Soils, *APL* 15, 87–124.

Bakker, J.A., & J.D. van der Waals 1973: Denekamp-Angelslo: Cremations, Collared Flasks and a Corded Ware Sherd in Dutch Final TRB Contexts, in: G. Daniel & P. Kjærum (eds), *Megalithic Graves and Ritual: Papers Presented at the III Atlantic Colloquium, Moesgård, 1969*, Copenhagen, 17–50.

Barker, G., 1985: *Prehistoric Farming in Europe*, Cambridge (New Studies in Archaeology).

Baudou, E., 1985: Archaeological Source Criticism and the History of Modern Cultivation in Denmark, in: K. Kristiansen (ed.), *Archaeological Formation Processes: the Representativity of Archaeological Remains from Danish Prehistory*, Copenhagen, 63–80.

Berg, A. van den, J. van Lith & J. Roos 1985: Toepassing van het computerprogramma MAP2 in het landschapsbouwkundig onderzoek, *Landschap* 2, 278–93.

Beuker, J.R., 1991: De pijlen van een stamhoofd, *NDV* 108, 97–103.

Binford, L.R., 1965: Archaeological Systematics and the Study of Culture Process, *American Antiquity* 31, 203–10.

Binford, L.R., 1972: Mortuary Practices: their Study and their Potential, in: L.R. Binford, *An Archaeological Perspective*, New York & London (Studies in Archeology), 208–43.

Binford, L.R., 1981: Behavioral Archaeology and the 'Pompeii Premise', *Journal of Anthropological Research* 37, 195–208.

Bloch, M., 1971: *Placing the Dead*, London, *etc.*

Bloch, M., 1975: Property and the End of Affinity, in: M. Bloch (ed.), *Marxist Analysis and Social Anthropology*, London, 203–28.

Bloemers, J.H.F., 1986: A Cart Burial from a Small Middle Iron Age Cemetery in Nijmegen, in: M.A. van Bakel, R.R. Hagesteijn & P. van de Velde (eds), *Private Politics: a Multi-disciplinary Approach to 'Big-man' Systems*, Leiden (Studies in Human Society, 1), 76–95.

Boeles, P.C.J.A., 1927: *Friesland tot de elfde eeuw: zijn oudste beschaving en geschiedenis*, The Hague.

Boeles, P.C.J.A., 1951: *Friesland tot de elfde eeuw: zijn vóór- en vroege geschiedenis* (2nd edn of Boeles 1927), The Hague.

Boersma, J.W., 1988: De datering van een vuurstenen sikkel van Middelstum-Boerdamsterweg, in: M. Bierma & A.T. Clason (eds), *Terpen en wierden in het Fries-Groningse kustgebied*, Groningen, 31–5.

Bogucki, P.I., 1982: *Early Neolithic Subsistence and Settlement in the Polish Lowlands*, Oxford (BAR Int. Ser., 150).

Boserup, E., 1965: *The Conditions of Agricultural Growth: the Economics of Agrarian Change under Population Pressure*, London.

Bourdieu, P., 1977: *Outline of a Theory of Practice*, Cambridge.

Bouwer, K., 1970: *Cultuurlandschapsvormen aan de westzijde van het Drents plateau*, Groningen.

Bradley, R., 1982: The Destruction of Wealth in Later Prehistory, *Man* n.s. 17, 108–22.

Bradley, R., 1984: *The Social Foundations of Prehistoric Britain: Themes and Variations in the Archaeology of Power*, London & New York (Longman Archaeology Series).

Bradley, R., 1990: *The Passage of Arms: an Archaeological Analysis of Prehistoric Hoards and Votive Deposits*, Cambridge.

Brandt, K.H., 1967: *Studien über steinerne Äxte und Beile der jüngeren Steinzeit und der Stein-Kupferzeit Nordwestdeutschlands*, Hildesheim (Münstersche Beiträge zur Vorgeschichtsforschung, 2).

Brandt, K.H., 1976: Derivate neolithischer Streitäxte im nordwestdeutschen Raum, *Jahresschrift für mitteldeutsche Vorgeschichte* 60, 263–84.

Brandt, R.W., 1987: Aardewerk uit enkele bronstijd-nederzettingen in West-Friesland, in: J.H.F. Bloemers (ed.), *Archeologie en oecologie van Holland tussen Rijn en Vlie*, Assen & Maastricht (Studies in Prae- en Protohistorie, 2), 206–67.

Briard, J., 1979: *The Bronze Age of Barbarian Europe: from Megaliths to the Celts*, London.

Brindley, A.L., 1986 (1988): The Typochronology of TRB West Group Pottery, *Palaeohistoria* 28, 93–132.

Broadbent, N., 1975–77: Perforated Stones, Antlers and Stone Picks: Evidence for the Use of the Digging Stick in Scandinavia and Finland, *TOR* 17, 63–106.

Broeke, P.W. van den, 1979: Een depot met vuurstenen bijlen uit het Eenerveld bij Een, gem. Norg, *NDV* 96, 105–15.

Broeke, P.W. van den, 1986: Zeezout: een schakel tussen west- en zuid-Nederland in de ijzertijd en de Romeinse tijd, in: M.C. van Trierum & H.E. Henkes (eds), *Rotterdam Papers, V: a Contribution to Prehistoric, Roman and Medieval Archaeology: teksten van lezingen, gehouden tijdens het Symposium Landschap en bewoning rond de mondingen van Rijn, Maas en Schelde te Rotterdam van 5 t/m 6 oktober 1984*, Rotterdam (Rotterdam Papers, 5), 91–114.

Brongers, J.A., 1976: *Air Photography and Celtic Field Research in the Netherlands*, Amersfoort (Nederlandse oudheden, 6).

Brunn, W.A. von, 1968: *Mitteldeutsche Hortfunde der jüngeren Bronzezeit*, Berlin (Römisch-Germanische Forschungen, 29).

Burrough, P.A., 1987: *Principles of Geographical Information Systems for Land Resources Assessment* (2nd edn), Oxford.

Bursch, F.C., 1936: Grafvormen van het noorden, *OML* 17, 53–72.

Butler, J.J., 1961: De Noordnederlandse fabrikanten van bijlen in de late bronstijd en hun produkten, *NDV* 79, 199–233.

Butler, J.J., 1963a: *Bronze Age Connections across the North Sea: a Study in Prehistoric Trade and Industrial Relations between the British Isles, the Netherlands, North Germany and Scandinavia*, Groningen (Palaeohistoria, 9).

Butler, J.J., 1963b: Ook in de oudere bronstijd bronsbewerking in Noord-Nederland?, *NDV* 81, 181–212.

Butler, J.J., 1969: *Nederland in de bronstijd*, Bussum (Fibula-reeks, 31).

Butler, J.J., 1973a: Einheimische Bronzebeilproduktion im Niederrhein-Maasgebiet, *Palaeohistoria* 15, 319–43.

Butler. J.J., 1973b: The Big Bronze Knife from Hardenberg, in: W.A. van Es *et al.* (eds), *Archeologie en historie: opgedragen aan H. Brunsting bij zijn zeventigste verjaardag*, Bussum, 15–27.

Butler, J.J., 1986 (1988): Drouwen: End of a 'Nordic' Rainbow?, *Palaeohistoria* 28, 133–68.

Butler, J.J., & J.D. van der Waals 1966 (1967): Bell Beakers and Early Metal-working in the Netherlands, *Palaeohistoria* 12, 41–139.

Butzer, K.W., 1982: *Archaeology as Human Ecology*, Cambridge.

Buurman, J., 1990 (1992): Carbonised Plant Remains and Phosphate Analysis of two Roman Period House Plans with sunken Byres at Oosterhout, *BROB*, 285–96.

Carlstein, T., 1982: *Time Resources, Society and Ecology: on the Capacity for Human Interaction in Space and Time*, I: *Preindustrial Societies*, London.

Carneiro, R.L., 1970: A Theory of the Origin of the State, *Science* 169, 733–8.

Casparie, W.A., 1990: Het veen, in: W.A.B. van der Sanden (ed.), *Mens en moeras: veenlijken in Nederland van de bronstijd tot en met de Romeinse tijd*, Assen (Monografieën van het Drents Museum, 1), 26–45.

Casparie, W.A., B. Mook-Kamps, R.M. Palfenier-Vegter, P.C. Struijk & W. van Zeist 1977: The Palaeobotany of Swifterbant: a Preliminary Report (Swifterbant Contribution, 7), *Helinium* 17, 28–55.

Casparie, W.A., & W. Groenman-Van Waateringe 1980: Palynological Analyses of Dutch Barrows, *Palaeohistoria* 22, 7–65.

Champion, T., C. Gamble, S. Shennan & A. Whittle 1984: *Prehistoric Europe*, London.

Chapman, R., 1981: The Emergence of Formal Disposal Areas and the 'Problem' of Megalithic Tombs in Prehistoric Europe, in: R. Chapman, I. Kinnes & K. Randsborg (eds), *The Archaeology of Death*, Cambridge (New Directions in Archaeology), 71–81.

Chatwin, B., 1987: *The Songlines*, London.

Clarke, D.L., 1972: A Provisional Model of an Iron Age Society and its Settlement System, in: D.L. Clarke (ed.), *Models in Archaeology*, London, 801–69.

Clarke, D.L., 1973: Archaeology: the Loss of Innocence, *Antiquity* 47, 6–18.

Clarke, D.L., 1976: The Beaker Network – Social and Economic Models, in: J.N. Lanting & J.D. van der Waals (eds), *Glockenbecher Symposium Oberried 1974*, Bussum & Haarlem, 459–77.

Clarke, D.L., 1978: *Analytical Archaeology* (2nd rev. edn), London.

Clason, A.T., 1981: *Voorlopige determinatie van de zoogdierbotten van Oldeboorn*, Groningen (unpublished report BAI).

Clason, A.T., 1983 (1986): Spoolde: Worked and Unworked Antlers and Bone Tools from Spoolde, de Gaste, the IJsselmeerpolders and Adjacent Areas, *Palaeohistoria* 25, 77–130.

Clason, A.T., & D.C. Brinkhuizen 1978: Swifterbant, Mammals, Birds, Fishes: a Preliminary Report (Swifterbant Contribution, 8), *Helinium* 18, 69–82.

Cleveringa, P., 1978: Pollenanalytische gegevens van de Wold Formatie in noordoost-Friesland, in: J.W. Griede, *Het ontstaan van Frieslands noordhoek: een fysisch-geografisch onderzoek naar de holocene ontwikkeling van een zeekleigebied*, Amsterdam, 140–7.

Cnossen, J., 1971: *De bodem van Friesland: toelichting bij blad 2 van de Bodemkaart van Nederland, schaal 1:200 000*, Wageningen.

Coles, J.M., & A.F. Harding 1979: *The Bronze Age in Europe: an Introduction to the Prehistory of Europe c. 2000–700 BC*, London.

Cowen, J.D., 1967 (1968): The Hallstatt Sword of Bronze: on the Continent and in Britain, *PPS* 33, 377–454.

Daniels, S.G.H., 1972: Research Design Models, in: D.L. Clarke (ed.), *Models in Archaeology*, London, 201–29.

Davidsen, K., 1978: *The Final TRB Culture in Denmark: a Settlement Study*, Copenhagen (Arkaeologiske studier, 5).

Deckers, P.H., 1986: *Coded Culture: Studies in Neolithic Flint*, I, *Constructing the Descriptive System*, Groningen.

Deckers, P.H., J.P. de Roever & J.D. van der Waals 1980 (1981): Jagers, vissers en boeren in een prehistorisch getijdengebied bij Swifterbant, *Jaarboek zwo* 1980, 111–44.

Demoed, H.B., 1989: De markeverdelingen in Drenthe in de 19de eeuw, *NDV* 106, 58–73.

Dodewaard, E. van, 1966: *De bodemgesteldheid van het ruilverkavelingsgebied Boornbergum*, Wageningen (Stibokarapport, 681).

Dodewaard, E. van, & G. Rutten 1977: *De bodemgesteldheid van het ruilverkavelingsgebied Midden-Opsterland*, Wageningen (Stibokarapport, 1278).

Dontje, K., & G. Rutten 1974: *De bodemgesteldheid van het ruilverkavelingsgebied Haulerwijk*, Wageningen (Stibokarapport, 1083).

Drenth, E., & E. Lohof in press: Burial Ritual in the Late Neolithic, the Early and Middle Bronze Age, in: L.P. Louwe Kooijmans, P.W. van den Broeke, H. Fokkens, & A.L. van Gijn (eds), *The Prehistory of the Netherlands*, Amsterdam.

Duinen, L. van, & W. van Zeist 1960: Some Pollen Diagrams from the Clay District in the Provinces of Groningen, Friesland and North-Holland (Netherlands), *Palaeohistoria* 8, 127–37.

Eekhof, W., 1849–59: *Nieuwe atlas van de provincie Friesland*, Leeuwarden.

Elzinga, G., 1964: *Fynsten út Fryske groun*, Leeuwarden (Bûnte liuwen, lân en folk yn wurd en byld, 9).

Elzinga, G., 1973: Een kringgreppelurnenveld bij Oosterwolde in Friesland, in: W.A. van Es *et al.* (eds), *Archeologie en historie: opgedragen aan H. Brunsting bij zijn zeventigste verjaardag*, Bussum, 29–47.

Es, W.A. van, 1960: *De Romeinse muntvondsten uit de drie noordelijke provincies: een periodisering der relaties*, Groningen (Scripta Academica Groningana).

Es, W.A. van, 1967: *Wijster: a Native Village Beyond the Imperial Frontier 150–425 A.D.*, Groningen (Palaeohistoria, 11).

Es, W.A. van, 1972: *De Romeinen in Nederland*, Bussum.

Es, W.A. van, H. Sarfatij & P.J. Woltering 1988: *Archeologie in Nederland: de rijkdom van het bodemarchief*, Amsterdam.

Flannery, K.V., 1976: Evolution of Complex Settlement Systems, in: K.V. Flannery (ed.), *The Early Mesoamerican Village*, New York, 162–73.

Fokkens, H., 1978: *Veldwerkverslag van een boorcampagne ten behoeve van nederzettingsonderzoek nabij Swifterbant (O.Fl.), 1–18 juni 1977*, Groningen (internal report BAI).

Fokkens, H., 1982 (1985): Late Neolithic Occupation near Bornwird (Province of Friesland), *Palaeohistoria* 24, 91–113.

Fokkens, H., 1986: From Shifting Cultivation to Short Fallow Cultivation: Late Neolithic Change in the Netherlands Reconsidered, in: H. Fokkens, P.M. Banga & M. Bierma (eds), *Op zoek naar mens en materiële cultuur: feestbundel aangeboden aan J.D. van der Waals ter gelegenheid van zijn emeritaat*, Groningen, 5–21.

Fokkens, H., 1991a: Nederzettingssporen uit de bronstijd en de vroege ijzertijd in Oss-Ussen, wijk Mikkeldonk, in: H. Fokkens & N. Roymans (eds), *Nederzettingen uit de bronstijd en de vroege ijzertijd in de Lage Landen*, Amersfoort (NAR, 13), 93–109.

Fokkens, H., 1991b: Bronze Age Settlements in the Netherlands, in: C. Chevillot & A. Coffyn (eds), *L'age du bronze Atlantique : ses faciès de l'Ecosse à l'Andalousie et leurs relations avec le bronze continental et la Méditerranée : actes du 1er colloque du Parc Archéologique de Beynac*, Beynac, 77–86.

Fokkens, H., & A.L. van Gijn in prep.: *Mesolithic, Neolithic and Bronze Age Extraction Camps near Oldeboorn (Friesland)*.

Fokkens, H., & C. Schinkel 1990: Neolithische slijpstenen uit de provincie Friesland, *De vrije Fries* 70, 39–52.

Foley, R., 1981: Off-Site Archaeology: an Alternative Approach for the Short-sited, in: I. Hodder, G. Isaac & N. Hammond (eds), *Pattern of the Past: Studies in Honour of David Clarke*, Cambridge, 157–83.

Fowler, P.J., 1983: *The Farming of Prehistoric Britain*, Cambridge.

Fried, M., 1967: *The Evolution of Political Society: an Essay in Political Anthropology*, New York.

Gerdsen, H., 1986: *Studien zu den Schwertgräbern der älteren Hallstattzeit*, Mainz a. R.

Giffen, A.E. van, 1918–19: Iets over terpen, *Jaarverslag van de Vereniging voor terpenonderzoek* 3, 9–31.

Giffen, A.E. van, 1924: Het verstoorde hunebed op de Eeze bij Steenwijk, *Verslagen en mededelingen van de Vereniging tot beoefening van Overijsselsch regt en geschiedenis* 41, 56–71.

Giffen, A.E. van, 1925a: Een kringgrepurnenveld te Oosterwolde, *Oudheidkundig jaarboek* 5, 152–7.

Giffen, A.E. van, 1925–27: *De hunebedden in Nederland*, vols I, II, and atlas, Utrecht.

Giffen, A.E. van, 1929: Grafheuvels in Oosterwolde: opgravingen in 1928, *De vrije Fries* 29, 37–60.

Giffen, A.E. van, 1938: Das Kreisgraben-Urnenfeld bei Vledder, Provinz Drente, Niederlande, *Mannus: Zeitschrift für Deutsche Vorgeschichte* 30, 331–84.

Giffen, A.E. van, 1951: De Havelterberg en omgeving bij Havelte, gem. Havelte: opgravingen in 1918, 1943, 1944 en 1946, *NDV* 69, 97–162.

Giffen, A.E. van, 1954: Praehistorische huisvormen op de zandgronden, *NKJ* 5, 11–40.

Giffen, A.E. van, 1958: Prähistorische Hausformen auf Sandböden in den Niederlanden, *Germania* 36, 35–71.

Gifford, D.P., 1978: Ethnoarchaeological Observations of Natural Processes Affecting Cultural Materials, in: R.A. Gould (ed.), *Explorations in Ethnoarchaeology*, Albuquerque, 77–101.

Gijn, A.L. van, 1988: The Use of Bronze Age Flint Sickels in the Netherlands: a Preliminary Report, in: S. Beyries (ed.), *Industries lithiques : tracéologie et technologie*, I : *aspects archéologiques*, Oxford (BAR Int. Ser., 411: I), 197–218.

Gijn, A.L. van, & H.T. Waterbolk 1984 (1986): The Colonization of the Salt Marshes of Friesland and Groningen: the Possibility of a Transhumant Prelude, *Palaeohistoria* 26, 101–22.

Goody, J., 1976: *Production and Reproduction: a Comparative Study of the Domestic Domain*, Cambridge.

Gregg, S.A., 1988: *Foragers and Farmers: Population Interaction and Agricultural Expansion in Prehistoric Europe*, Chicago (Prehistoric Archaeology and Ecology).

Gregory, C.A., 1980: Gifts to Men and Gifts to Gods: Gift Exchange and Capital Accumulation in Contemporary Papua, *Man*, 15, 626–52.

Gregory, C.A., 1982: *Gifts and Commodities*, London.

Griede, J.W., 1978: *Het ontstaan van Frieslands noordhoek: een fysisch-geografisch onderzoek naar de holocene ontwikkeling van een zeekleigebied*, Amsterdam.

Griede, J.W., & W. Roeleveld 1982: De geologische en paleogeografische ontwikkeling van het noordelijk kleigebied, *Geografisch tijdschrift*, n.r., 16, 439–55.

Groot, T.A.M. de, *et al.* 1987: *Blad Heerenveen West (11 W) en Heerenveen Oost (11 O)*, Haarlem, (Toelichtingen bij de Geologische Kaart van Nederland 1:50.000).

Haans, J.F.C.M., 1951: *De bodemgesteldheid van het DUW ontginningsobject Haskerveenpolder*, Wageningen (Stibokarapport, 258).

Haarnagel, W., 1965: Die Grabung auf der Heidenschanze bei Wesermünde im Jahre 1958, in: R. von Uslar (ed.), *Studien aus Alteuropa*, II, (Festschrift K. Tackenberg), Cologne (Beihefte der Bonner Jahrbücher, 10: II), 142–78.

Haarnagel, W., 1979: *Die Grabung Feddersen Wierde: Methode, Hausbau, Siedlungs- und Wirtschaftsformen sowie Sozialstruktur*, Wiesbaden (Feddersen Wierde, 2).

Haarnagel, W., & P. Schmid, 1984: Siedlungen, in: G. Kossack *et al.* (eds), *Archäologische und naturwissenschaftliche Untersuchungen an ländlichen und frühstädtischen Siedlungen im deutschen Küstengebiet vom 5.Jahrhundert v. Chr. bis zum 11.Jahrhundert n. Chr.*, I: *Ländliche Siedlungen*, Weinheim, 167–244.

Hamond, F.W., 1978: *The Simulation of Early Neolithic Settlement Development in the Lower Rhine Basin*, Cambridge.

Hamond, F.W., 1980: The Interpretation of Archaeological Distribution Maps: Biases Inherent in Archaeological Fieldwork, *Archaeo-Physika* 7, 193–216.

Hansen, M., 1985: Grave Mounds, Battle Axes and Pottery of the Single-grave Culture from South-west Jutland, in: K. Kristiansen (ed.), *Archaeological Formation Processes: the Representativity of Archaeological Remains from Danish Prehistory*, Copenhagen, 89–101.

Harck, O., 1987: Archäologisches zur Kenntnis des vor- und frühgeschichtlichen Ackerbaus, in: G. Kossack, O. Harck & J. Reichstein (eds), *Archsum auf Sylt*, II: *Landwirtschaft und Umwelt in vor- und frühgeschichtlicher Zeit*, Mainz a.R. (Römisch-germanische Forschungen, 44), 1–50.

Harrison, R.J., 1980: *The Beaker Folk: Copper Age Archaeology in Western Europe*, London.

Harsema, O.H., 1974: Archeologisch onderzoek op het Hijkerveld, gem. Beilen: voorlopig bericht van de campagnes 1969 en 1970, *NDV* 91, 161–8.

Harsema, O.H., 1979a: Het neolithische vuursteendepot, gevonden in 1940, bij Een, gem. Norg, *NDV* 96, 117–28.

Harsema, O.H., 1979b: *Maalstenen en handmolens in Drenthe: van het neolithicum tot ca. 1300 AD*, Assen (Museumfonds, 5).

Harsema, O.H., 1980: Het Drents plateau, in: M. Chamalaun & H.T. Waterbolk (eds), *Voltooid verleden tijd?: Een hedendaagse kijk op de prehistorie*, Amsterdam, 83–102.

Harsema, O.H., 1987: Change and Continuity in Rural Settlement in Drenthe from the Neolithic onwards: a Reconsideration of Traditional and Current Opinions, *Palaeohistoria* 29, 103–18.

Harsema, O.H., 1988: *Borger ruim 5000 jaar geleden: de Drentse samenleving in Europees perspectief*, Borger ('De Zwerfsteen' – Historisch tijdschrift voor de gemeente Borger, 88: 4; Flint'nhoesreeks, 4).

Harsema, O.H., 1991: De bronstijd-bewoning op het Hijkerveld bij Hijken, in: H. Fokkens & N. Roymans (eds), *Nederzettingen uit de bronstijd en de vroege ijzertijd in de Lage Landen*, Amersfoort (NAR, 13), 21–9.

Heidinga, H.A., 1987: *Medieval Settlement and Economy North of the Lower Rhine: Archeology and History of Kootwijk and the Veluwe (the Netherlands)*, Assen, Maastricht & Wolfeboro (USA) (Cingula, 9).

Henning, F.W., 1969: *Bauernwirtschaft und Bauerneinkommen in Ostpreussen in 18. Jahrhundert*, Würzburg (Beihefte zum Jahrbuch der Albertus-Universität Königsberg).

Heringa, J., 1985: Lijnen en stippellijnen in de geschiedenis van de buurschap, *NDV* 102, 69–93.

Heyink, W., 1960: *De bodemgesteldheid van het ruilverkavelingsgebied 'Gaasterland'*, Wageningen (Stibokarapport, 532).

Hodder, I., 1979: Economic and Social Stress and Material Culture Patterning, *American Antiquity* 44, 446–54.

Hodder, I., 1986: *Reading the Past: Current Approaches to Interpretation in Archaeology*, Cambridge.

Hodder, I., & C. Orton 1976: *Spatial Analysis in Archaeology*, Cambridge.

Hogestijn, J.W.H., 1990: From Swifterbant to TRB in the IJssel-Vecht Basin – Some Suggestions, in: D. Jankowska (ed.), *Die Trichterbecherkultur: neue Forschungen und Hypothesen*, I, *Material des internationalen Symposiums Dymaczewo, 20–24 September 1988*, Poznań, 163–80.

Hogestijn, J.W.H., 1992: Functional Differences between some Settlements of the Single Grave Culture in the Northwestern Coastal Area of the Netherlands, in: M. Buchvaldek & C. Strahm (eds), *Die kontinentaleuropäischen Gruppen der Kultur mit Schnurkeramik: Schnurkeramik-Symposium 1990*, Prague (Praehistorica, 19), 199–205.

Hole, F., & R.F. Heizer 1973: *An Introduction to Prehistoric Archaeology* (3d edn), New York, *etc.*.

Højlund, F., 1975: Stridsøksekulturens Flintøkser og -Mejsler, *Kuml* 1973–74, 179–96.

Huguenin, 1820–24: see Koeman 1963.

Hulst, R.S., & A.D. Verlinde 1976: Geröllkeulen aus Overijssel und Gelderland, *BROB* 26, 93–126.

Hulst, R.S., & A.D. Verlinde 1979: Spitzhauen aus den Niederlanden, *BROB* 29, 185–207.

Hurk, J.A. van den, & H. Makken 1964: *De bodemgesteldheid van het ruilverkavelingsgebied Jubbega-Schurega*, Wageningen (Stibokarapport, 607).

Hurk, J.A. van den, & J.H. Kalkdijk 1963: *De bodemgesteldheid van het ruilverkavelingsgebied Ooststellingwerf-zuid*, Wageningen (Stibokarapport, 600).

Huijts, C.S.T.J., 1992: *De voor-historische boerderijbouw in Drenthe: reconstructiemodellen van 1300 vóór tot 1300 na Chr.*, Arnhem.

Hvass, S., 1988: The Status of the Iron Age Settlement in Denmark, in: M. Bierma, O.H. Harsema & W. van Zeist (eds), *Archeologie en landschap: bijdragen aan het gelijknamige symposium gehouden op 19 en 20 oktober 1987, ter gelegenheid van het afscheid van H.T. Waterbolk...*, Groningen, 97–132.

IJzereef, G.F., 1981: *Bronze Age Animal Bones from Bovenkarspel: the Excavation at Het Valkje*, Amersfoort (Nederlandse oudheden, 10; Project Noord-Holland, 1).

IJzereef, G.F., & J.F. van Regteren Altena 1991: Nederzettingen uit de midden- en late bronstijd bij Andijk en Bovenkarspel, in: H. Fokkens & N. Roymans (eds), *Nederzettingen uit de bronstijd en de vroege ijzertijd in de Lage Landen*, Amersfoort (NAR, 13), 61–81.

Ingold, T., 1987: *Hunters in Transition*, London.

Iterson Scholten, F.R. van, & W.H. de Vries-Metz 1981: A Late Neolithic Settlement at Aartswoud, I, *Helinium* 21, 105–35.

Jager, S.W., 1981: Een grote vuurstenen bijl en een 'Plättbolzen' uit Fochteloo, gem. Ooststellingwerf, prov. Friesland, *Helinium* 21, 227–45.

Jager, S.W., 1992: *Havelte – rondom de Havelterberg – een archeologische kartering, inventarisatie en waardering*, Amersfoort (NAR, 14).

Janssen, L.J.F., 1850: Het hunebed te Rijs, in Gaasterland (1), *De vrije Fries* 5, 338–50.

Jelgersma, S., & J.B. Breewer 1975: Toelichting bij de kaart glaciale verschijnselen gedurende het Saalien, 1:600.000, in: W.N. Zagwijn & J.C. van Staalduinen (eds), *Toelichting bij geologische overzichtskaarten van Nederland*, Haarlem, 93–103.

Jensen, J., 1987 (1988): Bronze Age Research in Denmark 1970–1985, *Journal of Danish Archaeology* 6, 155–74.

Johansson, L., 1979: *Socio-ekonomiska strukturer i tidigt neolitikum och deras förutsättningar: Studier över Bistoft LA II – ett boplatsfynd fran Schleswig-Holstein*, Göteborg.

Johnson, G.A., 1982: Organizational Structure and Scalar Stress, in: C. Renfrew, M.J. Rowlands & B. Abott Segraves (eds), *Theory and Explanation in Archaeology: the Southampton Conference*, London, 389–421.

Jungerius, E., 1988: *Wassenaar-Weteringpark: een nederzettingsterrein en groepsbegraving uit de vroege bronstijd*, Leiden (internal report IPL).

Kaelas, L., 1983: Megaliths of the Funnel Beaker Culture in Germany and Scandinavia, in: C. Renfrew (ed.), *The Megalithic Monuments of Western Europe: the Latest Evidence Presented by Nine Leading Authorities*, London, 77–91.

Kastelijn, H.W., 1982: *Archeozoölogische vondsten van de opgraving in Oldeboorn 1980*, Groningen (internal report BAI).

Kersten, W., 1948: Die niederrheinische Grabhügelkultur: zur Vorgeschichte des Niederrheins im 1.Jahrtausend v.Chr., *BJ* 148, 5–80.

Kielman, D., 1986: The Postholes of Kolhorn (Northern Site): Preliminary Data Analysis and Pattern Recognition, in: H. Fokkens, P. Banga & M. Bierma (eds), *Op zoek naar mens en materiële cultuur: feestbundel aangeboden aan J.D. van der Waals ter gelegenheid van zijn emeritaat*, Groningen, 21–36.

Koeman, C, 1963: *Handleiding voor de studie van de topografische kaarten van Nederland 1750–1850*, Groningen.

Kooi, P.B., 1979: *Pre-Roman Urnfields in the North of the Netherlands*, Groningen.

Kooi, P.B., 1983 (1984): A Remarkable Iron Age Grave in Darp (Municipality of Havelte, The Netherlands), *OML* 64, 197–208.

Kooi, P.B., 1986: Peelo, 4000 jaar continuïteit?, *Westerheem* 35, 141–51.

Kooi, P.B., 1991: Een nederzetting uit de midden-bronstijd op het Huidsbergsveld bij Dalen, *NDV* 108, 104–17.

Kooi, P.B., G. Delger & K. Klaasens 1987: A Chieftain's Residence at Peelo?: A Preliminary Report on the 1987 Excavations, *Palaeohistoria* 29, 133–44.

Kooi, P.B., & G.J. de Langen 1987: Bewoning in de vroege ijzertijd op het Kleuvenveld te Peelo (gem. Assen), *NDV* 104, 151–65.

Kossack, G., K-E. Behre & P. Schmid (eds) 1984: *Archäologische und naturwissenschaftliche Untersuchungen an ländlichen und frühstadtischen Siedlungen im deutschen Küstengebiet vom 5.Jahrhundert v. Chr. bis zum 11.Jahrhundert n. Chr.*, 1: *Ländliche Siedlungen*, Weinheim.

Kristiansen, K., 1978: The Consumption of Wealth in Bronze Age Denmark, in: K. Kristiansen & C. Paludan-Müller (eds), *New Directions in Scandinavian Archaeologie, vol. 1*, Copenhagen, 158–90.

Kristiansen, K., (ed.) 1985: *Archaeological Formation Processes: the Representativity of Archaeological Remains from Danish Prehistory*, Copenhagen.

Kristiansen, K., 1989a: Value, Ranking and Consumption in the Bronze Age, in: H.-Å. Nordström and A. Knape (eds), *Bronze Age studies: Transactions of the British-Scandinavian Colloquium in Stockholm, May 10–11, 1985*, Stockholm (The Museum of National Antiquities, Stockholm, Studies, 6), 21–4.

Kristiansen, K., 1989b (1991): Prehistoric Migrations – the Case of the Single Grave and Corded Ware Cultures, *Journal of Danish Archaeology* 8, 211–25.

Kroll, H.J., 1975: *Ur- und frühgeschichtlicher Ackerbau in Archsum auf Sylt: eine botanische Großrestanalyse*, Kiel.

Kroll, H.J., 1987: Vor- und frühgeschichtlicher Ackerbau in Archsum auf Sylt: eine botanische Großrestanayse, in: G. Kossack, O.Harck & J. Reichstein (eds), *Archsum auf Sylt*, II: *Landwirtschaft und Umwelt in vor- und frühgeschichtlicher Zeit*, Mainz a.R. (Römisch-germanische Forschungen, 44), 51–158.

Kuiper, S.F., 1977: *Bodemkunde* (12th edn), Culemborg.

Laet, S.J. de, & W. Glasbergen 1959: *De voorgeschiedenis der Lage Landen*, Groningen.

Lanting, J.N., 1973: Laat-Neolithicum en Vroege Bronstijd in Nederland en N.W.-Duitsland: continue ontwikkelingen, *Palaeohistoria* 15, 215–317.

Lanting, J.N., 1986: Spoolde: onderzoek en vondsten binnendijks, in: H. Fokkens, P.M. Banga & M. Bierma (eds), *Op zoek naar mens en materiële cultuur: feestbundel aangeboden aan J.D. van der Waals ter gelegenheid van zijn emeritaat*, Groningen, 37–58.

Lanting, J.N., & J.D. van der Waals 1974 (1975): Oudheidkundig onderzoek bij Swalmen, I., praehistorie: opgravingen in de jaren 1936–38 en 1968–73, *OML* 55, 1–111.

Lanting, J.N., & J.D. van der Waals 1976: Beaker Culture Relations in the Lower Rhine Basin, in: J.N. Lanting and J.D. van der Waals (eds), *Glockenbecher Symposium Oberried 1974*, Bussum & Haarlem, 1–80.

Lanting, J.N., & W.G. Mook 1977: *The Pre- and Protohistory of the Netherlands in terms of Radiocarbon Dates*, Groningen.

Lévi-Strauss, C., 1949: *Les structures élémentaires de la parenté*, Paris.

Lévi-Strauss, C., 1962: *La pensée sauvage*, Paris.

Levy, J.E., 1982: *Social and Religious Organization in Bronze Age Denmark: an Analysis of Ritual Hoard Finds*, Oxford (BAR Int. Ser., 124).

Lohof, E., 1991: *Grafritueel en sociale verandering in de bronstijd van noordoost-Nederland*, Amsterdam.

Louwe Kooijmans, L.P., 1974: *The Rhine/Meuse Delta: Four Studies on its Prehistoric Occupation and Holocene Geology*, Leiden (APL, 7; OML, 53–4).

Louwe Kooijmans, L.P., 1976a (1977): Local Developments in a Borderland: a Survey of the Neolithic at the Lower Rhine, *OML* 57, 227–97.

Louwe Kooijmans, L.P., 1976b: The Neolithic at the Lower Rhine: its Structure in Chronological and Geographical Respect, in: S.J. de Laet (ed.), *Acculturation and Continuity in Atlantic Europe: mainly during the Neolithic Period and the Bronze Age*, Brugge (Dissertationes Archaeologicae Gandenses, 16), 150–73.

Louwe Kooijmans, L.P., 1990: Bronstijdstrijd, slachtoffers van een oeroorlog, *Natuur en Techniek* 58, 748–59.

Louwe Kooijmans, L.P., P.W. van den Broeke, H. Fokkens & A.L. van Gijn (eds) in press: *The Prehistory of the Netherlands*, Amsterdam.

Madsen, T., 1982: Settlement Systems of Early Agricultural Societies in East Jutland, Denmark: a Regional Study of Change, *Journal of Anthropological Archaeology* 1, 197–236.

Madsen, T., 1988: Causewayed Enclosures in South Scandinavia, in: C. Burgess, P. Topping, C. Mordant and M. Maddison (eds), *Enclosures and Defences in the Neolithic of Western Europe*, Oxford (BAR Int. Ser., 403: 2), 301–36.

Madsen, T., & H. Juel Jensen, 1982: Settlement and Land Use in Early Neolithic Denmark, *APL* 15, 63–86.

Makken, H.B., & J.A. van den Hurk 1969: *De bodemgesteldheid van het ruilverkavelingsgebied De Veenpolders*, Wageningen (Stibokarapport, 717).

Makken, H.B., & G. Rutten 1971: *De bodemgesteldheid van het ruilverkavelingsgebied Midden-Tjonger*, Wageningen (Stibokarapport, 835).

Makken, H.B., G. Rutten & J.F. Bannink 1975: *Modelonderzoek West-Groningen: het zuidelijk Westerkwartier bodemgesteldheid en bodemgeschiktheid*, Wageningen (Stibokarapport, 1176).

Malmer, M.P., 1962: *Jungneolithische Studien*, Bonn a.R., & Lund (Acta Archaeologica Lundensia, series in 8°: 2).

Mauss, M., 1923: *The Gift: The Form and Reason for Exchange in Archaic Societies* (edn 1990), London.

Minnis, P.E., 1985: *Social Adaptation to Food Stress*, London.

Monkhouse, F.J., & H.R. Wilkinson 1977: *Maps and Diagrams: their Composition and Construction*, London.

Müller, J., 1990: Die Arbeitsleistung für das Großsteingrab Kleinenkneten 1, in: M. Fansa, B. Renken & J. Döring (eds), *Experimentelle Archäologie in Deutschland*, Oldenburg (Archäologische Mitteilungen aus Nordwestdeutschland, Beiheft 4), 210–19.

Nielsen, P.O., 1977: Die Flintbeile der frühen Trichterbecherkultur in Dänemark, *Acta Archaeologica* 48, 61–138.

O'Shea, J., 1981: Coping with Scarcity: Exchange and Social Storage, in: A. Sheridan & G. Bailey (eds), *Economic Archaeology*, Oxford (BAR Int. Ser., 96), 167–83.

Pearson, G.W., J.R. Pilcher, M.G.L. Baillie, D.M. Corbett & F. Qua 1986: High-precision ^{14}C Measurement of Irish Oaks to Show the Natural ^{14}C Variations from AD 1840 to 5210 BC, *Radiocarbon* 28, 911–34.

Pearson, G.W., & M. Stuiver 1986: High-precision Calibration of the Radiocarbon Time Scale, 500–2500 BC, *Radiocarbon* 28, 839–62.

Piggott, S., 1965: *Ancient Europe: from the Beginnings of Agriculture to Classical Antiquity, a Survey*, Edinburgh.

Plassche, O. van de, 1979: Sea-level Research in the Province of South-Holland, Netherlands, in: K. Sugio *et al.* (eds), *Proceedings of the 1978 International Symposium on Coastal Evolution in the Quaternary*, Sao Paolo, 534–51.

Plassche, O. van de, 1982: *Sea-level Change and Water-level Movements in the Netherlands during the Holocene*, Haarlem (Mededelingen Rijks Geologische Dienst, 36: 1), 1–93.

Plassche, O. van de, 1985: Time-limit Assessment of Some Holocene Transgressive and Regressive Periods in the Northern Netherlands, *Eiszeitalter und Gegenwart* 35, 43–8.

Pleyte, W., 1877–1902: *Nederlandsche oudheden van de vroegste tijden tot op Karel den Groote*, vols I–III, Leiden.

Popping, H.J., 1929: De praehistorische vuursteen-werkplaatsen in Friesland (met een woord vooraf door Mr. P.C.J.A. Boeles), *De vrije Fries* 29, 1–36.

Popping, H.J., 1931: Nederlandsche praehistorische pijlspitsen, *Mens en maatschappij* 7, 121–38.

Popping, H.J., 1932a: Archeologische onderzoekingen in onze omgeving, *De Ooststellingwerver* 5.8.1932.

Popping, H.J., 1932b: *De bewoning van Friesland in voorhistorischen tijd*, Oosterwolde.

Popping, H.J., 1933a: *Voorhistorische vondsten in het Kuinderdal tusschen Oosterwolde en Donkerbroek*, Oosterwolde.

Popping, H.J., 1933b: Een graf van den IJstijdmensch, *De Ooststellingwerver* 22.9.1933.

Popping, H.J., 1933c: *Een neolithische nederzetting in de z.g. '150 bunder' te Appelscha*, Oosterwolde.

Popping, H.J., 1934: Praehistorie in een veengebied, *De Ooststellingwerver* 2.11.1934.

Popping, H.J., n.d.: *De nederzettingen langs den ouden verbindingsweg tusschen Friesland en Drente, over het Mandeveld bij Bakkeveen*, Oosterwolde.

Pott, R., 1990: Historische Waldnützungsformen Nordwestdeutschland, *Heimatpflege in Westfalen* 3, 1–9.

Rech, M., 1979: *Studien zu Depotfunden der Trichterbecher- und Einzelgrabkultur des Nordens*, Neumünster (Offa-Bücher, 39).

Renfrew, C., 1973: Monuments, Mobilization and Social Organization in Neolithic Wessex, in: C. Renfrew (ed.), *The Explanation of Culture Change: Models in Prehistory*, London, 539–58.

Renfrew, C., 1976: Megaliths, Territories and Populations, in: S.J. de Laet (ed.), *Acculturation and Continuity in Atlantic Europe: mainly during the Neolithic Period and the Bronze Age, Papers Presented at the IVth Atlantic Colloquium, Ghent 1975*, Brugge (Dissertationes Archaeologicae Gandenses, 16) 198–220.

Reynolds, P.J., 1987: *Butser Ancient Farm Year Book 1986*.

Roeleveld, W., 1974 (1976): *The Holocene Evolution of the Groningen Marine-clay District*, The Hague (supplement BROB, 24).

Roever, J.P. de, 1979: The Pottery from Swifterbant – Dutch Ertebølle? (Swifterbant Contribution, 11), *Helinium* 19, 13–36.

Rowlands, M.J., 1971: The Archaeological Interpretation of Prehistoric Metalworking, *World Archaeology* 3, 210–24.

Roymans, N., 1990: *Tribal Societies in Northern Gaul: an Anthropological Perspective*, Amsterdam, 1990 (Cingula, 12).

Roymans, N., 1991: Late Urnfield Societies in the Northwest European Plain and the Expanding Networks of Central European Hallstatt Groups, in: N. Roymans & F. Theuws (eds), *Images of the Past: Studies on Ancient Societies in Northwestern Europe*, Amsterdam (Studies in prae- en protohistorie, 7), 9–89.

Roymans, N., & F. Theuws (eds) 1991: *Images of the Past: Studies on Ancient Societies in Northwestern Europe*, Amsterdam (Studies in prae- en protohistorie, 7).

Roymans, N., & H. Fokkens 1991: Een overzicht van veertig jaar nederzettingsonderzoek in de Lage Landen in: H. Fokkens & N. Roymans (eds), *Nederzettingen uit de bronstijd en de vroege ijzertijd in de Lage Landen*, Amersfoort (NAR, 13), 1–19.

Sahlins, M.D., 1960: Evolution: Specific and General, in: M.D. Sahlins & E.R. Service (eds), *Evolution and Culture*, Ann Arbor, 12–44.

Sahlins, M.D., 1963: Poor Man, Rich Man, Big Man, Chief: Political Types in Melanesia and Polynesia, *Comparative Studies in Society and History* 5, 285–303 (reprinted in: M. Freilich (ed.) 1983, *The Pleasures of Anthropology*, New York, 383–99).

Sahlins, M.D., 1968: *Tribesmen*, Englewood Cliffs, N.J.

Sahlins, M.D., 1972: *Stone Age Economics*, London.

Sanden, W.A.B. van der, 1987: Oss-Ussen: de nederzettingen, in: W.A.B. van der Sanden & P.W. van den Broeke (eds), *Getekend Zand: tien jaar archeologisch onderzoek in Oss-Ussen*, Waalre, 53–67.

Sanden, W.A.B. van der, (ed.) 1990: *Mens en Moeras: veenlijken in Nederland van de bronstijd tot en met de Romeinse tijd*, Assen (Archeologische monografieën van het Drents Museum, 1).

Saxe, A., 1970: *Social Dimensions of Mortuary Practices*, Ann Arbor.

Schiffer, M.B., 1972: Archaeological Context and Systemic Context, *American Antiquity* 37, 156–65.

Schiffer, M.B., 1976: *Behavioral Archaeology*, New York, San Francisco & London.

Schiffer, M.B., 1983: Toward the Identification of Formation Processes, *American Antiquity* 48, 675–706.

Schotanus, C., 1664: *Beschrijvinge van de Heerlijckheydt van Frieslandt tusschen 't Flie end de Lauwers*, Franeker.

Schotanus à Sterringa, B., 1718: *Uitbeelding der Heerlijkheit Friesland; zoo in 't algemeen, als in haare xxx bijzondere Grietenijen*, Leeuwarden ('Halma atlas').

Schotanus à Sterringa, B., 1739: *Nieuwe Caert van Frieslant*, Amsterdam & Leeuwarden ('Vegelin map').

Service, E.R., 1971: *Primitive Social Organization: an Evolutionary Perspective* (2nd edn), New York.

Shanks, M., & C. Tilley 1987: *Re-Constructing Archaeology: Theory and Practice*, Cambridge.

Shaw, C.T., 1944: Report on Excavations carried out in the Cave known as 'Bosumpra' at Abetifi, Kwahu, Gold Coast Colony, *PPS* n.s. 10, 1–67.

Shennan, S.J., 1976: Bell Beakers and their Context in Central Europe, in: J.N. Lanting & J.D. van der Waals (eds), *Glockenbecher Symposium Oberried 1974*, Bussum & Haarlem, 231–9.

Shennan, S.J., 1977: The Appearance of the Bell Beaker Assemblage in Central Europe, in: R.J. Mercer (ed.) *Beakers in Britain and Europe*, Oxford (BAR Sup. Ser., 26), 51–70.

Shennan, S.J., 1982: Ideology, Change and the European Early Bronze Age, in: I.A. Hodder (ed.), *Symbolic and Structural Archaeology*, Cambridge, 155–61.

Sherratt, A.G., 1981: Plough and Pastoralism: Aspects of the Secondary Products Revolution, in: I. Hodder, G. Isaac & N. Hammond (eds), *Pattern of the Past: Studies in Honour of David Clarke*, Cambridge, 261–305.

Siebinga, J., 1944: *Overzicht van de voorgeschiedenis van de gemeente Smallingerland*, reprint with new pagination (3–31) from: *Smellingera-land: Proeve van een 'Geakinde' van de gemeente Smallingerland, uitgegeven ter gelegenheid van het driehonderdjarig bestaan van Drachten, 1641–1941)*, Drachten, 153–181.

Simons, A., 1989: *Bronze- und eisenzeitliche Besiedlung in den rheinischen Lößbörden: archäologische Siedlungsmuster im Braunkohlengebiet*, Oxford (BAR Int. Ser., 467).

Skaarup, J., 1973: *Hesselø-Sølager: Jagdstationen der süd-skandinavischen Trichterbecherkultur*, Copenhagen (Arkæologiske studier, 1).

Skaarup, J., 1975: *Stengade: ein langeländischer Wohnplatz mit Hausresten aus der frühneolithischen Zeit*, Rudkøbing.

Slicher van Bath, B.H., 1960: *De agrarische geschiedenis van West-Europa (500–1850)*, Utrecht (Aula-boeken, 32).

Slicher van Bath, B.H., 1978: *Bijdragen tot de agrarische geschiedenis*, Utrecht.

Slofstra, J., 1982: De regionaal-archeologische onderzoeksstrategie, in: J. Slofstra, H.H. van Regteren Altena, N. Roymans & F. Theuws, *Het Kempenproject: een regionaal-archeologisch onderzoeksprogramma*, Waalre (Bijdragen tot de studie van het Brabantse heem, 22), 22–43.

Slofstra, J., 1991: Changing Settlement Systems in the Meuse-Demer-Scheldt Area during the Early Roman Period, in: N. Roymans & F. Theuws (eds), *Images of the Past: Studies on Ancient Societies*, Amsterdam (Studies in Prae- en Protohistorie, 7), 131–99.

Slofstra, J., & W.A.B. van der Sanden 1987: Rurale cultusplaatsen uit de Romeinse tijd in het Maas-Demer-Scheldegebied, *APL* 20, 125–68.

Sørensen, M.L.S., 1989: Looking at Periferies: the Reproduction of Material Culture in Late Bronze Age Scandinavia and England, in: H.-Å. Nordström & A. Knape (eds), *Bronze Age Studies: Transactions of the British-Scandinavian Colloquium in Stockholm, May 10–11 1985*, Stockholm, 63–76.

Steenbeek, P., P. Cleveringa and W. de Gans 1981: Terreinvormen in Friesland uit de laatste ijstijd, *It Beaken* 43, 249–72.

Steensberg, A., 1980: *New Guinea Gardens: a Study of Husbandry with Parallels in Prehistoric Europe*, London.

Stein, J.K., 1983: Earthworm Activity: a Source of Potential Disturbance of Archaeological Sediments, *American Antiquity* 48, 277–89.

Stuiver, M., & B. Becker 1986: High-precision Decadal Calibration of the Radiocarbon Time Scale, AD 1950–2500 BC, *Radiocarbon* 28, 863–910.

Stuiver, M., & G.W. Pearson 1986: High-precision Calibration of the Radiocarbon Time Scale, AD 1950–500 BC, *Radiocarbon* 28, 805–38.

Taayke, E., 1988: Terpenaardewerk uit de ijzertijd en de Romeinse tijd, in: M. Bierma, A.T. Clason, E. Kramer & G.J. de Langen (eds), *Terpen en wierden in het Fries-Groningse kustgebied*, Groningen, 50–60.

Thrane, H., 1985: Bronze Age Settlements, in: K. Kristiansen (ed.), *Archaeological Formation Processes: the Representativity of Archaeological Remains from Danish Prehistory*, Copenhagen, 142–51.

Tilley, C., 1984: Ideology and the Legitimation of Power in the Middle Neolithic of Southern Sweden, in: D. Miller & C. Tilley (eds), *Ideology, Power and Prehistory*, Cambridge, 111–146.

Trier, B., 1989: Bericht über die Tätigkeit des Westfälischen Museums für Archäologie – Amt für Bodendenkmalpflege – im Jahre 1988, *Neujahrsgruß 1989; Jahresbericht 1988; Westfälisches Museum für Archäologie, etc.*, Münster.

Uil, H., 1987: Hoofdstuk 7: Hydrologie, in: T.A.M. de Groot *et al., Blad Heerenveen West (11 w) en Heerenveen Oost (11 o)*, Haarlem, (Toelichtingen bij de Geologische Kaart van Nederland 1:50.000), 177–84.

Vasbinder, A.C., & H. Fokkens 1987: Een bronstijd-huis uit Oss-Ussen, in: W.A.B. van der Sanden & P.W. van den Broeke (eds), *Getekend zand: tien jaar archeologisch onderzoek in Oss-Ussen*, Waalre, 131–5.

Veenenbos, J.S., 1950: *De bodemgesteldheid van het gebied tussen Lemmer en Blokzijl in het randgebied van de Noordoost polder*, The Hague (Verslagen van landbouwkundige onderzoekingen, 55.12; De bodemkartering van Nederland, 5).

Veenenbos, J.S., 1951: *De bodemgesteldheid van het D.U.W.-object Donkerbroek (Fr.)*, Wageningen (Stibokarapport, 266).

Velde, P. van de, 1979: *On Bandkeramik Social Structure*, The Hague, Boston & London (APL, 12).

Verlinde, A.D., 1979: Deponierte landwirtschaftliche Geräte aus Hirschgewei in der IJssel bei Deventer, *BROB* 29, 209–18.

Verlinde, A.D., 1987: *Die Gräber und Grabfunde der späten Bronzezeit und frühen Eisenzeit in Overijssel*, Amersfoort.

Verwers. G.J., 1969: The Beginning of the Late Bronze Age in the Lower Rhine Area, *BROB* 19, 17–25 (also: APL 4, 1971, 57–67).

Verwers, W.J.H., & L.I. Kooistra 1990 (1992): Native House Plans from the Roman Period in Boxtel and Oosterhout, *BROB* 40, 251–84.

Voss, J.A., 1982: A Study of Western TRB Social Organisation, *BROB* 32, 9–102.

Vynsrygg, S., 1987: Sex-roles and the Division of Labour in Hunter-gatherer Societies, in: R. Bertelsen (ed.), *Were they all Men?: an Examination of Sex Roles in Prehistoric Society: Acts from a Workshop Held at Utstein Kloster, Rogaland, 2–4 November 1979*, Stavanger (AMS-varia, 17), 23–32.

Waals, J.D. van der, 1962: Sporen van bewoning en begraving uit neolithicum en bronstijd bij Hoeve 'De Schipborg', gem. Anlo, *NDV* 80, 223–72.

Waals, J.D. van der, 1963: Een huisplattegrond uit de vroege ijzertijd te Een, gem. Norg, *NDV* 81, 217–29.

Waals, J.D. van der, 1964: *Prehistoric Disc Wheels in the Netherlands*, Groningen.

Waals, J.D. van der, 1965: Early Ceramics in the Netherlands: two Problems, in: F.R. Matson (ed.), *Ceramics and Man*, Chicago (Viking Fund Publications in Anthropology, 41), 124–39.

Waals, J.D. van der, 1972: Die durchlochten Rössener Keile und das frühe Neolithikum in Belgiën und in den Niederlanden, in: H. Schwabedissen (ed.), *Die Anfänge des Neolithikums vom Orient bis Nordeuropa*, V a, Cologne, 153–84.

Waals, J.D. van der, 1984 (1985): Discontinuity, Cultural Evolution and the Historic Event, *Proceedings of the Society of Antiquaries of Scotland* 114, 1–14.

Waals, J.D. van der, 1987: *De kolonisatie van het terpengebied: een ethno-archeologische benadering*, Haarlem (Kroon-voordracht, 10).

Waals, J.D. van der, & W. Glasbergen 1955: Beaker Types and their Distribution in the Netherlands, *Palaeohistoria* 4, 5–46.

Waals, J.D. van der, & H.T. Waterbolk 1976: Excavations at Swifterbant – Discovery, Progress, Aims and Methods (Swifterbant contribution, 1), *Helinium* 16, 3–14.

Wansleeben, M., 1988: Applications of Geographical Information Systems in Archaeological Research, in: S.P.Q. Rahtz (ed.), *Computer and Quantitative Methods in Archaeology*, Oxford (BAR Int. Ser., 446: 2), 435–51.

Waterbolk, H.T., 1957: Een kringgrepurnenveld te Wapse, *Van rendierjager tot ontginner: nieuwe oudheidkundige ontdekkingen in Drenthe* 2, 42–67 (in: NDV 75).

Waterbolk, H.T., 1958: Neolithische vlakgraven in Drenthe, *Van rendierjager tot ontginner: nieuwe oudheidkundige ontdekkingen in Drenthe* 3, 3–17 (in: NDV 76).

Waterbolk, H.T., 1959: Nieuwe gegevens over de herkomst van de oudste bewoners der kleistreken, *Akademiedagen* 11, 16–37.

Waterbolk, H.T., 1960: Preliminary Report on the Excavations at Anlo in 1957 and 1958, *Palaeohistoria* 8, 59–90.

Waterbolk, H.T., 1962: Hauptzüge der eisenzeitlichen Besiedlung der nördlichen Niederlande, *Offa* 19, 9–46.

Waterbolk, H.T., 1964a: Ein Grabhügel auf dem Gut 'De Eese', Gem. Vledder, Prov. Drenthe, *Palaeohistoria* 10, 71–86.

Waterbolk, H.T., 1964b: The Bronze Age Settlement of Elp, *Helinium* 4, 97–131.

Waterbolk, H.T., 1965: Ein eisenzeitliches Gräberfeld bei Ruinen, Provinz Drenthe, Niederlande, in: R. von Uslar (ed.), *Studien aus Alteuropa*, II, (Festschrift K. Tackenberg), Cologne (Beihefte der Bonner Jahrbücher, 10: II), 34–53.

Waterbolk, H.T., 1965–1966 (1967): The Occupation of Friesland in the Prehistoric Period, BROB 15–16, 13–35.

Waterbolk, H.T., 1968: Van rendierjagers tot terpbewoners, in: J. Kalma *et al.* (eds), *De geschiedenis van Friesland*, Drachten, 13–47.

Waterbolk, H.T., 1974: L'Archéologie en Europe: une reaction contre la 'New Archaeology', *Helinium* 14, 135–62.

Waterbolk, H.T., 1977: Walled Enclosures of the Iron Age in the North of the Netherlands, *Palaeohistoria* 19, 97–172.

Waterbolk, H.T., 1979: Siedlungskontinuität im Küstengebiet der Nordsee zwischen Rhein und Elbe, *Probleme der Küstenforschung in südlichen Nordseegebiet* 13, 1–21.

Waterbolk, H.T., 1982: Mobilität von Dorf, Ackerflur und Gräberfeld in Drenthe seit der Latènezeit, *Offa* 39, 97–137.

Waterbolk, H.T., 1985a: The Mesolithic and Early Neolithic Settlement of the Northern Netherlands in the Light of Radiocarbon Evidence, in: R. Fellmann, G. Germann & K. Zimmerman (eds), *Jagen und Sammeln: Festschrift für Hans-Georg Bandi zum 65. Geburtstag*, Bern (Jahrbuch des Bernischen historischen Museums, 63–64), 273–81.

Waterbolk, H.T., 1985b: Archeologie, in: J. Heringa, D.P. Blok, M.G. Buist & H.T. Waterbolk (eds), *Geschiedenis van Drenthe*, Meppel and Amsterdam, 15–90.

Waterbolk, H.T., 1987a: Terug naar Elp, in: F.C.J. Ketelaar (ed.), *De historie herzien: vijfde bundel 'Historische avonden' uitgegeven door het Historisch Genootschap te Groningen ter gelegenheid van zijn honderdjarig bestaan*, Hilversum, 183–215.

Waterbolk, H.T., 1987b: *Tussen Hunze en Eufraat: afscheidsrede uitgesproken op 20 oktober 1987 door dr. H.T. Waterbolk, hoogleraar in de prehistorie en de germaanse archeologie aan de Rijksuniversiteit Groningen*, Groningen.

Waterbolk, H.T., 1988: Zomerbewoning in het terpengebied?, in: M. Bierma, A.T. Clason, E. Kramer & G.J. de Langen (eds), *Terpen en wierden in het Fries-Groningse kustgebied*, Groningen, 1–19.

Waterbolk, H.T., 1989a: Elp, in: H. Beck, H. Jankuhn, K. Ranke & R. Wenskus (eds), *Reallexikon der Germanischen Altertumskunde von Johannes Hoops* (2nd edn), VII, Berlin & New York, 163–75.

Waterbolk, H.T., 1989b: Siebzig Jahre archäologische Siedlungsforschung durch das Biologisch-Archäologische Institut der Universität Groningen: unter besonderer Berücksichtigung der Untersuchungen Albert Egges van Giffen in der Provinz Drenthe, *Siedlungsforschung: Archäologie-Geschichte-Geographie* 7, 285–320.

Waterbolk, H.T., & J.W. Boersma 1976: Bewoning in vóór- en vroeghistorische tijd, in: W.J. Formsma *et al.* (eds), *Historie van Groningen: Stad en Land*, Groningen, 11–74.

Wee, M.W. ter, 1962: The Saalien Glaciation in the Netherlands, *Mededelingen van de Geologische Stichting, n.s.* 15, 57–76.

Wee, M.W. ter, 1975: Enkele momentopnamen uit de geologische geschiedenis van de Boorne, *It Beaken* 37, 334–40.

Wee, M.W. ter, 1976: *Blad Sneek (10 W, 10 O)*, Haarlem (Toelichtingen bij de Geologische Kaart van Nederland 1:50.000).

Wee, M.W. ter, 1981: The Saalian Glaciation in the Northern Netherlands, *Mededelingen Rijks Geologische Dienst* 34, 7–9.

Wensink, J.J., 1958: De jongpleistocene en holocene ontwikkeling van een deel van Westergoo, *Geologie en mijnbouw, n.s.* 20, 73–87.

Whittle, A., 1985: *Neolithic Europe: a Survey*, Cambridge.

Wijngaarden-Bakker, L.H., 1988: Zoöarcheologisch onderzoek in de west-Nederlandse delta 1983–1987, in: J.H.F. Bloemers (ed.), *Archeologie en oecologie van Holland tussen Rijn en Vlie*, Assen & Maastricht (Studies in prae- en protohistorie, 2), 154–85.

Willems, W.J.H., 1981: Romans and Batavians: a Regional Study in the Dutch Eastern River Area, I, *BROB* 31, 7–217.

Willems, W.J.H., & W. Groenman-van Waateringe 1988: Een rijk graf uit de vroege ijzertijd te Horst-Hegelsom, in: P.A.M. Geurts *et al.* (eds), *Horster Historiën*, 2, Horst, 13–29.

Wobst, H.M., 1977: Stilistic Behaviour and Information Exchange, in: C. Cleland (ed.), *For the Director: Research Essays in the Honour of James B. Griffin*, Ann Arbor (University of Michigan Museum of Anthropology Anthropological Papers, 61), 317–42.

Woltering, P.J., 1979: Occupation History of Texel, II the Archaeological Survey: Preliminary Report, *BROB* 29, 7–113.

Zagwijn, W.H., 1986: *Nederland in het Holoceen*, Haarlem (Geologie van Nederland, 1).

Zagwijn, W.H., & C.J. van Staalduinen 1975: *Toelichting bij geologische overzichtskaarten van Nederland*, Haarlem.

Zeiler, J.T., 1986: Swifterbant: Dwelling Place for a Season or throughout the Whole Year? An Archaeozoological Contribution, in: H. Fokkens, P. Banga & M. Bierma (eds), *Op zoek naar mens en materiële cultuur: feestbundel aangeboden aan J.D. van der Waals ter gelegenheid van zijn emeritaat*, Groningen, 85–95.

Zeiler, J.T., 1989: Archeozoölogisch onderzoek van de laat-neolithische vindplaats Kolhorn (N.-H.), *Paleo-aktueel* 1, 25–30.

Zeist, W. van, 1955: *Pollen Anlytical Investigations in the Northern Netherlands: with special reference to archaeology*, Utrecht (Acta Botanica Neerlandica, 4,1).

Zeist, W. van, 1991: Economic Aspects, in: W. van Zeist, K. Wasylikova & K.-E. Behre (eds), *Progress in Old World Palaeoethnobotany: a Retrospective View on the Occasion of 20 Years of the International Work Group for Palaeoethnobotany*, Rotterdam, 109–30.

Zimmermann, W.H., 1976: Die eisenzeitlichen Ackerfluren – Typ 'Celtic field' – von Flögeln-Haselhörn, Kr. Wesermünde, *Probleme der Küstenforschung im südlichen Nordseegebiet* 11, 79–90.

Zimmermann, W.H., 1980: Ein trichterbecherzeitlicher Hausgrundriß von Flögeln – Im Örtjen, Kr. Cuxhaven, in: T. Krüger & H.-G. Stephan (eds), *Beiträge zur Archäologie Nordwestdeutschlands und Mitteleuropas* (Festschrift K. Raddatz), Hildesheim, 479–89.

The maps I–VIII and I'–VIII'

On the following sixteen pages two series of eight maps of the western part of the Frisian-Drentian plateau have been reproduced: on the rectos eight coloured maps, numbered I–VIII; on the versos eight maps without colour, numbered I'–VIII'. Maps I–VIII show the palaeogeographical reconstruction of the successive periods, maps I'–VIII' the archaeological visibility. Both series show the distribution of the archaeological finds from the successive periods. The pairs of maps on opposite pages represent the same archaeological period. The legend pertaining to maps I–VIII has been printed on a fold-out (p. 181).

In terms of the Netherlands National Grid the surface of the maps is bordered in the west by the 150 abscissa, in the east by the 225 abscissa, in the south by the 530 ordinate and in the north by the 605 ordinate (maps I'–VIII') or the 606 ordinate (maps I–VIII). The distance between the west and east sides of the maps is 75 km in reality. The distance between the south and north sides of maps I'–VIII' is 75 km as well, that of maps I–VIII 76 km. (The distance between two successive co-ordinates with a whole number is 1 km.)

The different components of the two series of maps are discussed in the course of the book. For the archaeological finds the reader is referred to Chapters 2 and 8, for the palaeogeographical reconstructions to Chapter 3, and for the archaeological visibility to Chapter 6. All maps are discussed in Chapter 8.

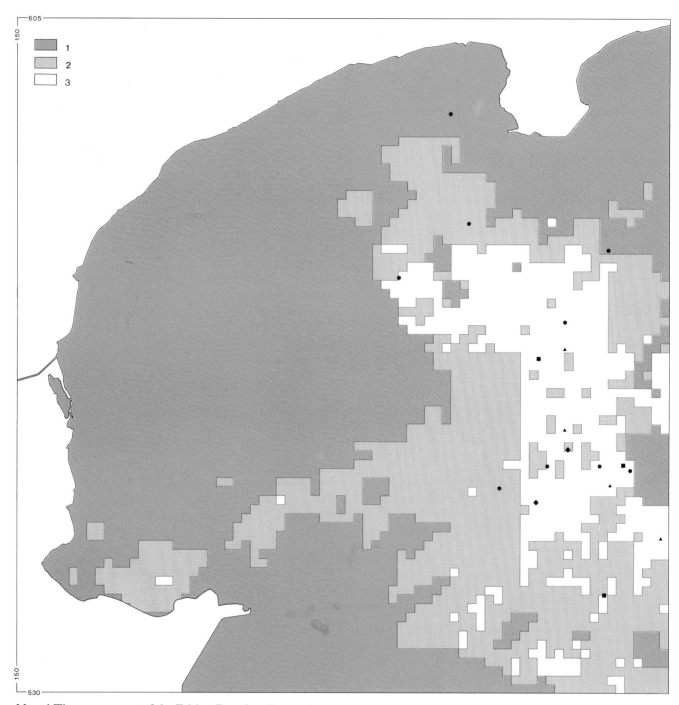

Map 1' The western part of the Frisian-Drentian plateau: the
distribution of finds from the Early Neolithic B in relation to
the archaeological visibility. Legend: 1 archaeological visibility
0–25%; 2 archaeological visibility 25–50%; 3 archaeological
visibility 50–100%.

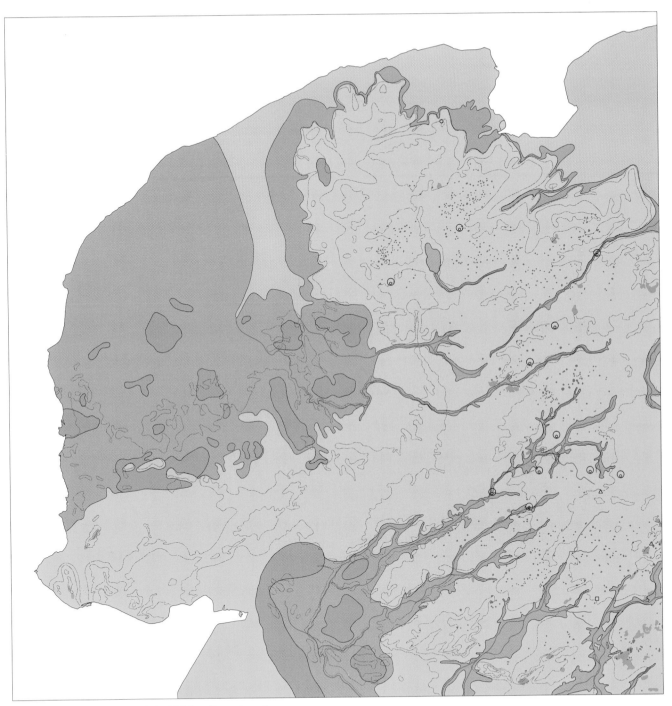

Map I The western part of the Frisian-Drentian plateau:
palaeogeographical map of the period 4400–4000 cal BC
(5550–5200 b.p.) with the distribution of the finds from the
Early Neolithic B.

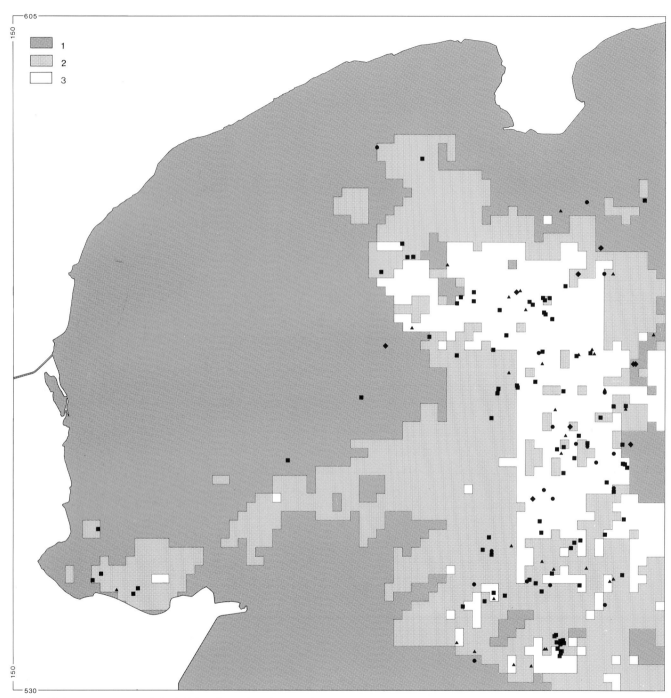

Map 11' The western part of the Frisian-Drentian plateau: the
distribution of finds from the Middle Neolithic B in relation to
the archaeological visibility. Legend: 1 archaeological visibility
0–25%; 2 archaeological visibility 25–50%; 3 archaeological
visibility 50–100%.

Map II The western part of the Frisian-Drentian plateau:
palaeogeographical map of the period 3400–2900 cal BC
(4700–4300 b.p.) with the distribution of finds from the
Middle Neolithic B.

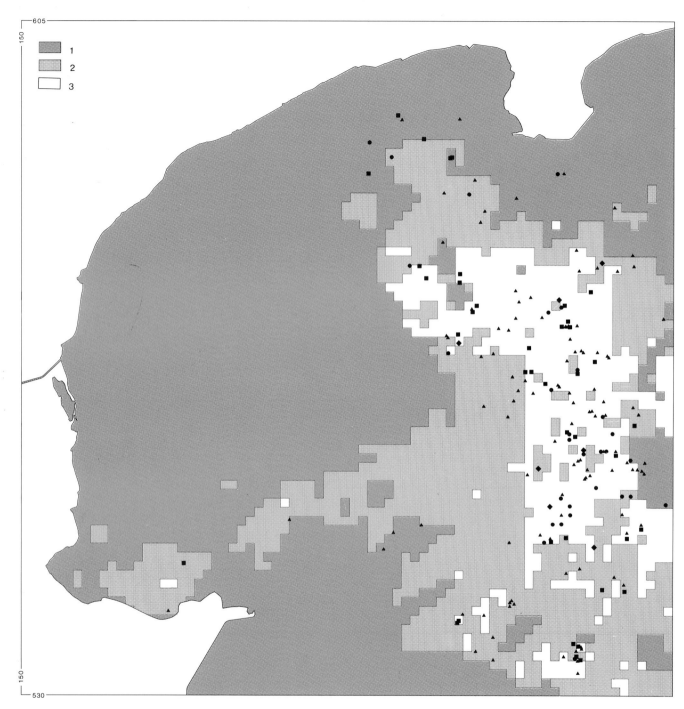

Map III' The western part of the Frisian-Drentian plateau: the distribution of finds from the Late Neolithic A in relation to the archaeological visibility. Legend: 1 archaeological visibility 0–25%; 2 archaeological visibility 25–50%; 3 archaeological visibility 50–100%.

Map III The western part of the Frisian-Drentian plateau:
palaeogeographical map of the period 2900–2500 cal BC
(4300–3950 b.p.) with the distribution of finds from the Late
Neolithic A.

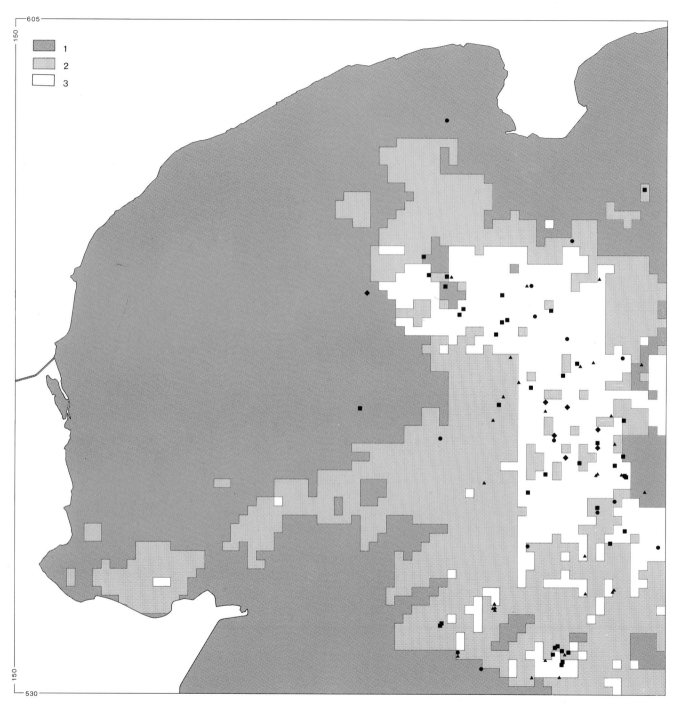

Map IV' The western part of the Frisian-Drentian plateau: the
distribution of finds from the Late Neolithic B and the Early
Bronze Age in relation to the archaeological visibility. Legend:
1 archaeological visibility 0–25%; 2 archaeological visibility
25–50%; 3 archaeological visibility 50–100%.

Map IV The western part of the Frisian-Drentian plateau:
palaeogeographical map of the period 2500–1800 cal BC
(3950–3450 b.p.) with the distribution of finds from the Late
Neolithic B and the Early Bronze Age.

Map V' The western part of the Frisian-Drentian plateau: the
distribution of finds from the Middle Bronze Age in relation to
the archaeological visibility. Legend: 1 archaeological visibility
0–25%; 2 archaeological visibility 25–50%; 3 archaeological
visibility 50–100%.

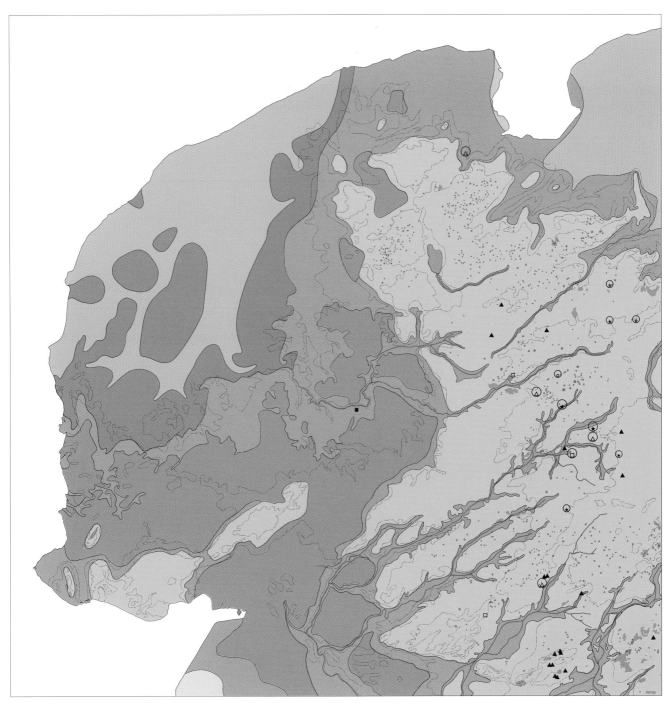

Map v The western part of the Frisian-Drentian plateau:
palaeogeographical map of the period 1800–1100 cal BC
(3450–2900 b.p.) with the distribution of finds from the
Middle Bronze Age.

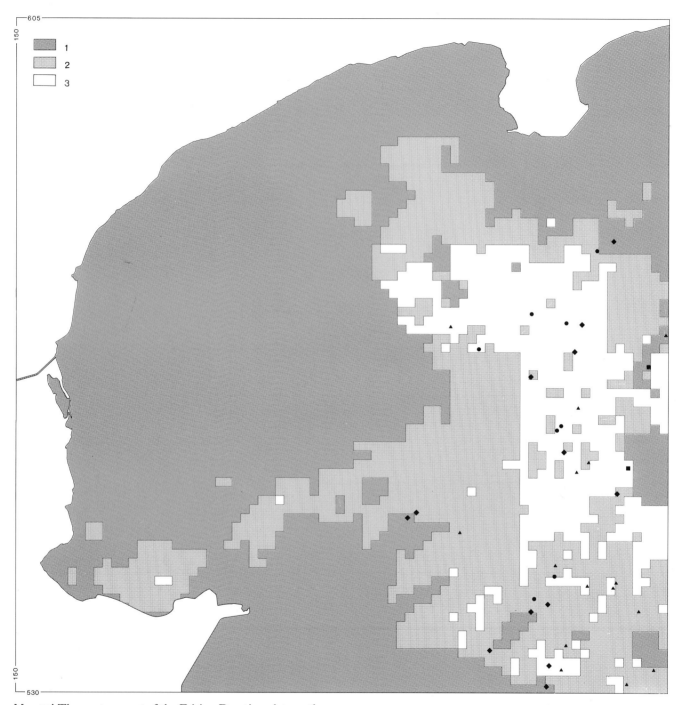

Map VI' The western part of the Frisian-Drentian plateau: the distribution of finds from the Late Bronze Age and the Early Iron Age in relation to the archaeological visibility. Legend: 1 archaeological visibility 0–25%; 2 archaeological visibility 25–50%; 3 archaeological visibility 50–100%.

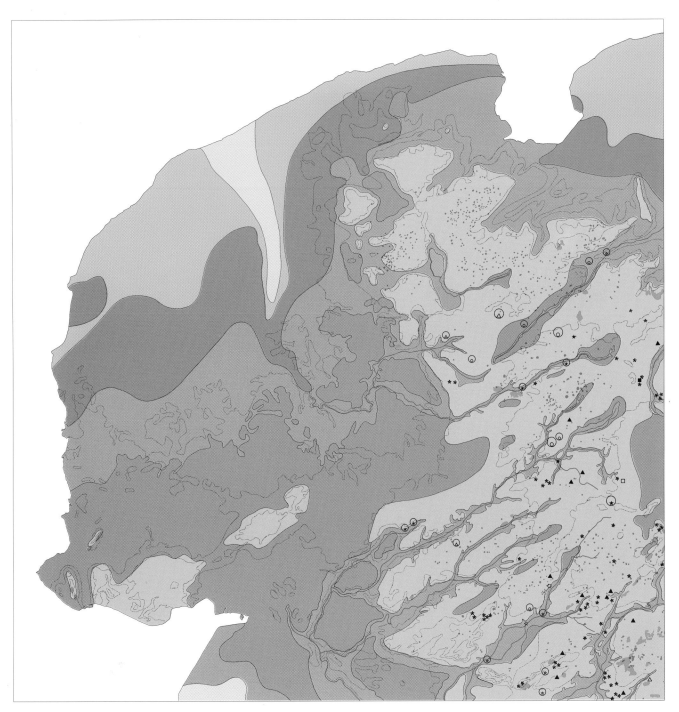

Map VI The western part of the Frisian-Drentian plateau:
palaeogeographical map from the period 1100–500 cal BC
(2900–2450 b.p.) with the distribution of finds from the Late
Bronze Age and the Early Iron Age.

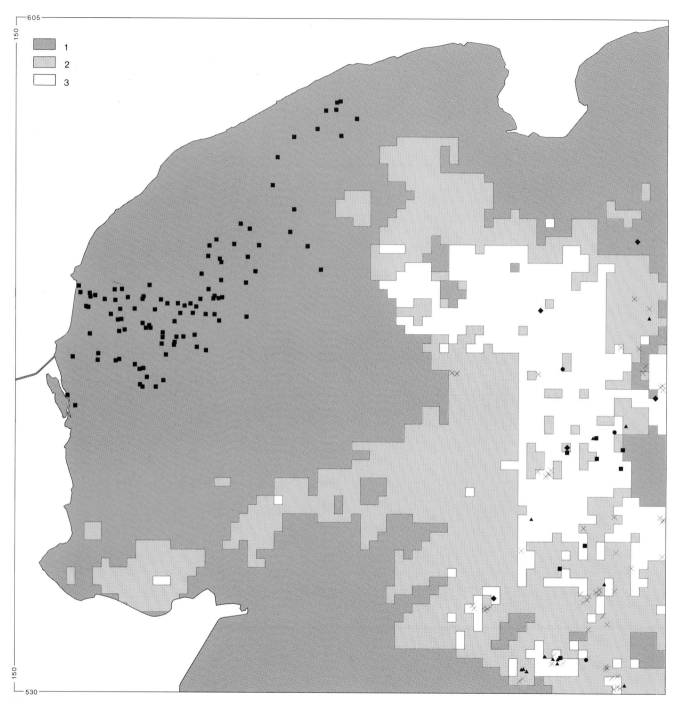

Map VII' The western part of the Frisian-Drentian plateau: the
distribution of finds from the Middle and Late Iron Age in
relation to the archaeological visibility. Legend: 1 archaeological
visibility 0–25%; 2 archaeological visibility 25–50%;
3 archaeological visibility 50–100%.

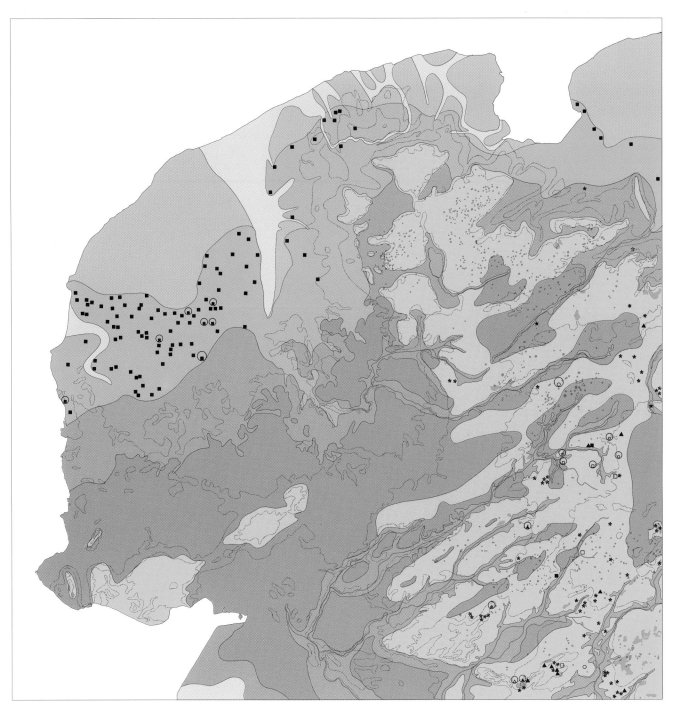

Map VII The western part of the Frisian-Drentian plateau:
palaeogeographical map of the period 500 cal BC – 12 BC
(2450–2000 b.p.) with the distribution of finds from the
Middle and Late Iron Age.

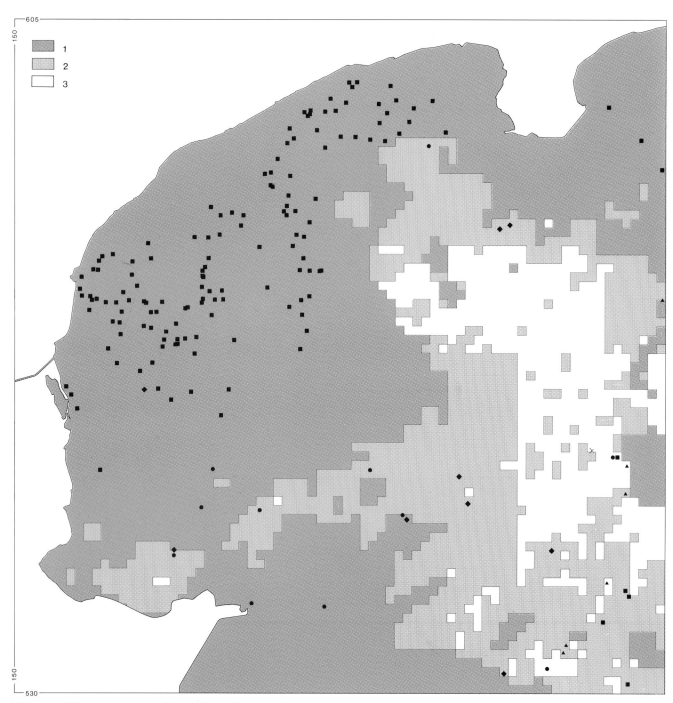

Map VIII' The western part of the Frisian-Drentian plateau:
the distribution of finds from the Roman period in relation to
the archaeological visibility. Legend: 1 archaeological visibility
0–25%; 2 archaeological visibility 25–50%; 3 archaeological
visibility 50–100%.

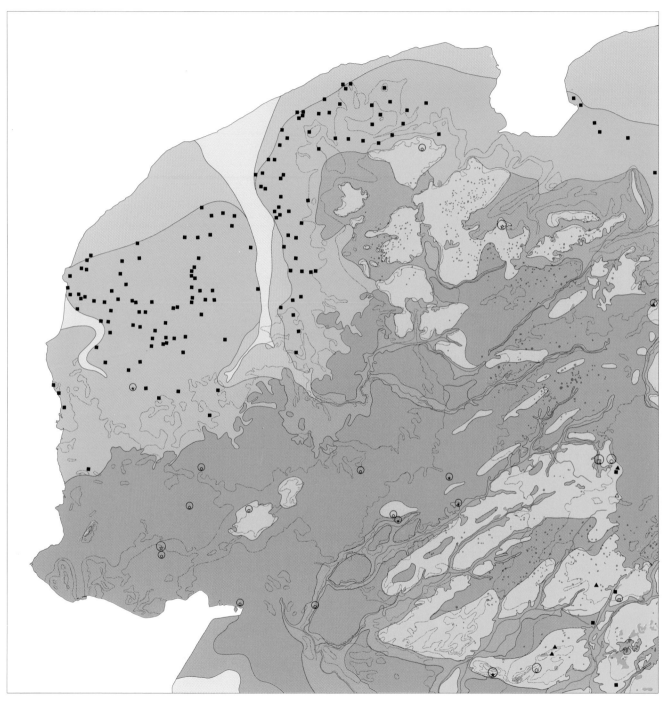

Map VIII The western part of the Frisian-Drentian plateau:
palaeogeographical map of the period 12 BC – AD 406
(2000–1650 b.p.) with the distribution of finds from the
Roman period.

LEGEND

geology: Holocene

. eutrophic and/or mesotrophic peat (including brook deposits)

. oligotrophic peat

. salt marsh

. tidal flat (or open water, maps I–V)

. clay on peat

geology: Pleistocene

. boulderclay at, or less than 0.4 m under the surface

. coversands

miscellaneous

. contour, height in metres (2 m interval below NAP, 4 m interval above NAP)

. tidal water

. lake

. river channels

. *dobben* (local depressions filled with peat)

archaeology

. settlement, exact location

. settlement, location within 500 m

. possible settlement, exact location

. possible settlement, location within 500 m

. possible settlement, location within the village boundary

. grave or cemetery, exact location

. grave or cemetery, location within 500 m

. possible grave or cemetery, exact location

. possible grave or cemetery, location within 500 m

. possible grave or cemetery, location within the village boundary

. hoard, exact location

. hoard, location within 500 m

. hoard, location within the village boundary

. possible hoard, exact location

. possible hoard, location within 500 m

. possible hoard, location within the village boundary

. site type undetermined, exact location

. site type undetermined, location within 500 m

. site type undetermined, location within the village boundary

. arable land, exact location

Abbreviations

*A*ms-varia	Arkeologisk museum i Stavanger-varia	IPL	Instituut voor Praehistorie Leiden
APL	*Analecta Praehistorica Leidensia*	IPP	Instituut voor Prae- en Protohistorische Archeologie Albert Egges van Giffen, Amsterdam
BAI	Biologisch-Archaeologisch Instituut, Groningen	NAP	(above) Normaal Amsterdams Peil (Dutch Datum Level)
BAR Int. Ser.	British Archaeological Reports International Series	-NAP	below Normaal Amsterdams Peil (Dutch Datum Level)
BAR Sup. Ser.	British Archaeological Reports Supplementary Series	NAR	Nederlandse Archeologische Rapporten
b.c.	before Christ (uncalibrated radiocarbon years BC)	*NDV*	*Nieuwe Drents(ch)e volksalmanak*
BJ	*Bonner Jahrbücher*	*NKJ*	*Nederlands Kunsthistorisch Jaarboek*
b.p.	before present (uncalibrated radiocarbon years before AD 1950)	n.r.	nieuwe reeks (new series)
		n.s.	new series
BP	b.p. (used in headings and running heads printed in small capitals)	NWO	Nederlandse Organisatie voor Wetenschappelijk Onderzoek, The Hague
BROB	*Berichten van de Rijksdienst voor het Oudheidkundig Bodemonderzoek*	O. Fl.	Oostelijk Flevoland
cal BC/AD	calibrated (radiocarbon years, expressed in years) BC or AD	*OML*	*Oudheidkundige Medede(e)lingen uit het Rijksmuseum van Oudheden te Leiden*
GrN	Groningen (laboratory code Centrum voor Isotopen Onderzoek, Groningen, formerly Physics Laboratory, University of Groningen, from 1.1.1961)	*PPS*	*Proceedings of the Prehistoric Society*
		ROB	Rijksdienst voor het Oudheidkundig Bodemonderzoek, Amersfoort
GRO	Groningen (laboratory code Physics Laboratory, University of Groningen, before 1.1.1961)	TRB	*Trichterbecher* (Culture)
		ZWO	Nederlandse Organisatie voor Zuiver-Wetenschappelijk Onderzoek (at present NWO), The Hague
GV	*Groningse volksalmanak*		